# Wirtschaftsethik in der globalisierten Welt

**Reihe herausgegeben von**
Ch. Luetge, München, Deutschland

Die Ordnungsethik analysiert die normativen Grundlagen moderner Gesellschaften einschließlich ihrer ökonomischen Aspekte und macht sie für die praktische Gestaltung zugänglich. Dies umfasst sowohl systematische als auch historische Perspektiven der Wirtschaftsethik sowie verwandter Gebiete der Philosophie, Ökonomik, Geistes- und Sozialwissenschaften.

**Reihe herausgegeben von**
Prof. Dr. Christoph Luetge
Technische Universität München
Deutschland

Weitere Bände in der Reihe http://www.springer.com/series/13464

Hiroshi Kabashima · Shing-I Liu
Christoph Luetge · Aurelio de Prada García
Editors

# The Idea of Justice in Literature

 Springer VS

*Editors*
Hiroshi Kabashima
School of Law
Tohoku University
Sendai, Japan

Christoph Luetge
Chair of Business Ethics and Global Governance
Technical University of Munich
München, Germany

Shing-I Liu
Center of Criminal Law
National Taipei University
New Taipei City, Taiwan

Aurelio de Prada García
Facultad de Ciencias Jurídicas y Sociales
Universidad Rey Juan Carlos
Madrid, Spain

ISSN 2524-3802          ISSN 2524-3810   (electronic)
Wirtschaftsethik in der globalisierten Welt
ISBN 978-3-658-21995-6          ISBN 978-3-658-21996-3   (eBook)
https://doi.org/10.1007/978-3-658-21996-3

Library of Congress Control Number: 2018942328

Springer VS
© Springer Fachmedien Wiesbaden GmbH, part of Springer Nature 2018

Responsible Editor: Frank Schindler

Printed on acid-free paper

This Springer VS imprint is published by the registered company Springer Fachmedien Wiesbaden GmbH part of Springer Nature
The registered company address is: Abraham-Lincoln-Str. 46, 65189 Wiesbaden, Germany

# Inhalt / Contents

# Introduction

Our project "Idea of Justice in Literature/ Die Idee der Gerechtigkeit in der Literatur" was firstly proposed by the chief editor, Shing-I LIU from Taiwan, and planed as an international dialogue joined by the co-editors, Aurelio de PRADA from Spain, Christoph LUETGE from Germany, and Hiroshi KABASHIMA from Japan. For this international collaboration, we organized five sessions in two days in English and German, on Monday, 27 July and Thursday, 30 July, 2015, in the form of a Special Workshop at the "XXVII World Congress of the International Society for the Philosophy of Law and Social Philosophy (IVR)" held at the Georgetown Law School in Washington D.C., the United States of America. In the sessions, we, the organizers, enjoyed so much our intellectual exchange with the excellent presenters and participants of all ages from all over the world who were engaged in the issue of "Justice in Literature", as it is now to trace in this editorial work on hand.

In fact, the editors as well as the authors are mostly active in law and social science, but not satisfied just with legal dogmatism and empirical positivism. They are willing to discuss legal and social themes rather in relation with philosophy, literature, and humanism than exclusively with legal authorities and scientific data. This shows that many scholars in law and social science are interested in literature, not only as an intellectual hobby in the private time, but also as an academic theme in the research, even though it is difficult to draw an objective, final, or decisive conclusion from interpreting literary works. The question is: How can it make sense for legal and social scientists to discuss the literature in their own subject?

The academic movement of Law and Literature can be found out already in the first two decades of the 20th century in the United States. Important authors would be named here: John H. Wigmore famous for "Sources of Ancient and Primitive Law" published in 1915, and Benjamin N. Cardozo for "The Nature of the Judicial Process" in 1921. Wigmore highlighted the ancient law expressed in the epic poetry and history like as the Iliad, the Plutarch's Lives, etc., whereas Cardozo compared the legal methodology with other academic methods of philosophy, history, sociology, etc. Seen from a current point of view, the former represented "Law 'in' Literature", and the latter "Law 'as' Literature". The both were, at any rate, involved in the movement of legal realism under the influence of the Justice Oliver W. Holms Jr., in opposition to the formalism represented by Christopher C.

© Springer Fachmedien Wiesbaden GmbH, part of Springer Nature 2018
H. Kabashima et al. (Hrsg.), *The Idea of Justice in Literature*,
Wirtschaftsethik in der globalisierten Welt,
https://doi.org/10.1007/978-3-658-21996-3_1

Langdell. The general standpoint of the legal realism is the assumption that it is necessary to pay attention to the context of the law in action so as to understand the substance of the law in books. So far as for this standpoint, our project of "Justice in Literature" adopts the same approach to law, justice, and literature as the legal realism did.

However, in the second half of the 20th century, the legal realism grew in a variety of versions especially in the United States: Law and Society, Law and Psychology, Law and Economy, and Law and whatever else. This expansion of the legal realism was driven by the common ambition for shaping up legal studies on the basis of solid, empirical, positivistic, and therefore objective methodology. For legal scholars in these new fields, law is not something normative any more, but merely an object of empirical analysis, so legal studies are not a normative discipline like ethics and philosophy, but an applied science like sociology, psychology, economics, etc. It is, for example, remarkable that one of the founders of Law and Economy, Richard Posner, does not consider literature relevant to legal studies, but economic calculation determinant in legal decisions (cf. Richard Posner: "Law and Literature: A Relation Reargued", Virginia Law Review vol. 72 No. 8, 1986, pp. 1351-1392).

Opposite to this tendency toward empirical science, our project takes a clear position that the idea of justice is one of the most essential components in law and social life, so that it is almost impossible to grasp what is law and society without knowing what is the human being that the literature expresses. Therefore, we adopt rather a hermeneutic than a scientific approach to the issue of law, justice, and literature in connection with the tradition of humanism, though this might vary according to the difference between our cultural backgrounds. So the goal of our project is to gain an illuminating insight into the inherent relation between law and justice, literature and human being.

In setting this goal, we are already aware that "Justice in Literature" is one of the most complex and profound themes. For the literature tells us that it is not an easy task for the humans to construct their common life in accordance with fairness and justice because their life is filled with contingency and absurdity. Especially since the existentialism brought the issue of alienation, isolation, senselessness, abyss, etc. in the second half of the 19th century, it has become more and more difficult for individuals to live with each other in an undoubted harmony, so easier and easier to fall into an identity crisis. The crisis is not only related to the personal life of individuals, but rather to the future of our civilization as a whole, because the mankind appears to have reached a deadlock between modernity and tradition, progress and senselessness. In our current circumstances, the more the world will be globalized, the deeper will be the gap between the personal life in family and community and the functional activity in business and profession. In the situation where the system colonizes the life-world, it would be meaningful to seek for a prescription in the literature to overcome the deadlock and to create a better world to live together in the future.

In this point, our project tries not only to develop the Law and Literature movement in a hermeneutic direction, but also to revive the original form of the Law and Literature in Germany, that is the Germanics, the Brothers Grimm. Here is only to suggest that the elder Jakob and the younger Wilhelm Grimm, who both were jurists and philologists, not only worked together in collecting folklore as crystallizing German spirits, but also engaged in the liberal protest action as members of the "Göttingen Seven" against the repressive lordship in 1837, which prepared for the first liberal constitution in Germany, the "Constitution of St. Paul's Church" proclaimed in Frankfurt am Main as the result of the March Revolution in 1849. In this history, we can find out that the scholarship of Law and Literature can have a revolutionary power to change the society in conformity with the idea of justice.

Whereas the issue that the Brothers Grimm tackled was to integrate the German people into one nation under the concept of freedom, the issue in our age of globalization would be to prepare the fair and just conditions for our co-existence in a single globe. Though there are a variety of cultural groups of the authors, the East- and the West European, the North- and the South American, and the East Asian, the outcome of our project shows that the difference between individual authors is larger than that between cultural backgrounds, and that we have nevertheless a sequence of intellectual concerns in common, from respect for the tradition of humanism to reflection on the limit of modernization. Satisfied with this fruitful achievement on hand, we, the editors of this project, are fully confident that it will be worthy to keep on discussing the issue "Idea of Justice in Literature" further in another form.

**I**

**The Idea of Justice in Drama**

# Widerstand im Namen der Gerechtigkeit

Shing-I Liu

## Zusammenfassung

Das Recht ist eine Erscheinung der Kultur. Die Rechtswissenschaft kennt in ihrem Bereich die Begriffe Recht und Gerechtigkeit und bedient sich keines Ausdruckes so häufig
wie des Begriffs „Recht und Gerechtigkeit". Die Legitimität der Staatsgewalt hängt mit
Gerechtigkeit und Recht eng zusammen. In der Frage des Widerstandsrechts und seiner
Erlaubtheit spiegeln sich Verständnisse von Politik, Recht, bürgerlicher Freiheit und
Verantwortung. Sie tauchen auch oft in der Kunst und Literatur auf. In diesem Aufsatz
werde ich zwei Beispiele erläutern: den Roman „Die Räuber vom Liang-Schan-Moor"
(14. Jahrhundert) und das Drama „Wilhelm Tell" (1804).

## Schlüsselbegriffe

Gerechtigkeit, Widerstandsrecht, Legitimität der Staatsgewalt, Literatur

## 1

Das Recht ist eine Erscheinung der Kultur. Wie wir das Recht in seinen kulturellen Zusam-
menhängen verstehen, so spiegelt sich auch die Kultur einer Zeit und eines Volkes im Recht.
Die Rechtswissenschaft kennt in ihrem Bereich der Begriff des Rechts und Gerechtigkeit
und bedient sich keines Ausdruckes so häufig wie des Wortes Recht und der Gerechtigkeit. Indessen gehört dasselbe nicht bloß dem Sprachschatz der Juristen als technischer
Terminus, sondern gleichzeitig auch der Alltagssprache an und zwar in mehreren, vom
gemeinen Sprachgebrauch zweifellos gestatteten Bedeutungen, die miteinander wie mit
den juristischen einigermaßen verwandt sind.[1]

---

1   Vgl. Adamek, S. A.: Die Ideologie des Rechts. I. Ursprung und Grundlagen des Rechts. Stock-
    holm o. J., S. 26; Bergbohm, K.: Jurisprudenz und Rechtsphilosophie. 1. Band: Einleitung –

© Springer Fachmedien Wiesbaden GmbH, part of Springer Nature 2018                                    7
H. Kabashima et al. (Hrsg.), *The Idea of Justice in Literature*,
Wirtschaftsethik in der globalisierten Welt,
https://doi.org/10.1007/978-3-658-21996-3_2

Die Terminologie, wie Recht oder andere verwandte Begriffe, gibt manchmal interessante Aufschlüsse über die ursprüngliche Rechtsauffassung vieler Völker. Die Griechen hatten bei ihrer hohen Kultur und ihrer wortreichen Sprache für Sitte, für Gewohnheit, für Recht und für Gesetz nur ein einziges, gemeinsames Wort: „nomos". Sie unterschieden diese Begriffe nicht von einander, anders als in der römischen Auffassung von „lex".[2]

Die Sprache dient eben nicht bloß wissenschaftlichen Zwecken und innerhalb der Wissenschaften nicht bloß einer Wissenschaft. Wir müssen es uns also gefallen lassen, dass manche Künste und Wissenschaften reichlichen Gebrauch von unserem vielsagenden Hauptterminus machen.

## 2

Die Kunst und die Literatur können auch Gegenstand von Recht sein. Das Verhältnis von Recht und Literatur ist aber nicht einseitig. Umgekehrt kann das Recht auch Gegenstand von Literatur und Kunst sein. Die beiden stehen in wechselseitiger Beziehung.[3] Dieser Beitrag befasst sich mit dem Verhältnis von Recht und Literatur und ist interdisziplinär zwischen Rechtswissenschaft und Literaturwissenschaft angesiedelt.

In der Dichtung, im Drama und in anderer Literatur sieht man oft, dass Recht enge Verbindung zum Gerechtigkeit, Staatsgewalt und Legitimität hat. Diese Begriffe gehören dem Kernbereich der Rechtswissenschaft, bzw. Rechtsphilosophie an. Die Themen Recht, Gerechtigkeit, Staatsgewalt, Widerstand und Gehorsamspflicht sind aber nicht nur Sache der Juristen.

Recht und Gerechtigkeit sind auch oftmals zentrales Themen in der Literatur und im Sprechtheater. Bereits im antiken griechischen Theater widmet Aischylos in der „Orestie" seine Aufmerksamkeit einem sehr schwer gerecht zu entscheidenden Strafprozess, in dem Götter und Menschen über einen Muttermörder, der durch seine Tat seinen von der Mutter ermordeten Vater rächen wollte, beraten und urteilen. Im deutschen Sprachraum thematisierte Friedrich Schiller die Gerechtigkeit in vielen seiner Werke von „Die Räuber" bis zum „Wilhelm Tell", aber auch in der Ballade „Die Kraniche des Ibykus". Berühmte Musterbeispiele hat Heinrich von Kleist mit seiner Erzählung „Michael Kohlhaas" und seinem Lustspiel „Der zerbrochne Krug" gegeben.

---

1. Abhandlung: Das Naturrecht der Gegenwart. Neudr. d. Ausgabe Leipzig 1892. Glashütten im Taunus 1973, S. 43.

2   Vgl. Böckenförde, E-W.: Geschichte der Rechts- und Staatsphilosophie. Antike und Mittelalter. Tübingen 2002, S. 135; 155.

3   Vgl. Kaufmann, Arthur: Beziehungen zwischen Recht und Novellistik. in: Weber, H. (Hrsg.): Annäherungen an das Thema „Recht und Literatur". Recht, Literatur und Kunst in der Neuen Juristischen Wochenschrift (1). Baden-Baden 2002, S. 65ff.

Weder können die Dichter, noch werden die Historiker, Geschichtsphilosophen usw. voraussichtlich je uns zuliebe darauf verzichten, sich des Ausdruckes Recht außer im juristischen auch in einem „höheren", jedenfalls nichtjuristischen Sinne zu bedienen, z. B. wenn sie einen tragischen Konflikt vorführen oder die Gerechtigkeit in den Schicksalen der Völker aufzeigen wollen.[4]

## 3

In der Frage des Widerstandsrechts und seiner Erlaubtheit spiegeln sich Verständnisse von Politik, Recht, bürgerlicher Freiheit und Verantwortung. Entsprechend unterschiedlich fällt die begriffliche Fassung von Widerstandsrecht und seine normative Untermauerung aus.

Die Legitimität der Staatsgewalt hängt mit Gerechtigkeit und Recht eng zusammen. Sie tauchen auch oft in der Kunst und Literatur auf. Vor allem dem Drama, und besonders der Tragödie, hat der Widerstand gegen Autorität immer wieder Modell gestanden. Dafür lassen sich Beispiele anführen: „Antigone" von Sophokles (5. Jh. v. Chr.), „Die Räuber vom Liang-Schan-Moor" von SHI Nai-An (1296 - um 1370), „Egmont" von Johann Wolfgang Goethe (1749-1832), „Wilhelm Tell" von Friedrich von Schiller (1759-1805), „Michael Kohlhaas" von Heinrich von Kleist (1777-1811).[5]

Nach konfuzianischer Lehre ist das Recht zu regieren keine absolute Macht, sondern ist bedingt durch die Tugend des Regenten. Die tyrannische Machtausübung wird als widernatürlich empfunden, wider die Natur des Menschen betrachtet. Meng Zi (372-289 v. Chr.) ist Schüler und Anhänger des Konfuzius. Er geht von der Gutartigkeit der menschlichen Natur aus und betrachtet Menschlichkeit, Gerechtigkeit, Sittlichkeit und Weisheit als die vier Haupttugenden.

Meng Zi ist ein Vorläufer der Widerstandslehre. Einmal redet er mit dem König Xüen von Qi und spricht: „Wenn einer von Euren Untertanen Frau und Kinder der Sorge eines Freundes anvertrauen und auf Reise in ferne Lande gehen würde, und wenn er bei seiner Rückkehr finden würde, dass sein Freund die Frau und Kinder hätte frieren und hungern lassen, was sollte mit ihm geschehen?" Der König antwortet: „Er sollte verstoßen werden." Meng Zi fährt fort: „Wenn der oberste Richter nicht imstande sein würde, die ihm

---

4   Vgl. Waider, H.: Zur Lehre vom Widerstandsrecht des Volkes nach Schillers „Wilhelm Tell", in: ZStrW 80 (1968), S. 389-408; Fleisch, N. H.: Ziviler Ungehorsam oder Gibt es ein Recht auf Widerstand im schweizerischen Rechtsstaat? Grüsch 1989, S. 35; Gierke, Julius von: Widerstandsrecht und Obrigkeit. Stuttgart 1956, 9; Hesse, B.: Querulatorischer Terrorist oder Kämpfer um's Recht? – Heinrich v. Kleists „Michael Kohlhaas", NJW 2003, 621-626; Holzer, W.: Politischer Widerstand gegen die Staatsgewalt. Historische Aspekte – Problemstellungen – Forschungsperspektiven. Wien 1985, S. 38.

5   Vgl. Kaufmann, Arthur: Beziehungen zwischen Recht und Novellistik. in: Weber, H. (Hrsg.): Annäherungen an das Thema „Recht und Literatur". Recht, Literatur und Kunst in der Neuen Juristischen Wochenschrift (1). Baden-Baden 2002, S. 65.

unterstehenden Untergebenen in Ordnung zu halten, was sollte mit ihm geschehen?" „Er sollte entlassen werden", antwortet der König. Meng Zi fährt fort: „Wenn Unordnung im ganzen Lande herrschte, was solle da geschehen?" Der König blickt verlegen nach rechts und nach links und redet von etwas anderem.[6]

Als einer der Vorläufer des Widerstandsgedankens ist Meng Zi ist der Meinung, dass, wenn ein Herrscher schwere Fehler hat, nämlich wider Recht, Gerechtigkeit und Humanität handelt, ihn seine Untertanen zurechtweisen sollen. Wenn er auf wiederholte Zurechtweisungen nicht hört, so zwingen die zu seiner Sippe gehörenden Untertanen ihn zur Abdankung und ersetzen ihn durch einen anderen. In demselben Fall verlassen die nicht zu seiner Sippe gehörenden Untertanen das Land.[7]

In der abendländischen Literatur sieht man auch oft den Gedanken über den Rechtfertigungsgrund des Staates. „Was anders sind also Reiche, wenn ihnen Gerechtigkeit fehlt, als große Räuberbanden (magna latrocinia)?" so meinte Aurelius Augustinus (354-430 n. Chr.).[8] Um Staaten von großen Räuberbanden zu unterscheiden, hat das politische, juristische Denken seit frühester Zeit nach den Rechtfertigungsgründen hoheitlicher Gewalt gefragt. Legitimität ist die Rechtfertigung des Staates, seiner Herrschaftsgewalt und seiner Handlungen durch höhere Werte und Grundsätze, im Unterschied zur Legalität (formellen Gesetzmäßigkeit) und zur rein faktischen Machtausübung.

Steht den Bürgern das Recht zu, sich gegen eine Regierung, die Freiheit und Menschlichkeit verletzt, zur Wehr zu setzen, um sich ein menschenwürdiges Dasein zu erkämpfen? Diese Frage hat die Geister viele Jahrhunderte bewegt. Die Bücher zahlreicher Völker besingen die Auflehnung gegen den Tyrannen als Heldentat. Die Bibel berichtet, wie Judith den Holofernes tötete; Sophokles preist den Mut der Antigone im Kampf gegen ein gottloses Gesetz; Cicero feiert den Mord an Cäsar als die schönste Tat des römischen Volks; Seneca hält es zum Wohle des Menschengeschlechts für geboten, den entarteten Tyrannen zu beseitigen; SCHI Nai-An hat den Aufstand gegen Ungerechtigkeit des Beamten rechtfertigt; Schiller legt im „Tell" dem Stauffacher sein Bekenntnis zum Widerstand und zur Freiheit in den Mund.

Die Lehre von den Menschenrechten ist der Anschauung, dass das Recht seinen Grund nicht in dem Staate oder in äußeren Verhältnissen, sondern in dem unwandelbaren Wesen des Menschen und der Menscheit hat. Die ganze neuere politische Geschichte stellt in wesentlicher Hinsicht einen Kampf zwischen Mensch und Staat dar, in dem das Streben der Staatsgewalt vielfach dahin geht, den Menschen und Bürger als Mittel für ihre Zwecke zu verwenden, der sich seiner bewusst werdende Mensch aber sich die Aufgabe stellt, den Staat zu einer Ordnung für den Schutz und die Pflege des Rechts und der Wohlfahrt umzubilden.

Seit dem frühen Mittelalter gehörte der aus einer innigen Verschmelzung von germanischem und christlichem Rechtsdenken geborene Gedanke des Widerstandsrechtes

---

6    S. das Werk von Meng Zi, Kap. 2 (Liang Hui Wang Xia), Abs. 6, S. 13.

7    Das Werk von Meng Zi, Kap. 10 (Wang Zhang Xia), Abs. 9, S. 82 f..

8    Vgl. Adomeit, K.: Rechts- und Staatsphilosophie. Bd.I: Antike Denker über den Staat. 3.Aufl. Heidelberg 2001, S. 151.

zu den Kristallisationspunkten der Staatsphilosophie. Je größer in einer Epoche die Unterdrückung von Seiten der Staatsgewalt wurde, desto stärker musste das Gefühl des Bewusstseins des angebornen menschlichen Rechts hervortreten, und endlich den kühnen Versuch hervorrufen, auf dem Grunde der Rechte des Menschen und Bürgers, eine völlig neue Staatsordnung aufzubauen.[9]

## 4

Das Widerstandsrecht ist deutlich ausgeprägt in der nordeuropäischen Rechtsauffassung. Der Staat ist nichts anderes als die Gesamtheit seiner Glieder. Es findet der Kampf gegen Tyrannei seinen letzten und härtesten Ausdruck in der Lehre und Praxis des sogenannten Tyrannenmordes. In der abendländichen Rechtsphilosophie hat Johann von Salisbury zwischen einem „tyrannus privatus" und einem „tyrannus publicus" unterschieden. Nur letzterer, gegen welchen es kein anderes gesetzliches Mittel gibt, darf getötet werden. Die Tötung des tyrannus publicus gilt nicht als Mord im üblichen Sinne, sondern als recht und billig.[10]

Auch in der Dichtkunst wird das Thema Recht literarisch behandelt. Speziell bei Schiller, der ja der Dichter der Revolution und des Rechtsgefühles ist, kommt es mehrfach vor. Schiller ist in der Periode seines Lebens revolutionär. Wilhelm Tell ist ein legendärer Schweizer Freiheitskämpfer, der um 1300 zur Befreiung der schweizerischen Urkantone von der habsburgischen Oberhoheit beigetragen hat. Seine Geschichte spielt in der Zentralschweiz und wird auf das Jahr 1307 datiert. Seit dem 15. Jahrhundert erwähnt, wird er zu einer zentralen Identifikationsfigur verschiedener, sowohl konservativer als auch progressiver Kreise der Eidgenossenschaft. Der Dichter Friedrich Schiller verfasste in seiner späten Schaffensphase das berühmte gleichnamige Bühnenwerk.[11]

Das Drama „Wilhelm Tell" (1804) behandelt am Tellstoff die Problematik des Freiheitskampfes und des Tyrannenmordes. In Etterlins Tell-Legende lässt der habsburgische Landvogt Gessler zu Altdorf einen Hut auf eine Stange stecken und befiehlt den einheimischen Untertanen, diesen jedes Mal zu grüßen, wenn sie an ihm vorübergehen. Wilhelm Tell, ein weithin bekannter Armbrustschütze, verweigert den Gruß, und der Vogt befiehlt ihm daraufhin, einen Apfel vom Kopf seines Sohnes Walter zu schießen. Sein Kind müsse

---

9   Vgl. Ahrens, H.: Naturrecht oder Philosophie des Rechts und des Staates auf dem Grunde des ethischen Zusammenhanges von Recht und Kultur. Bd.2, Neudr. d. 6. Aufl., Wien 1871, Aalen 1968, S. 14.

10  Vgl. Spörl, J.: Gedanken zum Widerstandsrecht und Tyrannenmord im Mittelalter, in: Kaufmann, Arthur (Hrsg.): Widerstandsrecht. Darmstadt 1972, S. 100ff.; Meinhold, P.: Revolution im Namen Christi. Ein Beitrag zur Frage von Kirche und Widerstandsrecht, in: Kaufmann, Arthur (Hrsg.) a. a. O., S. 254ff..

11  Vgl. Kübl, F.: Das Rechtsgefühl. Berlin 1913, S. 94; Radbruch, G.: Gesamtausgabe, Band 9: Strafrechtsreform. Heidelberg 1992, S. 389.

andernfalls mit ihm sterben. Tell tut widerstrebend, wie ihm geheißen, und trifft den Apfel. Er wird gefragt, wozu er sich einen zweiten Pfeil genommen hat und antwortet, wenn er sein Kind getroffen hätte, wäre dieser für den Vogt bestimmt gewesen.

„Wilhelm Tell" endlich beginnt damit, dass Konrad Baumgarten den Burgvogt von Wolfenschießen mit seiner Axt erschlagen hat, weil dieser Ungebührliches von seiner Frau verlangte. Die zuhörenden Hirten, Fischer und Jäger geben Baumgarten Recht und in allen beginnt zufolge dieses Ereignisses die Idee der Empörung aufzukeimen. Tell eilt über die Berge nach Küssnacht, erwartet den Vogt in einem Hohlweg, der Hohlen Gasse, und erschiesst ihn aus sicherem Versteck mit der Armbrust und wird so zum Tyrannenmörder.[12]

Die deutsche Widerstandsbewegung steht daher unter dem Stern der Überzeugung, die Schiller seinen Werner Stauffacher aussprechen lässt:

Nein, eine Grenze hat Tyrannenmacht,
Wenn der Gedrückte nirgends Recht kann finden.
Wenn unerträglich wird die Last – greift er
Hinauf getrosten Mutes in den Himmel
Und holt herunter seine ew'gen Rechte,
Die droben hangen unveräußerlich
Und unzerbrechlich wie die Sterne selbst.[13]

In „Wilhelm Tell" erhebt das unterdrückte Recht sich gegen tyrannisches Unrecht und wird die mitreißende Gewalt der Naturrechtsidee sichtbar. Schiller schildert die Befreiung von Fremdherrschaft, deren Tyrannenmacht eine Grenze hat. Seit Ende des 19. Jahrhunderts gilt Tell als der Nationalheld der Schweiz.[14]

# 5

Das Recht zu regieren ist keine absolute Macht, sondern ist auch bedingt durch die Tugend des Regenten. Für Konfuzianer liegt die Hauptaufgabe des Herrschers darin, gemäß dem Mandat des Himmels zu regieren. Im „Buch der Urkunde" („Shu Jing") heißt es: „Der

---

12  Kübl, F., a. a. O., S. 95.
13  S. Heuss, T.: Zur 10. Wiederkehr des 20. Juli, in: Kaumann, a. a. O. Fn. 10., S. 287; Eckhardt, W./Schmidt, L.: Einführung in die Rechtswissenschaft. Heidelberg 1977, S. 18. Kaulbach, F.: Plädoyer für ein transzendental-philosophisches Programm im Kontext der gegenwärtigen Rechtsphilosophie. in: Rechtstheorie 10 (1979), S. 50.
14  Vgl. Merkel, A.: Die Lehre von der Rechtskraft, entwickelt aus dem Rechtsbegriff. Eine rechtstheoretische Unzersuchung. Leipzig 1923, S. 479; Schmidt, H. G.: Lehre vom Tyrannenmord. Ein Kapitel aus der Rechtsphilosophie. Tübingen 1901, 120; Eckhardt, W./Schmidt, L, a. a. O., Fn. 13, S. 18.

Himmel liebt das Volk, und der Herrscher muss dem Himmel gehorchen."[15] Bewahrt ein Herrscher die Tugend nicht, dann zieht der Himmel seinen Auftrag zurück.[16] Also gilt der Herrscher als Beauftragter und hat den Willen des Himmels auszuführen. In diesem Gedanken liegt der Rechtfertigungsgrund für den Widerstand gegen einen tyrannischen Herrscher. Den Untertanen steht das Recht zu, ihn vom Throne zu stoßen. Das Volk betrachtet den die Menschlichkeit und die Gerechtigkeit vergewaltigenden Herrscher als Grausamen und als Feind und nennt ihn einen Verlassenen.[17]

Der Roman „Die Räuber vom Liang-Schan-Moor"[18] (wörtlich: Die Geschichte vom Flußufer; Outlaws of the Marsh, or Water Margin) ist von SCHI Nai-An geschrieben und ist der erste traditionell-chinesische Roman, der in Kapitel unterteilt ist. Das Werk erzählt den Aufstand einer Bande von 108 Männern und Frauen, die enttäuscht durch die Ungerechtigkeiten der Behörden und ihrer eigenen Lebenserfahrung sich zusammentun, um sich selbst ihr Recht zu verschaffen.

Die Rebellenarmee wird von Song Jiang angeführt, und kämpft gegen korrupte kaiserliche Beamte und Soldaten, was den Roman bis heute zu einer zeitlos brisanten Erzählung über Umsturz, Rebellion, Korruption, Loyalität, Verrat, Freundschaft macht.[19] Als der Kaiser Song Renzong sieht, dass die Pest über die Hauptstadt hergefallen ist, schickt er zwei seiner Untertanen auf die Reise, um den göttlichen Lehrer herbeizubringen, damit dieser für die Befreiung der Stadt von der Pest bete. Als einer der Untertanen, Marshal Hong, die Inschrift „öffnen, wenn Hong hier ist" auf einer der Stelen im Saal der Unterdrückten Dämonen sieht, befiehlt er, die Stele umzustoßen und den Boden darunter umzugraben. Schwarzer Rauch zischt aus dem Untergrund, der sich in über hundert goldene Blitze verwandelt. So ereignet sich die Geburt der 108 Helden von Liang-Schan-Moor und der Roman beginnt.

Geschildert werden dabei die Motivation und das Leben der zuletzt 36 Anführer und 72 Unterführer, die in einer Bergfeste mit ca. 30.000 namenlosen Anhängern am Liang-Schan-Moor leben. In dieser Bande finden sich Verfolgte und Geächtete, Bauern, Fischer, Kaufleute, Beamte, ehemalige Offiziere, Landadelige, Mönche und auch einige Frauen sowie Räuber. Sie werden zu einer Schwurbrüderschaft. Nach vielen siegreichen Feldzügen findet sie ein tragisches Ende. Hier denkt man auch an den tragischen Helden Michael Kohlhaas von Heinrich von Kleist.

---

15  Shu Jing (Das Buch der Urkunde), Buch 4 (Zhou Shu), Kap. 28 (Tai Shi Zhong), S. 67.

16  „Das Himmelsmandat währt nicht ewig; dem Auftrag gewährt er einem, der die Tugenden hat." S. Shu Jing (Das Buch der Urkunde), Buch 3 (Shang Shu), Kap. 17 (Xien You Yi De) S. 51; s. auch Shi Jing (Das Buch der Lieder), Buch 6 (Da Ya), Kap. 24 (Wen Wang), Abs. 1 (Wen Wang), S. 119.

17  Shu Jing (Das Buch der Urkunde), Buch 4 (Zhou Shu), Kap. 29 (Tai Shi Xia), S. 68.

18  In Deutschland ist der Roman erstmals 1934 durch Franz Kuhns gekürzte Adaption „Die Räuber von Liang-Schan-Moor" bekannt geworden.

19  Vgl, Bauer, W.: China und die Hoffnung auf Glück. München 1974, S. 561.

## 6

Gehorsamspflicht und Widerstand gelten lange als Komplementärbegriffe der politischen Ordnung. Gegen verbrecherische Befehle und ungerechte Gesetze Widerstand zu leisten, wird als Gehorsam gegenüber einem höheren Recht und Anerkennung höherer Werte angesehen. Konflikte zwischen dem staatlich positiven Gesetz und der Gerechtigkeit sind vielfach literarisch bearbeitet worden. Es gibt eine starke Ähnlichkeit zwischen jener Stelle in „Wilhelm Tell", an der Schiller den Stauffacher über die „Grenze der Tyrannenmacht" sprechen lässt und einer Stelle in SHI Nai-An's „Die Räuber vom Liang-Schan-Moor".

Nach der Naturrechtslehre stehen die Menschen einander gegenüber als gleichberechtigte Individuen, deren jedes den gleichen Anspruch auf Leben und Freiheit, Sicherheit und Eigentum, oder wie die Grundrechte sonst formuliert werden, besitzt. Freiheit als Pathos kommt nicht in der Utopie vor, sondern im Naturrecht, und in Verbindung mit dem aufrechten Gang, in Verbindung mit menschlicher Würde, die durch Freiheit gewährt ist. Das gesellschaftliche Verhältnis besteht eben darin, dass diese Rechte einander gegenseitig gewährleistet werden. Jeder Mensch besitzt bestimmte Ansprüche, die unverzichtbar sind – die ewigen Rechte, die droben hängen am Himmelszelt, heißt es in Schillers „Tell" und SCHI Nai-Ans „Die Räuber vom Liang-Schan-Moor", sind unverlierbar; – und für diese Ansprüche finden sie Anerkennung. Wir sehen, dass Gerechtigkeit, Widerstand und Gehorsamspflicht ewige Hauptthemen in der Rechtswissenschaft und Literaturwissenschaft sind, auch wenn es für die Konflikte keine Patentlösung gibt.

## The Author

Der Autor ist Professor am Institut für Kriminologie, Nationale Taipei Universität, Taiwan.

# The Heads of Justice
## "ANTIGONE-ISMENE"?, "ANTIGONE and ISMENE"?, "ANTIGONE-"?, "-ISMENE"?...

Aurelio de Prada García

**Abstract**

Antigone, as one of the greatest characters in Greek Tragedy, has attracted great attention throughout history. Other characters in the homonymous tragedy by Sophocles have not attracted the same attention though. This is especially surprising in the case of Ismene, –the sister of Antigone–, who faces the same problem as her and, consequently, has the opportunity of becoming protagonist along with Antigone, changing in the process the very title of the play and even its tragic character. As a result, in the present paper we shall analyze from our praxis horizon, among all concepts of justice included in Sophocles' tragedy, only those represented by Antigone and Ismene.

**Keywords**

Antigone, Ismene, legal justice, natural justice, praxis horizon

> *"Oh my very own sister's shared, common head of Ismene."*
> Sophocles, *Antigone*

## 1    Introduction

*CREON*
*Tell me briefly—not in some lengthy speech—*
*were you aware there was a proclamation*
*forbidding what you did?*

*ANTIGONE*
*I'd heard of it.*
*How could I not? It was public knowledge.*

© Springer Fachmedien Wiesbaden GmbH, part of Springer Nature 2018
H. Kabashima et al. (Hrsg.), *The Idea of Justice in Literature*,
Wirtschaftsethik in der globalisierten Welt,
https://doi.org/10.1007/978-3-658-21996-3_3

*CREON*
*And yet you dared to break those very laws?*

*ANTIGONE*
*Yes. Zeus did not announce those laws to me.*
*And Justice living with the gods below*
*sent no such laws for men. I did not think*
*anything which you proclaimed strong enough*
*to let a mortal override the gods*
*and their unwritten and unchanging laws.*
*They're not just for today or yesterday,*
*but exist forever, and no one knows*
*where they first appeared. So I did not mean*
*to let a fear of any human will*
*lead to my punishment among the gods.*[1]

The famous dialogue between Creon, King of Thebes, and Antigone, his niece, has become one of the founding moments of Western legal thought. In fact, two different and opposite concepts of law or two different faces of justice appear here: positive and natural law. The idea represented by Creon according to which only positive law matters and has to be obeyed without any other consideration and the idea represented by Antigone, according to which, above the positive laws, there are unwritten, unchanging laws that have to be obeyed even though they do not agree with positive law. This confrontation underlies the history of Western legal thought to the present.

However, the contraposition between Antigone and Creon, between natural law and positivism is far from crystal clear but full of subtleties. It includes loads of features, even contradictory ones. In fact, we are not facing just two faces of justice because Antigone— daughter of Oedipus and Yocasta, sister of Polinices, Eteocles and Ismene- is also Creon's niece and is engaged to his son, Haemon. On the other hand, Creon is also Polinices' uncle and therefore is obliged too to fulfill the familiar duties of burying the relatives [2]. Precisely the duties Antigone appeals to when disobeying the law established by Creon.

In this context, it is not surprising that the tragedy Antigone by Sophocles has fascinated the Western mind for over two millennia, giving birth to new Antigones not only in the field of legal theory but also in literature, art, thought… It is not difficult either to predict the appearance of more new Antigones because new subtleties can be added to the original

---

1    We follow here, with some minor changes, the translation by Ian Johnston, Vancouver Island University, Nanaimo, British Columbia, Canada. We deeply thank Prof Johnston for letting us make use of his translation.

2    Vid. NUSSBAUM, M.C.: The fragility of Goodness. Luck and Ethics in Greek tragedy and Pholosophty. Cambridge University Press, 2001, p. 55.

contraposition positivism-natural law mentioned above. For instance, the contraposition between male-female, old and young, family and state…. in such a way that:

> "But these are conjectures and books as yet unwritten. All I can be certain of is this: what I have tried to say is already in need of addition. New 'Antigones' are being imagined, thought, lived now; and will be tomorrow."[3]

New 'Antigones' and therefore new "Creons", since the recreation of the character that gives title to Sophocles' tragedy requires the recreation of her main antagonist. We are talking about new "Creons" and, consequently, about new "other antagonists", because Creon is not the only antagonist of Antigone, whereas Antigone is not Creon's unique antagonist. In fact, Creon has also Haemon, -his own son engaged to Antigone-, and Tiresias, the fortune teller, as antagonists. On the other hand, Antigone has at least another antagonist besides Creon: her own sister Ismene. But, surprisingly, all these other antagonists have scarcely got the attention of later authors[4].

This lack of attention could be explained by the intensity of the conflict between Antigone and Creon or by the limited interventions of the remaining characters in the tragedy but it is especially surprising in the case of Ismene, the sister of Antigone, who faces the same problem as her.

As a result, in the following pages we are not going to analyze all the faces of justice implicated in Sophocles' tragedy but the ones represented by Antigone and Ismene. Sure enough, this analysis cannot be done in the abstract since we are part of the tragedy by reading it. Precisely, we are part of it from our own present, from our own praxis horizon as Gadamer [5] would state it and, maybe, the face of justice represented by Ismene is the closest to our own point of view, to our praxis horizon.

## 2    One or Two Protagonists?

ANTIGONE
Now, dear Ismene, my own blood sister,
do you have any sense of all the troubles
Zeus keeps bringing on the two of us,
as long as we're alive? All that misery
which stems from Oedipus? There's no suffering,

---

3   STEINER, G.: Antigones: How the Antigone legend has endured in Western literature, art and thought. Oxford University Press, New York 1985.

4   MARTÍNEZ DÍEZ; A. 'Introducción' a Sófocles Antígona, p. 9. Ediciones clásicas, Madrid 2015.p. 9.

5   GADAMER, H .G : Verdad y método, vol. I, Salamanca 1977, p. 453.

*no shame, no ruin—not one dishonour—*
*which I have not seen in all the troubles*
*you and I go through. What's this they're saying now,*
*something our general has had proclaimed*
*throughout the city? Do you know of it?*
*Have you heard? Or have you just missed the news?*
*Dishonours which better fit our enemies*
*are now being piled up on the ones we love.*

This is the way Sophocles begins his recreation of the tradition[6] in front of his contemporaries and in front of us: with a prologue in which, immediately before daybreak, Antigone
and her sister, Ismene, -to whom she has just brought outside the gates of the royal palace
in Thebes-, are speaking.

A very innovative beginning, not only because the prologue in the form of a dialogue is
an exception in Greek tragedy[7], but because it was the place usually reserved to secondary
characters[8].Now Sophocles, among the many possibilities he had[9], chooses to place in it
the two more affected characters by Creon's ban to bury the traitors to the city: Antigone
and Ismene, the only survivors of Layo's family.

The two more affected characters, we say, but neither with the same consciousness nor
with the same appreciation of the facts, nor with the same perspective. Actually, Antigone's
first words *"Oh my very own sister's shared, common head of Ismene"* [10] are not a mere
invocation but a reminder and an exhortation.

Antigone reminds Ismene that both of them have the same blood; both of them belong
to the same family and, over all, both of them are sisters with a special and unique sorority.
They are sisters between themselves and they are Oedipus' sisters too and thus they are
her mother's, -Yocasta-, granddaughters as well.

---

6    GIL, L.: Introducción cit. p. 19 y 20.

7    STEINER Antigones, cit. p 70.

8    GIL, L.: Introducción a SOFOCLES, Antígona cit. p.21.

9    GIL, L.: Introducción, cit. p. 23-24.

10   Following STEINER, G., we have to modify here the translation we are making use of: "The
     opening line consists of five words of which two, 'O', and 'Ismene' are straightforward. The other
     three have been the object of voluminous exegesis. The semidarkness in which they are spoken
     seems to cling to them. Literally -and literally always begs the question- we read something like
     this: "Oh my very own sister's shared, common head of Ismene." See: Antigones: cit. p. 208.

All this, as Antigone's words imply, would make them a common being, with a *shared, common head*[11] with the same way of thinking. Obviously, this is something that denies any trace of individuality[12].

Such a common being, such a special sorority would carry the two of them, dually[13], to suffer the same afflictions stemming from Oedipus. Antigone is really very aware of it, but she hesitates whether Ismene is conscious as well or not; whether she knows about it or not:

*... do you have any sense of all the troubles*
*Zeus keeps bringing on the two of us,*
*as long as we're alive? All that misery*
*which stems from Oedipus? There's no suffering,*
*no shame, no ruin—not one dishonour—*
*which I have not seen in all the troubles*
*you and I go through...*

But Antigone not only doubts about Ismene's knowledge as to *all that misery which stems from Oedipus*. She doubts too about Ismene's awareness regarding the immediate future waiting for the two of them. This is something evident for Antigone, as we can deduct from her famous dialogue with Creon:

*How could I not? It was public knowledge,*

but she doubts about Ismene's knowledge:

*...What's this they're saying now,*
*something our general has had proclaimed*
*throughout the city? Do you know of it?*
*Have you heard? ...*

---

11   BERNARDETE, S.: A Reading of Sophocles 'Antigone' in Interpretation: A journal of Political Philosophy. I, 1975, p. 148.

12   "Both physically and metonymically, the head of an individual is taken to incarnate him or her individuality. In the shadow-ligth before dawn, Antigone recognizes Ismene by the shape or bent of her head. To claim this head as being 'common to us both' and as 'shared in the totality of sisterhood', is to negate, radically, the most potent, the most obvious differentiation between human presences." STEINER, Antigones... cit., p 209.

13   "When Antigone invokes the afflictions which Zeus is unleashing and will unleash upon 'us both', she uses the dual. This is a grammatical marker in common colloquial use, as we know from Aristofanes, for the ending of those verbs, nouns and adjectives used only when two subjects are acting, are being designated, or are being qualified. We are unable to reproduce this particular linguistic instrument. It's nevertheless, pivotal. After Ismene's initial refuse to help bury Polyneices, Antigone will not again resort to any dual forms." STEINER, Antigones..., cit. 210.

*What's this...? Do you know of it? Have you heard?* A triple question that ends up by insinuating Ismene does not want to realize what it is going on:

*Or have you just missed the news?*

And once again without giving Ismene the very possibility of answering, Antigone states:

*Dishonors which better fit our enemies are now being piled up on the ones we love.*

With such a gradation in the questioning, we can see clearly that Antigone, -beyond the doubt about whether Ismene knows or does not know the troubles they, dually, are going through- suspects Ismene prefers not to know what is going to be. Something Ismene confirms immediately with her answer:

*ISMENE*
*I've had no word at all, Antigone,*
*nothing good or bad about our family,*
*not since we two lost both our brothers,*
*killed on the same day by a double blow.*
*And since the Argive army, just last night,*
*has gone away, I don't know any more*
*if I've been lucky or face total ruin.*

Ismene confirms so Antigone's suspicions and, at the same time, shows a completely different perspective. Although she makes allusion to the dual, common features of what is happening to them, to the two of them:

*our family,... we two lost both our brothers, killed on the same day by a double blow,*

she addresses Antigone by her name, Antigone, without any reference to a special sorority, stating in such a way her individuality; her own, -not shared-, head. An affirmation of individuality that she reinforces with her last words

*I don't know any more*
*if I've been lucky or face total ruin.*

Opposite to the dual used by Antigone[14]; opposite to the invocation of a shared head, of a common being... Ismene persistently puts forward the first person pronoun[15] and that, certainly, obliges Antigone to uncover her purposes:

*ANTIGONE*
*I know that. That's why I brought you here,*
*outside the gates, so only you can hear.*

Now we begin to "know" the purpose of the first lines of this innovative prologue. Antigone knew perfectly well that Ismene did not know what it was impossible not to know and, therefore, she brought Ismene outside the gates of the royal palace in Thebes before daybreak, in order her to know what she had to know; what, perhaps she preferred not to know; what now, despite her distrusts:

*ISMENE*
*What is it? The way you look makes it seem*
*you're thinking of some dark and gloomy news,*

she will know from Antigone's mouth:

*ANTIGONE*
*Look—what's Creon doing with our two brothers?*
*He's honouring one with a full funeral*
*and treating the other one disgracefully!*
*Eteocles, they say, has had his burial*
*according to our customary rites,*
*to win him honour with the dead below.*
*But as for Polyneices, who perished*
*so miserably, an order has gone out*
*throughout the city—that's what people say.*
*He's to have no funeral or lament,*
*but to be left unburied and unwept,*
*a sweet treasure for the birds to look at,*
*for them to feed on to their heart's content*
*That's what people say the noble Creon*
*has announced to you and me—I mean to me—*
*and now he's coming to proclaim the fact,*
*to state it clearly to those who have not heard.*

---

14   Vid., note 13.
15   STEINER, *Antigones*, cit., p. 165.

*For Creon this matter's really serious.*
*Anyone who acts against the order*
*will be stoned to death before the city.*
*Now you know, and you'll quickly demonstrate*
*whether you are nobly born, or else*
*a girl unworthy of her splendid ancestors.*

"Now you know", now Ismene knows and, apparently, she knows the implications of what she knows: she has to decide whether she is nobly born, or else a girl unworthy of her splendid ancestors. And now we know too the last meaning of these first verses of the tragedy. In a very unusual way, Sophocles starts with suggesting that the tragedy could have "two" protagonists, Antigone and Ismene, instead of just only one, Antigone.

We think of "two protagonists", Antigone and Ismene, but we are not being precise enough because we should rather consider a dual one: "Antigone-Ismene", a single being, with a shared head. Then, we should talk about a different title for the tragedy and maybe a different approach to the controversy on positive versus natural law.

In other words, we should not be considering two conflicting individual characters, two different and easily recognizable heads of justice: Antigone against Creon, natural law against positive law, but a dual one Antigone-Ismene against an individual one: Creon. In such a case, natural law would have appeared from a dual perspective-, without individuals as such, but as shared heads-, meanwhile positive law would have appeared individually, with a single head: Creon.

But Ismene does not seem very willing to accept becoming protagonist along with Antigone. She does not seem ready to assume the shared head, the common being that would include too her twin brothers: Polyneices and Eteocles[16]. She does not seem very willing to change either the title of the tragedy, its character or the original approach of the controversy positive -natural law.

Actually, as we have seen so far, she "did not know", she "missed the news", she addressed her sister by her name, Antigone, without any mention to special sorority. Though she points out the common, dual characteristics of what is happening to them, she affirms her individuality; her individual, -not shared-, head, by putting forward persistently the first person pronoun and the singular possessive and now, facing the dilemma Antigone has just put,

*Now you know, and you'll quickly demonstrate*
*whether you are nobly born, or else*
*a girl unworthy of her splendid ancestors.*

she still does not know,

---

16   STEINER, Antígones, cit., p. 164 y 165.

*ISMENE*
*O my poor sister, if that's what's happening,*
*what can I say that would be any help*
*to ease the situation or resolve it?*

what, obviously, she had to know,

*ANTIGONE*
*Think whether you will work with me in this*
*and act together.*

*ISMENE*
*In what kind of work?*
*What do you mean?*

*ANTIGONE*
*Will you with these hands*
*take up Polyneices' corpse and bury it?* [17]

Now Ismene knows and now we begin to detect the last implications of Antigone's perspective. The common being, the shared head implies shared hands too so that "with these hands", "with Antigone's hands" Ismene can take up Polyneices' corpse and bury it. But once again, Ismene rejects that special sorority, taking sides this time with Creon, for positive law:

*ISMENE*
*What? You're going to bury Polyneices,*
*when that's been made a crime for all in Thebes?*

*ANTIGONE*
*Yes. I'll do my duty to my brother—*
*and yours as well, if you're not prepared to.*
*I won't be caught betraying him.*

*ISMENE*
*You're too rash.*
*Has Creon not expressly banned that act?*

---

17   Following MARTINEZ DIEZ, A. in SÓFOCLES, Antígona cit., p. 20., we have modified the translation we are making use of. Instead of "Will you help these hands…", we translate "Will you with these hands…"

*ANTIGONE*
*Yes. But he's no right to keep me from what's mine.*

*ISMENE*
*O dear. Think, Antigone. Consider*
*how our father died, hated and disgraced,*
*when those mistakes which his own search revealed*
*forced him to turn his hand against himself*
*and stab out both his eyes. Then that woman,*
*his mother and his wife—her double role—*
*destroyed her own life in a twisted noose.*
*Then there's our own two brothers, both butchered*
*in a single day—that ill-fated pair*
*with their own hands slaughtered one another*
*and brought about their common doom.*
*Now, the two of us are left here quite alone.*
*Think how we'll die far worse than all the rest,*
*if we defy the law and move against*
*the king's decree, against his royal power.*
*We must remember that by birth we're women,*
*and, as such, we shouldn't fight with men.*
*Since those who rule are much more powerful,*
*we must obey in this and in events*
*which bring us even harsher agonies.*
*So I'll ask those underground for pardon—*
*since I'm being compelled, I will obey*
*those in control. That's what I'm forced to do.*
*It makes no sense to try to do too much.*

As we can see, although Ismene underlines the dual features of all what is happening to them, -both of them-, she does not accept the dual perspective and the lineage as the last behavior's criteria:

*whether you are nobly born, or else*
*a girl unworthy of her splendid ancestors.*

Instead of that, she calls her by her name, Antigone, without any sign of special sorority and she justifies her obedience to Creon's law by her male condition and the law of the jungle, the law of the strongest. Therefore, the question of the protagonist of the tragedy is solved: just one protagonist, Antigone.

But it is not so easy because, after hearing Ismene, Antigone says:

*ANTIGONE*
*I wouldn't urge you to. No. Not even*
*if you were keen to act. Doing this with you*
*would bring me no joy. So be what you want.*
*I'll still bury him. It would be fine to die*
*while doing that. I'll lie there with him,*
*with a man I love, pure and innocent,*
*for all my crime. My honours for the dead*
*must last much longer than for those up here.*
*I'll lie down there forever. As for you,*
*well, if you wish, you can show contempt*
*for those laws the gods all hold in honour.*

"*I wouldn't urge you to*". Antigone starts recognizing that it does not make any sense to keep pretending a dual protagonist Antigone-Ismene, since Ismene does not share the common being, the common head and defends expressly her individuality, her "I". However, Antigone realizes that Ismene's perspective could lead her, Ismene, to the opposite decision: to bury Polyneices, *if you were keen to act*, so that the tragedy could have two protagonists: Antigone and Ismene.

In other words, the protagonists could be two individual beings, Antigone and Ismene, and not a dual one, "Antigone-Ismene", with a shared head. But that possibility,—two separated heads-, conflicts with the dual perspective Antigone upholds so that she expressly rejects it

*Not even*
*if you were keen to act. Doing this with you*
*would bring me no joy. So be what you want.*

As a result, the question of the protagonist of the tragedy seems to be definitively solved. Once rejected as the dual protagonist, "Antigone-Ismene", as the double one, "Antigone and Ismene", we only have one protagonist, Antigone, who expressly accepts it: *I'll still bury him.*

But once again, it is not so easy. After all we have seen, it is compulsory to ask whether Antigone is Antigone or not. This sounds as an illogical question from our grammar, from our way of thinking; but it is absolutely coherent from Antigone's perspective; from Antigone's point of view. Taking it into account, we have to conclude that Antigone is not Antigone, but a mutilated dual being, so to speak, who has no other choice but to assume itself, very much to its regret [18], as an individual. In other words, Antigone is not Antigone but "Antigone-", the mutilated half of the dual being "Antigone-Ismene".

A mutilated half that keeps talking with her previous other half, now turned into an individual, Ismene, who tries to justify her obedience to Creon's law:

---

18   STEINER, Antigones, cit., p. 212

*ISMENE*
*I'm not disrespecting them. But I can't act*
*against the state. That's not in my nature*

*ANTIGONE*
*Let that be your excuse. I'm going now*
*to make a burial mound for my dear brother*

And who shows she is worried about "Antigone-" being punished and, therefore, advises her to keep purpose as a secret

*ISMENE*
*Oh poor Antigone, I'm so afraid for you.*

ANTIGONE
*Don't fear for me. Set your own fate in order*

ISMENE
*Make sure you don't reveal to anyone*
*what you intend. Keep it closely hidden.*
*I'll do the same.*

A piece of advice that "Antigone-"rejects in anger:

*ANTIGONE*
*No, no. Announce the fact—*
*if you don't let everybody know,*
*I'll despise your silence even more*

*ISMENE*
*Your heart is hot to do cold deeds.*

*ANTIGONE*
*But I know*
*I'll please the ones I'm duty bound to please.*

And then, finally, Ismene reveals the very reason she has to reject helping "Antigone-"with the burial of Polynices:

*ISMENE*
*Yes, if you can. But you're after something*
*which you're incapable of carrying out.*

*ANTIGONE*
*Well, when my strength is gone, then I'll give up.*

*ISMENE*
*A vain attempt should not be made at all.*
This a very famous exhortation[19] to which "Antigone-" answers asking Ismene to leave her
and her foolishness alone in such a way that she agrees:

*ANTIGONE*
*I'll hate you if you're going to talk that way.*
*And you'll rightly earn the loathing of the dead.*
*So leave me and my foolishness alone—*
*we'll get through this fearful thing. I won't suffer*
*anything as bad as a disgraceful death.*

*ISMENE*
*All right then, go, if that's what you think right.*
*But remember this—even though your mission*
*makes no sense, your friends do truly love you.*

Now, after a key prologue in which Sophocles has placed the two more affected characters
by Creon's ban to bury the traitors to the city: Antigone and Ismene, we already know that
the tragedy could have had up to four different protagonists though our grammar only
allows expressing properly three of them.

Now we know too that the controversy positivism/natural law does not appear for the
first time in the famous dialogue between Antigone and Creon, but in the dialogue between Antigone and Ismene, placed in that key prologue. The controversy does not appear
originally between the ban's author and one of the subjects obliged by it, but between two
of those subjects. Lastly, it does not appear in theory but in practice; in Antigone's natu-
ral-law proposal directed to Ismene in order to disobey Creon's ban. A proposal rejected
by Ismene who prefers to adhere to positivism:

*since I'm being compelled, I will obey*
*those in control. That's what I'm forced to do*

But it does not make any sense to keep investigating how natural law would have appeared
dually and positivism individually, because so far we have analyzed only the prologue of
the tragedy and that is not the only place in which Sophocles makes Ismene act.

---

19   STEINER, Antígones, cit., p. 212.

## 3      Two Individualities?

CREON

>                                  ... *She may be*
> *my sister's child, closer to me by blood*
> *than anyone belonging to my house*
> *who worships Zeus Herkeios in my home,*
> *but she'll not escape my harshest punishment—*
> *her sister, too, whom I accuse as well*
> *She had an equal part in all their plans*
> *to do this burial. Go summon her here.*
> *I saw her just now inside the palace,*
> *her mind out of control, some kind of fit.*
> *When people hatch their mischief in the dark*
> *their minds often convict them in advance,*
> *betraying their treachery. How I despise*
> *a person caught committing evil acts*
> *who then desires to glorify the crime*

Thus, with a double death penalty *not to escape my harshest punishment*, ends up Creon after his famous dialogue with Antigone we reproduced above[20], becoming in such a way the first representative of positivism and that not as Ismene, from the perspective of the subject obliged to obey the norm, but from the point of view of the applicator of it.

However, we are talking about a first representative of positivism that, paradoxically, assumes the natural law position implicit in the dual protagonist "Antigone-Ismene" we analyzed before. In fact, the threat is a double one –a dual one- even though Antigone is the only one who has been surprised trying to bury Polyneices.

In other words, for Creon, Antigone is not Antigone, an individual being with an only, unique head, with her own name but, literally, *my sister's child*, Yocasta's child. For Creon, Antigone is just a member of his house, a member of his family *closer to me by blood than anyone belonging to my house*. Ismene, on the other hand, to whom he has seen with *her mind out of control*, is not Ismene either. He does not mention her making use of her name, but calling her *her sister*, the sister of *my sister's child*.

For Creon, then, Antigone and Ismene are not such, individual beings, individual not shared heads, but just two sisters, daughters of the same mother. For him, "they" are a dual being, "Antigone-Ismene", with a shared head in such a way that it is perfectly coherent to punish it, -both of them-, even though only one, -only one half-, has been found disobeying the law. Actually, Creon addresses to Ismene, once she has been summoned in front of him, as one part of a dual being, as a "you" part of a "two you".

---

20   See above, Introduction

*CREON*
*You there—you snake lurking in my house,*
*sucking out my life's blood so secretly.*
*I'd no idea I was nurturing two pests,*

And thus makes Sophocles appear, for the second and last time, Ismene in the tragedy: sentenced to *Creon's harshest punishment*. But that sentence is not going to be executed without giving her the possibility of defensing herself:

*CREON*
                                    *... Come here.*
*Tell me this—do you admit you played your part*
*in this burial, or will you swear an oath*
*you had no knowledge of it?*

A possibility Ismene does not reject:

*ISMENE*
*I did it—*
*I admit it, and she'll back me up.*
*So I bear the guilt as well*

Now we realize that maybe we have not taken into account the ambiguity of Ismene's character. Got wrong by her affirmation of individuality that her refusal to disobey Creon's law implied, perhaps we did not emphasize properly the dual features of her answers to her sister's questions in the prologue: whether she knew or not, whether she was *nobly born, or else a girl unworthy of her splendid ancestors...*

Maybe we undervalued those dual features and we jumped too hasty to the conclusion that Ismene was already Ismene. The second half of the dual being "Antigone-Ismene" would have already rejected that duality turning into a complete "I", a single head able to refuse individually to bury Polineices and obeying so, in a positivistic way, to those *who rule, who are in control.*

But now her answer to Creon's question proves the opposite: her evolution, so to speak, towards individuality, towards a not-shared head, a separated "I" was not as definitive as we had concluded. The dual aspects of her personality, -if we are allowed to make use of this term-, would have reemerged with Antigone-'s attempt to bury Polyneices, putting Ismene's mind out of control and making her assume that attempt. As a result, we have to conclude now that Ismene is not Ismene anymore but "-Ismene", the second half of a previous dual being trying to restore the previous unity, the previous dual being. And for this, obviously, "-Ismene" needs the other half, needs "Antigone-".

However, the other half does not seem very willing to collaborate in the restauration of the previous dual being. Moreover, we could doubt about its very existence, about the existence of the other half "Antígone-". In fact, if Antigone-'s natural law disobedience to Creon's law has put Ismene's mind out of control until making her reject her individualistic positivistic obedience, until turning her into "-Ismena", that very disobedience seems to have put "Antigone-" in the opposite situation regarding her individuality.

Actually, her disobedience to Creon's law seems to have made her progress from the impossible individuality "Antígone-", (to which she was forced, very much to her regret, due to Ismene's refusal to disobey Creon), to a complete individuality, to an individual "I", to "Antígone". And so, she answers the Ismene's petition,

*I did it—*
*I admit it, and she'll back me up*

with these words:

*ANTIGONE*
*No, no—*
*justice will not allow you to say that.*
*You didn't want to. I didn't work with you.*

It is difficult to imagine a flatter refusal to Ismene's demand *back me up* than these words said by Antigone. In fact, there is not any reference to a special sorority, there is not any trace of a half of a dual being… and, therefore, there is no possibility of any help to restore that dual being. Instead of that we only find in Antigone's answer a persistent use of the personal, individual pronouns: *you… you… I… you*

But that flat refusal does not finish with "-Ismene's" attempt to restore the shared head, the previous dual being. On the contrary, forgetting Creon and addressing only to her "sister", "-Ismene" reiterates her demand by saying that she only pretends to respect the dead and to die with the other half of the dual being "Antigone-Ismene", with "Antigone-".

*ISMENE*
*But now you're in trouble, I'm not ashamed*
*of suffering, too, as your companion.*

*ANTIGONE*
*Hades and the dead can say who did it—*
*I don't love a friend whose love is only words.*

*ISMENE*
*You're my sister. Don't dishonour me.*
*Let me respect the dead and die with you.*

Such a demand of common death is, however, denied by Antigone

ANTIGONE
*Don't try to share my death or make a claim*
*to actions which you did not do. I'll die—*
*and that will be enough.*

A few lines above we wrote that it was difficult to imagine a flatter refusal to Ismene's demands but obviously we were wrong and really, leaving aside the use by Antigone of personal pronouns we have seen several times so far, it is impossible to imagine a flatter refusal to the demand of restoring the previous dual being "Antigone-Ismene", than these words *Don't try to share my death.*

A dual being, a shared head… lives and dies together, so to speak, in such a way that these words *my death* are the most evident proof that "Antigone-" has already turned into Antigone. She is not anymore one half of the dual being "Antigone-Ismene", nor the impossible individual "Antigone-" but she is now "Antigone", an individual being who is going to die her own death and does not allow anyone to share her individual death.

All this leads "-Ismene" to wonder what kind of life she, "- Ismene", is going to live without "Antigone-":

ISMENE
*But if you're gone,*
*what is there in life for me to love?*

An extreme complaint that is cruelly answered by Antigone:

ANTIGONE
*Ask Creon. He's the one you care about.*

And really, to propose as an alternative to the already impossible dual being, "Antígone-Is-mene", a new one, "Creon-Ismene", is hurtful until torture as "-Ismene" states, offering at the same time her help:

ISMENE
*Why hurt me like this? It doesn't help you.*

ANTIGONE
*If I am mocking you, it pains me, too.*

ISMENE
*Even now is there some way I can help?*

An individualistic offer, "I", that gives place to a final dialogue between them in which personal and possessives pronouns are the dominant ones:

*ANTIGONE*
*Save yourself. I won't envy your escape.*

*ISMENE*
*I feel so wretched leaving you to die*

*ANTIGONE*
*But you chose life—it was my choice to die.*

*ISMENE*
*But not before I'd said those words just now.*

*ANTIGONE*
*Some people may approve of how you think—*
*others will believe my judgment's good.*

*ISMENE*
*But the mistake's the same for both of us.*

*ANTIGONE*
*Be brave. You're alive. But my spirit died*
*some time ago so I might help the dead*

Thus makes Sophocles finish "-Ismene's" attempt to restore the common being, the shared head and all that before Creon, who is astonished by the struggle between his sister's two daughters. One of them tries to share death with the other one and the other one rejects that possibility.

*CREON*
*I'd say one of these girls has just revealed*
*how mad she is—the other's been that way*
*since she was born.*

This remark is answered by "-Ismene", stating once again that for her there is no life without "Antigone-"

*ISMENE*
*My lord, whatever good sense*
*people have by birth no longer stays with them*

*once their lives go wrong—it abandons them.*

CREON
*In your case, that's true, once you made your choice*
*to act in evil ways with wicked people.*

ISMENE
*How could I live alone, without her here?*

And really as, in a lucid and ambiguous moment, Creon says "Antigone-"does not exist anymore:

CREON
*Don't speak of her being here. Her life is over*

Facing this situation, "-Ismene" makes a last attempt to save "Antigone-", not the "Antigone-" half of the dual being "Antígone-Ismene", but the half of the dual being "Antigone-Haemon"; Haemon, the Creon's son, to whom Antigone was engaged. A last attempt that is rejected by Creon with the chorus leader's help:

ISMENE
*You're going to kill your own son's bride?*

CREON
*Why not? There are other fields for him to plough.*

ISMENE
*No one will make him a more loving wife*
*than she will.*

CREON
*I have no desire my son*
*should have an evil wife.*

ANTIGONE
*Dearest Haemon,*
*how your father wrongs you.*

CREON
*I've had enough of this—*
*you and your marriage.*

*ISMENE*
*You really want that?*
*You're going to take her from him?*

*CREON*
*No, not me.*
*Hades is the one who'll stop the marriage.*

CHORUS LEADER
*So she must die—that seems decided on.*

CREON
*Yes—for you and me the matter's closed.*

And so, trying unsuccessfully to be useful to "Antigone", makes Sophocles disappear definitely "-Ismene" from the scene, but not from the tragedy. In fact, he makes us reminds of her twice. The first time is immediately after the dialogue between Creon and his son Haemon who tries to save Antigone from death without getting it. Then he goes away so furious that the chorus leader warns Creon in these terms:

*CHORUS LEADER*
*My lord, Haemon left in such a hurry.*
*He's angry—in a young man at his age*
*the mind turns bitter when he's feeling hurt.*

And Creon answers

*CREON*
*Let him dream up or carry out great deeds*
*beyond the power of man, he'll not save these girls—*
*their fate is sealed.*

*He'll not save these girls*, once again we see that, for Creon, Antigone and Ismene are not Antigone and Ismene, two individual beings without a common, shared head but his sister's daughters, the two halves of the dual being "Antigone- Ismene". Although he has sentenced only Antigone, he still thinks he has sentenced the dual being. But after the chorus leader's question:

*CHORUS LEADER*
*Are you going to kill them both?*

He rectifies immediately:

*CREON*
*No—not the one whose hands are clean. You're right.*

The second and the last time Sophocles makes us remind of Ismene is really a dramatic one: Antigone's last words in the tragedy

*ANTIGONE*
*O city of my fathers*
*in this land of Thebes-*
*and my ancestral gods,*
*I am being led away.*
*No more delaying for me.*
*Look on me, you lords of Thebes,*
*the last survivor of your royal house,*
*see what I have to undergo,*
*the kind of men who do this to me,*
*for paying reverence to true piety.*

## 4    To Conclude: Ismene and Us

*The last survivor of your royal house.* Therefore, in Antigone's opinion, Ismene, the other survivor of the royal house, has disappeared completely. She has disappeared too in Sophocle's opinion because he does not mention her explicit or implicitly anymore. But, has she disappeared too in our opinion? In the opinion of complete individuals, not shared heads that, however, following Hobbes, -the father of modern natural law and modern positivism too- , have created, for our protection and defense, the State, an artificial man[21], with just

---

21  "NATURE (the art whereby God has made and governs the world) is by the art of man, as in many other things, so in this also imitated, that it can make an artificial animal. For seeing life is but a motion of limbs, the beginning whereof is in some principal part within, why may we not say that all automata (engines that move themselves by springs and wheels as does a watch) have an artificial life? For what is the heart, but a spring; and the nerves, but so many strings; and the joints, but so many wheels, giving motion to the whole body, such as was intended by the Artificer? Art goes yet further, imitating that rational and most excellent work of Nature, man. For by art is created that great LEVIATHAN called a COMMONWEALTH, or STATE (in Latin, CIVITAS), which is but an artificial man, though of greater stature and strength than the natural, for whose protection and defence it was intended;" HOBBES, TH, Leviathan, Introduction. Peguin, Classics, London, 1979, p. 81.

one head, a shared head so that we authorize all his actions and judgments, in the same manner as if they were our own[22].

Maybe not, maybe we already know that Ismene's evolution from the individualistic-positivistic rejection to disobey Creon's law, to the attempt to recover the natural law disobedience from a rebuilt dual being is closer to us than the natural law-individualistic position with which Antigone ends up. But, to discover definitively who, *Antigone-Ismene?*, *Antigone and Ismene?*, *Antigone?*, *-Ismene?* …, is closer to us is something that goes beyond our forces.

## The Author

Aurelio de Prada García is professor of philosophy of law at Rey Juan Carlos University in Madrid, Spain. Current research lines: Confucianism, glocalism, human rights, rights of nature, right to facts and post-justice. Main publications in English: *Human Rights and Rights of Nature: The individual and Pachamama* (2014), *Confucianism and Democracy: Dogs, Princes, Individuals* (2013), *Between Confucianism and Human Rights*: 君 人 *Individuals and Kings* (2012) and *Glocal justice* (2011). aurelio.deprada@urjc.es

---

22  "A State is said to be instituted when a multitude of men do agree, and covenant, everyone with everyone, that to whatsoever man, or assembly of men, shall be given by the major part the right to present the person of them all, that is to say, to be their representative; every one, as well he that voted for it as he that voted against it, shall authorize all the actions and judgments of that man, or assembly of men, in the same manner as if they were his own, to the end to live peaceably amongst themselves, and be protected against other men." HOBBES, TH, Leviathan, II, cap. XVII, cit. p. 228.

# Taming the Anger
## A Jurisprudential Reading of Two Greek Dramas

You-Da Pan

**Abstract**

In the final play of Aeschylus' trilogy "Eumenides", the court, which is established by Athena and the citizens of Athens, stopped the pursuit of Furies, and made them rested in the newly found Athens. In Aeschylus' view, the law in its beginning is to end the endless turmoil of vendetta, providing an acceptable solution for both sides. However, since Furies are "rested in" rather than "expelled from Athens", law did not exclude Fury; What the drama plot may indicate is that the Furies, being worshipped in the polis, are necessary for Justice. On the one hand, law tames anger, and on the other hand, law needs anger. In this tragedy regarding the conflict between anger and prudence, oikos and polis, father and son, law as justice is considered as a synthesis of them. But in the Aristophanes' Comedy "Wasps", law makes the conflict begin: it is the law that makes a father being in conflict with his own son, it is the law that makes his fellow juries anger. Law as synthesis ended up broken apart. Law is the end of tragedy, but the beginning of comedy. In Hegel's Phenomenology of Spirit, after the tragic conflict the legal status (Rechtszustand) appeared; but the comedy appears from the self-contradiction of it. Following these analyses, we may conclude that law needs emotion as well as reason; but emotion, tied with real human situation, i. e. oikos and polis, is bound to be untamable in legal way. The legal status is rather a conclusion of stability than its ground.

**Keywords**

Law, Reason, Emotion, Greek Drama, legal status.

In the end of May, 2015, during the writing of this paper, a tragic incident happened in Taiwan: a young man entered an elementary school and cut a school girl's throat. As the crowd surrounded police station, angrily demanding justice, the girl passed away in hospital. Until now the hatred toward murderer has transferred to the debate on death

© Springer Fachmedien Wiesbaden GmbH, part of Springer Nature 2018
H. Kabashima et al. (Hrsg.), *The Idea of Justice in Literature*,
Wirtschaftsethik in der globalisierten Welt,
https://doi.org/10.1007/978-3-658-21996-3_4

penalty.[1] Although Taiwan does not abolish capital punishment yet, and if so, it would be a long way to go; nevertheless the atmosphere now is who promote the abolishment of death penalty are responsible for this tragedy. This paper will not make any analysis to capital punishment, nor will try to make any legal, philosophical argument about it. What will I do in this paper is to see: from where comes this anger? How can it be tamed? Why this anger aims at death penalty?

In order to answer these questions, we may first look into Aeschylus' *Eumenides*, the last play of *Oresteia* trilogy. In the play, Erinyes, who aroused by Clytemnestra's accusation, chasing Orestes for his matricide into Athens. Athena set up a court with 11 Athenian citizens for this case, with Erinyes as accuser, Apollo as defender; because the votes are equal, Orestes is acquitted. After the following debate between Athena and Erinyes, Erinyes accepted her offer, giving bless rather than curse to Athens and enshrined as "Eumenides", the kindly one.

The background of this trilogy is polis in turmoil: when the play was originally performed at the Dionysian festival in Athens in 458 BC, Athens was facing perils both aboard and at home. By 459 Athens was committed to a war with Corinth, which is bound to be a war against entire Peloponnesian League under Spartan Leadership (Thuc. 1.105.1). And she is also at war in Aegina, Megara ( Thuc. 1.105.2-106 ), Cyprus, and Egypt(Thuc. 1.104). This is the year now usually called the First Peloponnesian War (Sommerstein, 1989: 28-9). In Athens, however, the fight between oligarchs and democrats continues: the democrat leader Epilates was assassinated in 461 BC after a reform of Areopagus, and few years earlier, the oligarch leader Cimon was ostracized by the democrats (Sommerstein, ibid: 26-7).

The oligarchs were encouraging Peloponnesian army invades Athens before the Long Walls completed. Though the plan was failed ( Thuc. 1.107.4, Sommerstein, ibid: 29). Athens was at crossroad of her history, from which she might go on to greatness or to ruin in the spring of 458 (Sommerstein, ibid.). There were many anxieties during those days, which are reflected and reserved in this play that can be seen between lines : 1)the Argive alliance (line 289-91, 669-73, 762-74), which at that time is established no more than 3 years, now has a origin dated back to heroic age; 2) the wars, which on line 864 were promised by Athena : "may you have external war, and plenty of it"; 3[2]) civil strife mentioned by Athena (858-66) and by Erinyes (976-87). One passage (980-3) may indicate the political murder of Epilates; 4) the Areopagus council, which at that time was in a rapid

---

1    For the news report about this incident, see "Man allegedly cuts young girl's throat", Taipei Times, Sat, May 30, 2015, available at http://www.taipeitimes.com/News/front/archives/2015/05/30/2003619485; "Eight-year-old who had throat cut dies in hospital", Taipei Times, Sun, May 31, 2015, available at http://www.taipeitimes.com/News/front/archives/2015/05/31/2003619557;" Death penalty debate revived", Taipei Times, Sun, May 31, 2015, available at http://www.taipeitimes.com/News/taiwan/archives/2015/05/31/2003619580.

2    The english translations of all greek texts are mainly based on the translation in Perseus Digital Library, which can be found at www.perseus.tufts.edu/.

change (Sommerstein, ibid: 30-1). Aeschylus, also a citizen at his time, publicly espouses one principle concerning internal affairs: the vital importance of avoiding anything that might lead to civil conflict. Whatever his private view is, the public message for Athenian people is clear: unity and victory (ibid, 32).

What Aeschylus tried to do is to show the importance of judicial role, which is to stop vendetta. But what is his method? We can discover his intention in two respects. First, there are some interesting changes in the last play of trilogy: the first two plays are mythology stories which are far away. But the last play, followed by the first two's context, explains the origins of Areopagus, now it has a heroic age origin. The tale about Orestes' trial in Athens has several versions: who is the accuser? Some say Erinyes, some say a relative of Clytemnestra; who were the judges? Some say Areopagus council itself, a human tribunal; some say a jury of gods. What was the result of the trial? The details varied in many respects (ibid, 4). So before Aeschylus, many materials can be chosen and edited for him. He choose a version with human jury, Erinyes as accusers, Apollo as a defense witness, all these details are probably new to the Athenians who are familiar with the story in 458 BC, thus this play has some Aeschylean innovations in it (ibid, 5). In this version, gods are handing over their case to a human tribunal, its significance with its political-historical background mentioned earlier, leads us to Aeschylus' support on Areopagus: even the gods have to stop by there to make the dispute among them settled.

And there is another change worth mentioning. In the first two plays of trilogy, chorus are belonged to main actors , ex. Elders of Argos, they are doing merely more than giving advice and warning, or leading the actor, helping the plot go on. However, in Eumenides, chorus is Erinyes, i.e. the main feature of whole drama. Chorus in tragedy is unique existence. They can be recognized by the alternation of song and speech, "the contrast between sung lyrics meters and spoken meters parallels to a large extent the contrast between chorus and actors" (Mastronarde, 2002: 74). The language of lyrics in tragedy is also given a superficial Doric coloring style (such as replace many "eta" with "alpha"), but of dialogue, it has a common Greek or Ionic coloring (ibid, 82-3); in short, when a tragedy performed, the actors and the chorus, through their words, rhythms, and sound, would make a quite different impression toward audience, making them felt like the chorus lives in another world.

From the distinctive feature among tragic actors and chorus, the chorus' function in tragedy is also in dispute. A romantic critic Schlegel said chorus is the "ideal spectator", offering back a lyrical and musical expression of his own emotion to spectators; while Aristotle argued that the chorus should be treated as one of the actors (Wiles, 2000: 142); despite the two opposite opinions, various theories are offered: the voice of myth, worshippers of Dionysus, the body politic, the feminized other, counter-weight to the actor (ibid., 142-4). All these theories are backed by the awkward position of chorus: sometimes they just watch and do nothing; sometimes they act, and sometimes they are trying to act. When they are not acting but watching, their function is like "ideal spectator" or only a mouthpiece of someone/something; while they are trying to act, they are more like the actor. But in general, among the existing tragedies chorus is doing little. Even in some situations that they might have chance to act to alter the plot, the real action nevertheless would not occur due to various reasons. For example, in Euripides' *Medea*, when Medea is killing her sons, the chorus (Corinthian women) is saying that they have determined to enter the house (line 1275, "Shall I enter the house? I am determined to stop the death of the children."), but the result is still unchanged, chorus did not go on stage after their determination.

The chorus' function and role in *Eumenides* is very uncommon. Among surviving Greek tragic plays, only three plays have their chorus as main character. Apart from *Eumenides*, the other two are Aeschylus' Suppliants and Euripides' *Trojan Women*. (Lexikon der Antike Welt, 1965: 582) Yet *Eumenides*' uniqueness is strengthened by the fact that it is part of the trilogy. The three plays of *Oresteia* were all performed as a trilogy on a single day in 458 B.C., just two years before Aeschylus' death (Taplin, 2003: 15). Thus the chorus' transformation, i.e. from spectator to a more active role, can be noticed by the audience during the performance on stage. The myth story in theater, the chorus as spectators, the regular remoteness set by tragedy suddenly disappears in *Eumenides*: myth has become reality, and chorus has become main character. For what reason does such a change occur? For what purpose does Aeschylus manage to arrange such transformation? These unusual features may lead us to author's intention.

In *Poetics*, Aristotle argued that while watching tragedy the audience may acquire the effect of "catharsis" (purification). The purpose of tragedy is to purify fear and pity among audience: "Those who are influenced by pity and fear, and every emotional nature, must have a like experience, and others in so far as each is susceptible to such emotions, and all are in a manner purged and their souls lightened and delighted"(1341b 32- 1342a 16). In order to acquire such an effect, one must first see through the play's plot and its arrangement. The plot aims to imitate actions arousing pity and fear, and what lies in the center of plot, according to Aristotle, is the idea of tragic hero. By watching the action of tragic hero, we may experience actual emotions without experiencing actual actions. Therefore, the type of tragic hero is central to tragic play. This tragic hero must be the intermediate kind of personage, "a man not pre-eminently virtuous and just, whose misfortune, however, is brought upon him not by vice and depravity but by some error of judgement (1453a7-10)." Tragic hero is someone better than us, but similar to us at the same time, so that what he undergoes on stage may arouse audience's emotion.

Therefore, myth story in theater is actually all about real life in polis, yet it is something distant from reality. The action of tragic hero may lead us to emotion change, thereby purifies us while watching. With this knowledge about tragedy, we can ask: what is to be purified in *Eumenides*? In order to answer this question, we must ask first: who is the tragic hero in this play? When Orestes had been acquitted, he immediately left the stage, the latter part of play has nothing to do with him; as a defendant he also has fewer lines, Apollo made most of his defense. Athena is the mediator, suffering nothing in play. The remaining option is Erinyes, i.e. the chorus.

*We can boldly interpret the chorus as the tragic hero in Eumenides.* Aeschylus purposely break up the rule that the chorus should be the spectator, rather he made them to be the main character; in doing so, chorus is dragged into the drama, what Aeschylus break is the distinction between world in drama and world outside drama. The line between theater and audience has become blurred. There are also some distinct features relevant to this observation in *Eumenides*, which also contribute to the elimination of this borderline: there are some lines, such as 566, 997, 1039, and 1047, made to speak directly to the audience, which is a unique way in tragedy. For example, line 566 spoken by Athena: "Herald, give the signal and restrain the crowd", the only crowd present in theater is the audience (Sommerstein, 1989: 34). It seems that Aeschylus made tragedy come into reality in the last play of trilogy. If so, then the role Erinyes represent is easy to understand: they are the anger of crowd. The ancient Greek geographer Pausanias thought their name (Ἐρινύς) are connected with an Arcadian usage ἐρινύω, "to be angry" (Pausanias. 8.25.6). The anger toward shocking crime, such as matricide, may lead to endless vendetta, like the restless Erinyes. But vendetta is not an option beneficial for polis, rather it must be stopped. The crime, which stirs up anger, must be handed over to an Arbitration, rather to be devoured by the anger itself.

According to Aristotle, a tragic hero's end is not due to his" villainy but to some great flaw" (Poetics, 1453a15-16), i. e. his own tragic flaw, and the end must be "from happiness to misery" (1453a15). Following this instruction, we can proceed to discover Erinyes' tragic flaw and their misfortune, so that we may get better understanding to the catharsis effect this play has. Since the end in *Eumenides* is somehow a happy ending for us in 21th century, we must look closer to find out its tragic part. The most obvious misfortune for Erinyes is their failure to revenge. First they failed to revenge on Orestes, then they failed to poison Athens, where Orestes is acquitted. All their intentions are failed. Furthermore, their act is directed to opposite direction, i. e. giving blessing rather than poisoning the place which has just denied their demand for justice. With this foreknowledge, the tragic flaw may be easier to find. The most distinct feature of Erinyes is their stubbornness. After Orestes left the stage, the two chorus songs which immediately followed by are worth mentioned (line 778-92, 808-22; 837-47, 870-80), because each pair's strophe and antistrophe are identical word for word. As Sommerstein said, "there could be no better way of indicating the stubborn resistance of the Erinyes to all persuasion." (Sommerstein, ibid: 240). Their stubbornness resisted Athena' words, however, led them to the opposite of what they have intended before. By persuasion and intimidation (ex. line 827-8, "and I alone of the gods know the keys to the house where his thunderbolt is sealed"), Athena "forced" them "willingly" to carry out her will. As we have shown, if Erinyes represent the anger of crowd, then in short, *the tragic part of this play is that only through anger natural justice can never be fulfilled in a civilized society like Athens.* The stubbornness to demand justice when terrible crime occurred ought to be failed. However, as Athena's speech shows, this anger is needed, rather to be expelled. If the anger stays, it can be good for the rest of the polis. Anger should be tamed, in order to be beneficial for the state.

Aeschylus seems to be confident in his goal to purify anger and the function of Areopagus. This is the faith that many jurists have, thus many jurists do not understand the anger when terrible crime appears to the public. But what if the catharsis fails? What if the

"Kindly ones" return to "Furies", poisoning Athens rather than blessing? In Aristophanes'
*Wasps*, it is the story that was told: a crazy father who has court-mania is held at home
by his son, triggered a series of events both absurd and ridiculous. The costume of chorus
(jurors) is like wasp with sting, being ready to sting anyone at any time. The picture of
judicial role in democratic state depicted by Aristophanes is quite the opposite. We may
also have some insights toward the same issue from this comedy.

*Wasps* can be divided into three parts: on the first part of the play, two slaves who
were ordered by Bdelykleon, the son, to guard his father, fell asleep. When they are awaked,
interpreting each other's dream, Philokleon, the crazy juror, is escaped. He even called his
colleagues (chorus) to help, after the chaos and court debate, Philokleon is under arrested.
Afterwards Bdelykleon, who cares about his father, set up a court for his father to judge: the
case is about a dog who has stolen cheese at house. For the case the son summons two
dogs as both parties in court, pots and pans as witnesses. Under the persuasive speech
by Bdelykleon, Philokleon reluctantly made the dog acquitted then fall unconscious. In
the last part, Bdelykleon decided to educate his father, bringing him to banquet and telling
him how to behave like a gentleman, by telling jokes and anecdotes. However, the education
failed. The banquet is a mess, and the play ended in Philokleon's frenzy.

Philokleon's love toward court is crazy, even erotic. Aristophanes uses many words have
sexual-content in play, applying them on law courts. In line 607-9, Philokleon said that
when he carried his fee (3 obols) home for his service as juryman in his mouth, his daughter would kiss him and fish the obols out of the mouth. The kiss was known to be highly
erotic to the Greeks (Dover, 1972: 172). The sting of wasps, according to some scholars,
is also sexual-implied, because the sting's position makes it like phallus (Reckford, 1977:
305-7). Why he is so zealous about it? It is the power that has made him high: "When my
lighting flashes, the rich and the proudest of men gasp and shit them" (line 626-7). The
pleasure is like sex organism for him when he and other jurors made those defendant
guilty, imposing harm on them. Also there is a theme about education: a son teaches his
father how to live a good life. Leo Strauss thought that the play is about a failed education
imposed by Bdelykleon: he wants to educate his father, but only partly succeed: Philokleon
has learned how to enjoy good things, but failed not to harm others. (Strauss, 1980: 134)
The more his nature is being oppressed, the more violently it rebounds.

But why do those jurors have to make others feel bad, in order to be satisfied? Unlike his
colleagues, Philokleon is wealthy enough to live a good life without payment from court,
by which most of the jurors make a living (every juror got paid 3 obols after attendance).
However the wasp-like jurors have indicated where their anger originated from: they established democracy, they have driven out the Persians, "Oh! At that time I was terrible, I
feared nothing; forth on my galleys I went in search of my foe and subjected him. Then we
never thought of rounding fine phrases, we never dreamt of calumny; it was who should
prove the strongest rower. And thus we took many a town from the Medes," (line 1091-1098);
but younger generation has stolen their efforts:"…the tribute, which the younger men
steal it."(Line 1100-1). These people are like drones without sting, staying out of trouble
and "seize on our revenues as they flow past them and devour them (line 1115-6)". In the

past those jurors threw themselves into battlefield with spear and shield, now they threw themselves into court with peddle vote. In other words, because feeling hurt, they crazily impose anger and harm on others.

The craziness of wasps resulted from a generation war between old and new, which has made the jurors turned in to beasts (κνώδαλον); κνώδαλον means the beast in a state of frenzy. Coincidentally, this word is used to describe Erinyes by Apollo, and it is the first case that this word was used in metaphorical purpose (Beta, 1999: 136). The anger pre-law is like beast uncontrollable (chorus in Eunmenides), but the anger law should tame is crawling back through democratic jury system (chorus in Wasps). Law is the end of tragedy, but the beginning of comedy. Law should eliminate dispute, but dispute is now covered with juristic robe and keeps rolling. Erinyes' anger ended up in peace, but the wasps' anger was being manipulated. By Bdelykleon's mouth Aristophanes has indicated that the jurors thought they are omnipotent, but they were actually manipulated by orators; they are sheep in ecclesia, the Athenian assembly, devoured by politician, as Sosias' dream showed (line 31-6).

Since law is considered to settle dispute, we may focus on the dispute which these two plays have depicted, and the role law plays in them. For Hegel, in an ethical community lie two different laws: the law of gods and the laws of men, the latter is represented by the law imposed by polis (state), and the former is natural law, its domain is oikos (family). After these two laws being in conflict with each other, as the plot in Sophocles' *Antigone* has shown, something new has emerged: legal status (Rechtszustand). Legal status is the stage of spirit that "the universal being ... split up in to a mere multiplicity of individuals, this lifeless Spirit is an equality, in which all count the same, i. e. as persons (Hegel, 1977: 290)". In legal status, the real struggle within ethical substance is replaced by "multitude of separate atoms (ibid: 289)". Law is a necessary immediacy for nature and its opposite, after the ruin of ethical substance. And also in his reading on *Eumenides*, the function of law is similar: law mediates the force of state, represented by Apollo, and the force of family, represented by Erinnyes. (Hegel, 1986: 495-6). Following this way of reading Eunmenides, law in play is a neutral arbitrator between oikos and polis, which have dispute against each other.

It is the story tragedy has told, yet the comedy tells a different story. We can take a look on the *Wasps'* two agons (debate or contest scene of old comedy). The first agon(334-402)[3] is a debate between Philokleon and his son. The than what they argue is that the role of jurors. Philokleon is on their side, but as the law demands neutrality as arbitrator, his juror colleagues betray him, rendered a judgment favored his son. In this way the jurors, embodiment of democratic legal system, betray the idea of law in order to fulfill the

---

3    Line 334-402, according MacDowell, is not an agon, although it has some features and elements; while Gelzer considered it as an agon. See MacDowell, 1971: 179. Since this paper does not focus on the formal structure, which is philologist's work, but on the content that matters for the topic we have discussed. Nevertheless it is a debate scene. So I consider it as an agon in broader meaning.

idea of law. Before first agon the jurors accuse Bdelykleon of being the enemy against democracy, for he hindered his father doing his duty. Since the law is imposed by state, it is easy to accuse the one who disobeys law as the traitor of state. These two are connected together, hardly being neutral. Therefore, the neutrality of law in fact is mocked by two respects: it is swaying indecisive between two views, even one of which could be law's own view; it is the creation of state, thus hardly remains neutral toward its creator. The second agon(526–630 & 631–724) is something more absurd. The dispute is created by the son to please his father. Law is creating dispute rather than solving it. Just as Hegel's view, comedy lacks the true struggle against fate or other, rather his opponent is imagined by himself (Hegel, 1986: 498).Law is against law, and creates more unreal strife by itself. It is like the random collision of atoms.

After the analysis of both dramas, we may return to the questions in the beginning. What makes the crowd anger is the demand of natural justice, or more specifically, the demand of retributive justice. Yet the demand can never be fulfilled under a state with legal system, so *Eumenides* is a tragedy in this way. It is also the reason why there are so many super-hero comics and movies, in novels people can fulfill their fantasy desire to natural justice. And for many people, death penalty is the sacred cow for ultimate retribution, abolishment of death penalty is like closing the door to natural justice, even though in reality death penalty could have many problem both in execution and in its own legitimacy. As for the jurists who are discussing this event, they may just like the plot in *Wasps,* making their own straw man, in fact it is the public grief that must be dealt with. Nussbaum in her recent book *"Political Emotion: Why Love Matters for Justice (2013)"* has indicated that tragedy focuses on the vulnerability of man, making audience feel compassion (Nussbaum, 2013: 261-266); comedy makes them accept their fragility (ibid, 272-275). When Athenians watch Eumenides, they knew the limits of anger; when they watch Wasps, they knew the anger is funny. Both in opposite ways purify the emotions and benefit public life. In reading these two dramas, we may have known that although we have created legal system in the price of tragedy, but it can function like a comedy occasionally. The analysis of Greek comedy and tragedy, as Nussbaum put it, is beneficial for us in modern days because "Large modern nations cannot precisely replicate the dramatic festivals of ancient Athens, but they can try to understand their political role and find their own analogues- using political rhetoric, publicly sponsored visual art... (Nussbaum, ibid: 261)." And it is also the conclusion of this paper.

# Reference

ANDERSON, CARL (hrsg). Lexikon der alten Welt. Zürich: Artemis Verlag, 1965.
DOVER, KENNETH JAMES. Aristophanic Comedy. Berkeley: University of California Press, 1972.
HEGEL, G. W. F. Phenomenology of Spirit. Translated by A. V. Miller. Oxford: Oxford University Press, 1977.
HEGEL, G. W. F. Werke 2, Jenaer Schriften 1801-1807. Frankfurt am Main: Suhrkamp Verlag, 1986.
KASSEL, RUDOLFUS. Aristoteles De arte poetica liber. Oxford: Clarendon Press 1965.
MACDOWELL, DOUGLAS M. Aristophanes Wasps. Edited with Introduction and Commentary. Oxford: Clarendon Press 1971.
MASTRONARDE, DONALD J. Euripides Medea. Edited with Introduction and Commentary. New York: Cambridge University Press, 2002.
NUSSBAUM, MARTHA. Political Emotion: Why Love Matters for Justice. Cambridge; Harvard University Press, 2013.
RECKFORD, KENNETH J. *Catharsis and Dream-Interpretation in Aristophanes' Wasps*, Transactions of the American Philological Association Vol. 107 (1977), 283-312.
SOMMERSTEIN, ALAN H.. Aeschylus Eumenides. Edited with Introduction and Commentary. New York : Cambridge University Press, 1989.
STRAUSS, LEO. Socrates and Aristophanes. Chicago: University of Chicago Press, 1980.
TAPLIN, OLIVER. Greek Tragedy in Action. London: Routledge.
WILES, DAVID. Greek Theatre Performance: An Introduction. New York: Cambridge University Press, 2000.

# The Author

**You-Da Pan**, PhD Student at Faculty of Law, National Taiwan University, Taiwan.

**II**

**The Idea of Justice in Narrative Literature**

# Democracy, Law, Judges and Solitude
## Some Reflections from Walden and the Lake Isle of Innisfree

Donald Bello Hutt

**Abstract**

The paper reflects upon Henry David Thoreau's *Walden; or, Life in the Woods* and W.B. *Yeats' The Lake Isle of Inisfree*. It aims at suggesting that the image of solitude and insulation pervading both works of literature functions as a good metaphor for the paradigm of judicial reasoning which is dominant among legal scholars, particularly among those who champion a prominent role of the judiciary in the interpretation of constitutional norms, as well as a control exercised by judges on other branches of government. This last assertion works as a methodological constraint for the paper, as I shall only be concerned with the way in which judges perform their duties in polities where judicial supremacy is the norm, i.e., where judges hold the final word in the interpretation of a constitution.

**Keywords**

Judicial Review, Judicial Supremacy, Solitude, Yeats, Thoreau, Democracy

This paper focuses on a question familiar to most legal theorists who engage with political theory or political philosophy. The question is basically one about the reasons one could provide to justify an institutional practice which places a great amount of power in the judiciary, giving it the faculty of what champions of popular constitutionalism have referred to as "having the final word" in constitutional interpretation (Tushnet, 1999; Kramer, 2004; 2004; 2007; Donnelly, 2012).

This political problem must be analytically specified by distinguishing two different phenomena raised by the question of "the final word". The first of these categories is traditionally known as *judicial review* of legislation, which in the words of Keith Whittington "refers to the authority of a court, in the context of deciding a particular case, to refuse to give force to an act of another governmental institution on the grounds that such an act is

© Springer Fachmedien Wiesbaden GmbH, part of Springer Nature 2018    49
H. Kabashima et al. (Hrsg.), *The Idea of Justice in Literature*,
Wirtschaftsethik in der globalisierten Welt,
https://doi.org/10.1007/978-3-658-21996-3_5

contrary to the requirements of the Constitution" (Whittington, 2007, p. 7). The doctrine of judicial review was most famously depicted by John Marshall in his 1803 decision *Marbury vs Madison* where he claimed that

> It is emphatically the province and duty of the judicial department to say what the law is. Those who apply the rule to particular cases, must of necessity expound and interpret that rule. If two laws conflict with each other, the court must decide on the operation of each.
> So if a law be in opposition to the constitution; if both the law and the constitution apply to a particular case, so that the court must either decide that case conformably to the law, disregarding the constitution; or conformably to the constitution, disregarding the law; the court must determine which of these conflicting rules governs the case. This is of the essence of judicial duty.
> If, then, the courts are to regard the constitution, and the constitution is superior to any ordinary act of the legislature, the constitution, and not such ordinary act, must govern the case to which they may both apply.[1]

The notion is quite clear, and it puts emphasis on the idea that the judiciary—just as any other institution—is bound by the constitution and, to the extent that there is a normative conflict between legal sources, that it is the one with the highest hierarchy must prevail, in this case, the constitution. Not doing so would imply, in Marshall's own words, that "written constitutions [be] absurd attempts on the part of the people to limit a power in its own nature illimitable".

However, this thesis does not imply in itself granting judges a privileged role or position with respect to other organs of the state, at least not in the way the doctrine of judicial review has pervaded political practice thorough the 20th century, which is closer to a second concept or model, labeled as *judicial supremacy*. The difference was already clear to Thomas Jefferson who in a letter to Spencer Roane noticed that his understanding of the institutional dialogue as framed by the constitution was one in which

> each department is truly independent of the others, and has an equal right to decide for itself what is the meaning of the constitution in the cases submitted to its action; and especially , where it is to act ultimately and without appeal. (1819; 2008, pp. 134-135)

In the same vein, Madison begged to know

> upon what principle it can be contented that any one department draws from the constitution greater powers than another, in marking out the limits of the powers of the several departments. The constitution is the charter of the people to the government; it specifies certain powers as absolutely granted, and marks out the departments to exercise them. If the constitutional boundary of either be brought into question, I do not see that any one of

---

1    Likewise, Hamilton, 1948, p. 398.

these independent departments has more right than another to declare their sentiments on that point (Madison, 1789).[2]

These contentions by both *framers* suggest that judicial review should be distinguished from the different category of *judicial supremacy*. In such model courts' decisions do not limit themselves to settle a specific case, but also that the meaning they give to the constitutional provisions they apply to decide binds other political agents authoritatively towards the future (Hirschl, 2004). The theory 'culminates in the extreme position that (a) there is no constitutional problem that cannot be solved by the courts and (b) no constitutional problem is truly solved until is solved by a court' (Tomkins, 2010, p. 3).

Two different elements of both accounts are important: one *intrinsic* to judicial decision-making, and another *extrinsic,* and both have to do with the effects of the judicial decision. The intrinsic element of the decision relates to its *inter pares* effects, that is, to the fact that the decision generates rights and obligations for the litigants in a concrete case and for no one else, for a judge could refuse to give force to (say) an act of the legislature because she considered it unconstitutional in that specific case. Judicial review does not exclude this possibility. However in a model of judicial supremacy, judicial decisions include an extrinsic feature, in the sense that they generate obligations for other institutions which are not derived from the concrete case at hand, — e. g. "the court finds this person to be guilty", or "the court considers this contract to be void", etc. — but from abstract and general considerations regarding the *meaning* of constitutional clauses and from the *reasoning* employed by the court — e. g. "the clause of the constitution that guarantees the protection of the right to life does not include a permission to congress to ban abortion" —. This extrinsic element explains the position of courts in the interpretation of the constitution. Thus defined, judicial supremacy involves the determination of constitutional meaning together with the imposition of obligations on other governmental agents and citizens, resulting from that interpretive process.

Now, provided that there are different arguments in favour and against judicial review and judicial supremacy, in this paper I will sidestep a general overview of those arguments and instead focus on one of them, to wit, the contention that judicial supremacy is a desirable thing given the judiciary's insulation from politics—call this, the *insulation argument*. To do so, I will rely on two literary works, namely W.B. Yeat's *The Lake Isle of Inisfree* and H.D. Thoreau's *Walden; or, Life in the Woods*, in order to asses why these author's eagerness of being isolated from the world in order to reach knowledge, cannot be transported into the political and legal domain. In a nutshell, my claim is that in law as well as in politics, the kind of knowledge needed to solve the problems raised within the core of those disciplines, cannot and should not arise in insulation.

In its traditional form, the insulation argument is linked to the principle of the independence of the judiciary. It highlights the value of isolating courts from electoral pressure.

---

2    The same idea is reaffirmed in Helvidius I (August 24, 1793) JAMES MADISON, REPÚBLICA Y LIBERTAD 119-129 [Liberty and Republic], (Jaime Muñiz ed., 2005).

Hamilton underscored this in the *Federalist 78* when he claimed that if the courts are to be deemed "the bulwarks of a limited constitution against legislative encroachments", it follows that the an independent judiciary is "requisite to guard the constitution and the rights of individuals, from the effects of those ill-humours which [may] occasion dangerous innovations in the government an serious oppression of the minor party in the community" (1948, p. 400).

The insulation argument rests on the hope that this seclusion "helps generate better outcomes than would a system of legislative supremacy" (Doherty & Pevnick, 2013, p. 1). It entails that it is preferable that some decisions be made in a judicial venue because it can help better protect rights and ease distortions in the democratic process (Doherty & Pevnick, 2013, p. 2). That is to say, roughly, that the kind of knowledge necessary to decide cases of constitutional salience, where rights and liberties are involved, is not of the kind that the judiciary, because of its insulation, is able to produce. The argument needs to meet two sort of requisites in order to reach that constitutional or essential knowledge: first, it needs individuals who are willing and able to live in that isolated setting and, second, it needs the existence of the proper institutional conditions where insulation can produce those outcomes we consider to be fundamental. The consequence, once such conditions are met, is that we will be in the presence of an epistemically competent subject, fit for making decisions about constitutional essentials, placed in a higher stage with regard to other bodies of government, a sort of institutional *Inisfree* or *Walden Pond*. Let's recall Yeat's poem:

> I will arise and go now, and go to Innisfree,
> And a small cabin build there, of clay and wattles made:
> Nine bean-rows will I have there, a hive for the honey-bee;
> And live alone in the bee-loud glade.
>
> And I shall have some peace there, for peace comes dropping slow,
> Dropping from the veils of the morning to where the cricket sings;
> There midnight's all a glimmer, and noon a purple glow,
> And evening full of the linnet's wings.
>
> I will arise and go now, for always night and day
> I hear lake water lapping with low sounds by the shore;
> While I stand on the roadway, or on the pavements grey,
> I hear it in the deep heart's core.

The very first line assumes that there is an ascension from the ordinary world towards a higher place, which Yeats envisions as the lake isle of Inisfree. For what he does when he imagines himself living in that place is *arising*, moving from an ordinary setting, i. e., the city, where noise, tumults, vain and trivial talk that impede a person from reaching philosophical and aesthetical knowledge, to one where that knowledge is possible to be attained. Indeed, Yeat's desire to move from the city to the country side, where the lake isle of Inisfree is located, is a sign of ascending to a morally and epistemically superior place—"I will arise and go now and go to Inisfree"—after which he proceeds to build those epistemic conditions—"*and* a small cabin build there, of clay and wattles made — nine bean-rows will I have there, a hive for the honey bee — and live alone in the bee loud glade". The insulation provoked by the solitude longed by Yeats puts him in a position where no noises are heared but those of what's essential for a life of contemplation.

Let's move now to the main influence Yeats had when he wrote this poem, namely Thoreau's *Walden*. In this work, he also praised the advantages of living in this sort of setting, in a place where contemplation and (relative) insulation from the city where possible:

> Let us consider for a moment what most of the trouble and anxiety which I have referred to is about, and how much it is necessary that we be troubled, or, at least, careful. It would be of some advantage to live a primitive and frontier life, though in the midst of an outward civilization, if only to learn what are the gross necessaries of life and what methods have been taken to obtain them; or even to look over the old day-books of the merchants, to see what it was that men most commonly bought at the stores, what they stored, that is, what are the grossest groceries. For the improvement of ages have had but little influence on the essential law of man's existence; as our skeletons, probably, are not to be distinguished from those of out ancestors (Thoreau, 1995, p. 7).

I think there are good reasons to identify this sort of reasoning with the way we usually envision the work of judges, even more especially in a setting where judicial supremacy is the norm, which takes judges to be the embodiment of the ideal procedural and deliberative conditions for making decisions involving pervasive constitutional disagreements and that, conversely, holds a discredited image of legislatures (Rawls, 1996, pp. 231-240; Habermas, 1996, pp. 240-224; Eisgruber, 2001, p. 171). Jeremy Waldron famously dedicated a book to make this claim explicit:

> People have become convinced that there is something disreputable about a system in which an elected legislature, dominated by political parties and making its decisions on the basis of majority-rule, has the final word on matters of right and principle. It seems that such forum is thought unworthy of the gravest and most serious issues of human rights that a modern society conforms. The thought seems to be that the courts, with their wigs and ceremonies, their leather-bound volumes, and their relative insulation from party politics, are a more appropriate place for resolving matters of this character (1999, p. 5).

Now compare Waldron's statement with Dworkin's claim in what follows:

> We have an institution that calls some issues from the battleground of power politics to the forum of principle. It holds out the promise that the deepest, most fundamental conflicts between individual and society will once, someplace, finally become questions of justice. I do no call this religion or prophesy. I call it law (1981, p. 518).

Champions of the insulation argument would say that there is an additional feature of this argument which is of benefit for democratic government. They would claim that the exercise of strong judicial review can correct distortions in the democratic process. Ely famously made an analogous argument in *Democracy and Distrust*. There, he claimed that the function of the US Supreme Court is to police the processes of representation and exercise its reviewing powers when the political process excluded discrete and insular minorities, echoing the wording of the also famous footnote four of Justice Stone's *Carolene Products* decision (1980, pp. 77-78) . According to this feature of the insulation argument, judges would police the democratic process in order to avoid the discrimination of those minorities during the process of decision making, deciding without pressure from electoral politics, which was what originated the problem in the first place. Examples include legislation related to term limits, campaign finance and gerrymandering (Doherty & Pevnick, 2013, p. 2).

The key claim of the insulation argument is that there are reasons "grounded in the ideals of individual rights and democratic governance—that speak in favour of having certain kinds of policy decisions made in an environment in which actors are immersed in a legal framework and to some degree insulated from electoral pressure" (Doherty & Pevnick, 2013, p. 3).

There is, perhaps, some truth in these remarks. It may be the case that these admittedly important decisions require a deeper level of reflection, time to discuss them, willingness to hear others and—although this is more arguable—a certain level of expertise which would aid the decision maker to adopt those delicate rulings. It requires, the insulation argument goes, some peace and time to perform this duty, which explains why we have come up with an image of the judiciary as "the forum of principles" (Dworkin, 1981), as scepters of reason (Hamilton, 1948, p. 284) and the like. Legislatures and citizenries are far from living up to this ideal, as the notions we have created of them are "pervaded by imagery that presents ordinary legislative activity as deal-making, horse trading, log-rolling, interest-pandering, and pork-barreling—as anything, indeed, except principled political decision making" (Waldron, 1999, p. 2). Insulation thus provides us the possibility to cope with those deliberative vices.

Living in a small cabin, of clay and wattles made, where one shall have a peace that does not come fast through checkerboard legislation, but slow, dropping from the veils of the tranquil court-room from where reason speaks, a place where the adjudicator arises and lives unaware of the noisy world of politics; where he (yes, usually he) stands afar from those mundane things, hearing in his deep heart's core, the enlightened reasoning of constitutional thinking. This is the aesthetical model that here seems to be followed.

My claim is that the analogy fails precisely because the insulation argument neglects one fundamental trait of democratic government: that democratic decisions are collective decisions, and such sphere of decisions should be distinguished from individual decisions and personal choices which are not binding on others. In short, the realm of democracy is the realm of collective decisions (Beetham, 1999, p. 4).

The fact that judicial decisions in contexts of judicial supremacy affect large groups of individuals jeopardizes the insulation argument. Both Thoreau and Yeats wanted to achieve a sort of knowledge that affects no one but them, not other individuals. Likewise, in their isolation, courts loose sight of certain elements of moral discourse for the sake of respecting features that are internal to the practice of law. Put another way, the higher one goes in the hierarchical structure of judicial procedures, the more judges distract themselves from the parties affected by a certain case. Highr courts, supreme courts, or constitutional courts, when placed in a position of judicial supremacy, find themselves in a position regarding their audiences which is in tension with their functional orientation towards individual cases. On the one hand, they need to decide and settle a dispute between two individual parties. On the other, judicial suprecist schemes force courts to take into account the systemic effects of their decisions. This requires a standoff from the specific process that ingnited the decision in the first place. Higher courts then become interpreters of constitutional provisions whose linguisitc indeterminacy and normative abstraction have thin conversational context, for "constitutions do not form part of an ordinary conversation between parties sharing a great deal of background knowledge" (Marmor, 2014, p. 149).

In the constitutional context, where the effects of a decision extend beyond those who are parties at one specific trial, courts leave their isolation, come back to the world, and abandon Walden pond, as it were. Decisions cease being a matter of private conversation, solvable through the private language of law, and become of the interest of many other agents affected by the court's decision. No more isolation is permissible in that context.

What follows from the recognition that courts need to leave their insulation when cases reach higher courts? In a context of judicial supremacy, two alternatives comes to mind. First, the rejection of the idea of judicial supremacy as such. This would lead researchers to think of ways in which instituional dialogue can be reframed, so that courts no longer have the final word in constitutional interpretation. Settlement would then be provided by a different institution. Second, to the extent that our empirical research tells us that the rule of law is better secured when embodied in the courtroom, we should drop the insulation argument. As I have argued, the context in which courts decide at the constitutional level puts them in a position of deciding with little conversational context, in the abstract and with reference to an array of indviduals who shall become recipients of the their decisions. Granting this power is incompatible with a rather naïve view that sees courts as impervious to politics. More importantly, should we take this second path, we should be willing to accept a loss in democracy.

## Coda

By employing a metaphor, I have attempted to show that the insulation of courts from the political process is a desideratum pervading a good number of scholarly accounts. I have also provided reasons to reject such argument when the exercise of judicial powers is made against other branches of government or against *the people themselves,* to use Madison's wording.

I believe the metaphor is a plausible and correct one. It clearly relates in aesthectic terms the virtues that legal and political theorists see in courts with the idea that knowledge is reached away from social and political presures, without hearing others. There are good reasons to challenge this view, which are not exclusevily limited to the philosophy of aesthetics or to literature. Law, as Dworkin himself argued, can be read in literary terms, that is true. What I claim, however, is that judges are not the only readers and writers of the chain-novel of law that he thinks represents the best way to understand our legal and political systems in terms of constitutional interpretation (1982).

The idea of living on the edge of the world of politics, isolated from society, safeguarding fundamental values and reaching the ideally best moral answers to hard cases is, I have suggested, a flawed conception of how justice should be distributed in a contemporary democracy. In *Walden* and in *The Lake Isle of Inisfree*, wisdom is achieved via running away from the world of others, escaping from society. Thus conceived, this process, if arguably adequate for aesthetic reflection, distorts the kind of justice imparted in a judicial setting insofar as such an account of justice implies not only wisdom of a specific kind, but knowledge of, and concern for others. Accordingly, political wisdom and political justice are better achieved in a democratic deliberative setting.

Admittedly, these lines are insufficient to cover the whole debate brought about by judicial review, judicial supremacy, the relationship of courts with other branches of the state and so forth. I am not suggesting otherwise. What I do suggest is that this is a helpful metaphorical way of understanding those categories. More research is, nonetheless, necessary to explore them in their entirety.

### References

Alexy, R. (2005). Balancing, constitutional review, and representation. *International Journal of Constitutional Law, 3*(4), 572-581. doi:10.1093/icon/moi040

Alexy, R. (2014). Constitutional Rights and Proportionality. *Revus, 22*, 51-65. doi:10.4000/revus.2783

Beetham, D. (1999). Defining and Justifying Democracy. In D. Beetham, *Democracy and Human Rights* (pp. 1-29). Polity Press.

Doherty, K., & Pevnick, R. (2013). Are There Good Procedural Objections to Judicial Review? *The Journal of Politics*, 1-12. doi:10.1017/S0022381613001084

Donnelly, T. (2012). Making Popular Constitutionalism Work. *Wisconsin Law Review, 2012*, 159-194.

Dworkin, R. (1981). The Forum of Principle. *New York University Law Review*(56), 469-518.

Dworkin, R. (1982). Law as Interpretation. *Critical Inquiry, 9*(1), 179-200.

Eisgruber, C. (2001). *Constitutional Self-Government*. Cambridge, Massachusetts & London: Harvard University Press.

Ely, J. (1980). *Democracy and Distrust. A Theory of Judicial Review*. Cambridge, Massachusetts and London, England: Harvard University Press.

Ferejohn, J., & Pasquino, P. (2002). Constitutional Courts as Deliberative Institutions: Towards an Institutional Theory of Constitutional Justice. In W. Sadurski (Ed.), *Constitutional Justice: East and West* (pp. 21-36). The Hague: Kluwer Law International.

Fish, S. (1982). Working on the Chain Gang: Interpretation in The Law and in Literary Criticism. *Critical Inquiry, 9*(1), 201-216.

Habermas, J. (1996). *Between Facts and Norms: Contributions to a Discourse Theory of Law and Democracy.* (W. Rehg, Trans.) Cambridge, Massachusetts: M.I.T. Press.

Hamilton, A. (1948). The Federalist LXXXIII. In *The Federalist, or The New Constitution* (pp. 424-436). Oxford: Basil Blackwell.

Hirschl, R. (2004). *Towards Juristocracy. The Origins and Consequences of the New Constitutionalism.* Harvard University Press.

Jefferson, T. (1819, September 6). *Letter to Spencer Roane.* Retrieved from Electronic resources from the University of Chicago Press Book Division: http://press-pubs.uchicago.edu/founders/documents/a1_8_18s16.html

Jefferson, T. (2008). *The Essential Jefferson.* (J. Dewey, Ed.) Mineola, New York.

Kramer, L. (2004). Popular Constitutionalism circa 2004. *California Law Review, 92,* 959-1012.

Kramer, L. (2004). *The People Themselves. Popular Constitutionalism and Judicial Review.* New York: Oxford University Press.

Kramer, L. (2007). "The Interest of the Man": James Madison, Popular Constitutionalism, and the Theory of Deliberative Democracy. *Valparaiso Law Review, 41*(2), 697-754.

Madison, P. o. (1789). *Speech to the House of Representatives on the Removal Power of the President.*

Marmor, A. (2014). *The Language of Law.* Oxford: Oxford University Press.

Muñiz, J. (2005). Estudio preliminar. República y libertad en el pensamiento político de James Madison. In J. Madison, & J. Muñiz (Ed.), *República y libertad* (J. Muñiz, Trans., pp. XI- LIII). Madrid: Centro de estudios políticos y constitucionales.

Rawls, J. (1996). *Political Liberalism.* New York: Columbia University Press.

Thoreau, H. D. (1995). *Walden; or, Life in the Woods.* New York: Dover Publications.

Tomkins, A. (2010). The Role of the Courts in the Political Constitution. *University of Toronto Law Journal, 60,* 1-22.

Tushnet, M. (1999). *Taking the Constitution Away from the Courts.* Princeton: Princeton University Press.

Waldron, J. (1999). *The Dignity of Legislation.* Cambridge: Cambridge University Press.

Whittington, K. (2007). *Political foundations of Judicial Supremacy. The Presidency, the Supreme Cout, and Constitutional Leadership in U.S. History.* Princeton: Princeton University Press.

Zurn, C. (2007). *Deliberative Democracy and The Institutions of Judicial Review.* Cambridge: Cambridge University Press.

## The Author

**Donald Bello Hutt,** Doctor in Philosophy, Universidad de Valladolid, Spain; PhD (c) in Politics, King's College London. I thank Nuria López for her comments on earlier versions of this paper. I also thank Aurelio de Prada and the rest of the participants of the Special Workshop on "The Idea of Justice in Literature"—2015 IVR Conference in Washington D.C.

# The Idea of the Honest Businessman in Literature

Christoph Luetge

**Abstract**

The idea of the honest businessman is a very old one in the European tradition. Its roots go back to medieval Northern Europe and Italy. This idea has also been taken up in literature: prominent writers have included depictions, analysis and criticism of the honest businessman in their works, such as Thomas Mann („Buddenbrooks", "Joseph the Provider"), Goethe ("Wilhelm Meister") and others. Some of these depictions are presented, along with a discussion of the concept's relevance for today's globalized economy.

**Keywords**

business ethics, honest businessman

## 1    The Concept of the Honest Businessman

One of the oldest concepts of business ethics is the concept of the honest businessman. It has a long history, especially (but not exclusively) in Europe: its roots go back to the times of the Hanseatic League and to medieval Northern Italy. Handbooks and guides for business people taught the idea of keeping to certain values in the business world as early as the 12th century. One example of this is the still existing "Versammlung eines Ehrbaren Kaufmanns zu Hamburg" (Association of an honest businessman in Hamburg), which goes back to the 16th and 17th century, but was re-established in 1955.

Comparable concepts or ideals existed in other, non-European countries, such as Japan (Shibusawa 1916, cf. Shimazu 2017) and China (cf. Chun 2012).

The concept of the honest businessman belongs to the tradition of virtue ethics. In this (neo-) Aristotelian tradition, certain virtues are identified as being of positive value both to their bearers as well as to others, in particular the bearers' own community. This

© Springer Fachmedien Wiesbaden GmbH, part of Springer Nature 2018          59
H. Kabashima et al. (Hrsg.), *The Idea of Justice in Literature*,
Wirtschaftsethik in der globalisierten Welt,
https://doi.org/10.1007/978-3-658-21996-3_6

idea however relies on the social background of pre-modern times, which I will explore in section 2 of this article.

The elements listed as forming part of the honest businessman vary, but common points are the following:

- Be faithful, e. g., keep your contracts!
- Be sincere in your business!
- Be discrete in your business!
- Be dedicated to your business!
- Have a sense of decency and/or sobriety!
- Show prudence in running your business!

As an exemplification of the virtues of the honest businessman, the façade of Nuremberg Chamber of Commerce's building (originally built in 1560) says:

> *"Der Handel begehrt solche Leut*
> *Bei denen sei Aufrichtigkeit*
> *In Wort und Werk das wohl vernimm*
> *auch Herz und Mund zusammenstimm."*
>
> (This can be translated into English as follows: "Trade will covet people of a kind whose sincerity in words and action corresponds to their heart and mouth.")

The question is whether this ideal is just an ideal of the past, or whether it still holds bearing for today. During the last years, several organizations in Germany have promoted a revival of the honest businessman, in particular some Chambers of Commerce (see for example, IHK für München und Oberbayern 2012). While I think that this revival is in general a good idea, one should be cautious that the concept of traditional business virtues and customs cannot be directly applied to the modern economy in times of globalization. To name but one example: Being discrete is nowadays, for most parts, *not* seen as a virtue, but rather as a vice. Instead, it is transparency what is being called for.

In the modern globalized economy, a revival of the honest businessman should be put into a broader context of business ethics and Corporate Social Responsibility. Structural and organizational measures, incentives schemes and others are mechanisms that can serve as implementation mechanisms for the honest businessman in the world of today: Mechanisms like reputation and social capital have become decisive in the globalized world—and corporations are well advised not to put them at risk for short-run reasons (cf., e. g., Luetge/Mukerji 2016).

To put this into a clearer perspective, some remarks about the historical and social background of the concept of the honest businessman are necessary.

## 2      The Historical Background of the Honest Businessman

In order to put the honest businessman into a historical perspective, it must be taken into account that in most of their evolutionary history and during pre-modern times, human beings have lived in small societies. Until the year 1000, there were only 10 cities in the world with more than 100,000 inhabitants (like Rome (the largest in 100 AD), Cordoba (the largest in 1000) and Beijing (the largest from 1500 – ca. 1800)).

If the framework is a traditional pre-modern society with small groups, then fierce and intense competition can have disastrous consequences, both for businesspeople as well as for others. More precisely, pre-modern societies played zero-sum games in which people could only gain significantly at the expense of others (cf. Luetge, 2012, Luetge, 2015, Luetge et al., 2016). These societies lacked sustained economic growth.

In such societies without systematic, sustained growth, the view of the 15th century Florentine merchant Giovanni Rucellai (written about 1450) concisely expresses the situation of ethics and economics: "by being rich, I make others (which I might not even know) poor". Under the conditions of zero-sum societies, this is true. Here, an ethics of temperance is needed that, for example, prohibits the lending of money at interest (cf. Luetge, 2014, Luetge, 2015). Such an ethos can be found in Christian as well as in Islamic and other traditions. The ideal of the honest businessman exemplifies such an ethos.

There may have been one (disputable) historical exception to zero-sum society: Part of the Roman period might have been a non-zero sum society. And interestingly, the evaluation and moral reputation of businesspeople changed during that time. As Cicero wrote in 44 BC in his *De Officiis*:

"Trade, if it is on a small scale, is to be considered vulgar; but if wholesale and on a large scale, importing large quantities from all parts of the world and distributing to many without misrepresentation, it is not to be greatly disparaged. *Nay, it even seems to deserve the highest respect.*" (http://perseus.uchicago.edu/perseus-cgi/citequery3.pl?dbname=LatinAugust2012&-getid=1&query=Cic.%20Off.%201.151)

In historical perspective, this is an unusual positive ethical evaluation of (at least parts of) business activity.

In modern societies however, the social and economic conditions are substantially different from the pre-modern ones: Modern societies are anonymous and large societies, and they are especially societies with systematic growth. The concept of growth employed here can be framed in different ways, it can be qualitative growth, growth in an ecological sense, but growth nevertheless. Under these conditions, positive sum games are played.

However, one key ethical problem remains or even becomes more prominent: Those who behave ethically in a costly way run into disadvantages in competition with others. The prisoner's dilemma and the free rider dilemma describe exactly this situation, in which those who act ethically on the basis of ethical values etc. ultimately might be forced out of business (cf. Luetge, 2015, Luetge et al., 2016). To give an example from the financial crisis:

A manager who discouraged his clients to invest in funds with a proposed, but—as he knew, in the longer run unrealistic—return of 20 %, put his job in jeopardy as others offered 20 %, and so was forced by competition to offer the same. (The situation actually gets worse the more people are acting ethically: the greater the incentives become for unethical acts, like the examples of illegal arms trade or drug trafficking show.)

At this point, critics like Marx insist that the ethical actors are forced out of the market: We end up with a dog eat dog society. Though the exact wording differs, this is nonetheless equally accepted by less anti-market authors like Max Weber (1905/2005), however, the lessons drawn from it are quite different. Eventually, it turned out that the Marxist attempt to completely abandon economic competition was not viable. Instead, we have to find adequate order frameworks for markets to make them work in the direction we want (Luetge/Mukerji 2016). The honest businessman is still an honorable ideal under these conditions. However, it should be implemented via structures and incentives rather than primarily through individual virtues (cf. Luetge/Strosetzki 2017).

This is the systematic account. But what about the impact of the ideal on literature? Has there been an impact on (German) literature? I will focus on two writers here: Thomas Mann and Goethe. Both, in contrast to many others, deal with economic subjects, at least occasionally.

## 3    The Honest Businessman in Literature

Many prominent German writers have had difficulty dealing with business and economics as subjects. Thomas Mann (1875-1955) is a notable exception, however. In his famous novel "Buddenbrooks", written in 1901, he lets the old Lübeck merchant gives an advice to his son and future owner:

> "*My son, show zeal for each day's affairs of business, but only for such that makes for a peaceful night's sleep.*" ("Mein Sohn, sey mit Lust bey den Geschäften am Tage, aber mache nur solche, daß wir bey Nacht ruhig schlafen können.")

This quote is not a simple call for conducting one's business in a moderate way (sleeping peacefully at night), but also for *enjoying* doing business at day. This implies taking risks in order to expand one's company, and not just aiming for moderate profits. It is what the merchants of the Hanseatic League, in Lübeck and elsewhere, had been doing for centuries, but which got lost or at least reduced in some companies, as the story of the "Buddenbrooks" tells.

In "Joseph the Provider" (written much later, in 1943), Thomas Mann further describes the "honorable political economist" as a desirable objective. Mann's book is about the biblical Joseph, who, by the end of the four-volume novel cycle "Joseph and His Brothers," administrates Egypt for the Pharaoh. He does this by means of "a combined system that exploits the business environment and exercises benevolence" (Mann 1943/2004, 308). He has enormous stocks of seeds accumulated for times of need, which are then either distributed free of charge to the poor or sold to the rich. The latter are met with an additional requirement: They have to "update their irrigation system" and can no longer let it "waste away into a state of feudal backwardness" (ibid., 310). Here, economics and ethics are of a piece. Towards the end of the novel, we further read that the biblical Joseph was "neither a divine hero, nor a messenger of spiritual salvation, [...] only an economist" (ibid., 410). If I may take the liberty of saying so, to be an economist led by a sense of business ethics is a laudable goal.

Another notable writer who had a rather unique—if unusual—relationship to economics was Johann Wolfgang von Goethe. The Weimar poet laureate holds a special status in the German literary pantheon in this regard. While other Weimar Classicist authors—from Schiller to Hölderlin, Wieland, Kleist, and others—rarely grappled with supposedly "base" economic questions, if at all, Goethe had a personal interest in economic issues. He also dealt with them directly in his work, especially in "Faust" (most of all Part II):

In the first act of "Faust II," a fraud involving paper money plays a prominent role. Mephistopheles convinces the emperor to pay his debt with fiat money. When the swindle is finally revealed, Faust and Mephistopheles are forced to hastily leave the court. From our vantage point today, this act reads—at least on the surface—like a commentary on the recent financial crisis. Even the dike project described in the 5th Act, in which the old Faust tries to reclaim land from the sea, is clearly economic in nature.

In other works, such as in "Wilhelm Meister's Apprenticeship" and in the "Journeyman Years," Goethe deals with issues ranging from agriculture to land-ownership rights, the beginning of industrialization, and monetary theory. Certainly, Goethe had read many economic classics, not only the Physiocrats who traced wealth exclusively to agriculture, but also Adam Smith, the founder of modern economics. More than that, he also put his knowledge to use. Firstly, he amassed his own personal wealth—not only for its own sake, but also to participate in the period's social life in a way that was otherwise barred to his fellow poets and writers. At the same time, Goethe was exposed to novel ideas that allowed him to profit more from his work—compared not only to his contemporaries, but also later writers.

Moreover, Goethe was in charge of economic and financial policy for the indebted Duchy of Saxe-Weimar, whose debts at least did not increase under his watch. Goethe also enacted massive austerity measures, which ultimately allowed the Duke to construct new palatial structures. In his own economic dealings, Goethe auctioned off his epic poem "Hermann and Dorothea." By means of an economically ingenious auction process, his publishers were required to submit bids in sealed envelopes. Far from condemning competition, Goethe understood how to use it for his own purposes.

Of course, it is necessary to add the caveat that Goethe was not in favor of modern economics in every respect. In all likelihood, his engagement with the Physiocrats contributed to his very conservative view of the economy—one which tends to view capital and its function sceptically and instead looks at the real economy as the only true source of wealth. He refused to take on any debt. In his review of "Goethe und das Geld" (Goethe and Money), Gustav Seibt writes that Goethe was "middle-class (bürgerlich) in a sturdy and honorable sense," and even adds: "this [posture] should become modern once again." At best, however, one can only follow Goethe's example on an abstract level.

For many reasons, and even despite the repeated financial crises, a return to physiocratic economics, which relies exclusively on the real economy and generally distrusts financial markets or denies them legitimacy, has become unthinkable. Financial markets have their function: They serve in the procurement of venture and risk capital; they contain risks (when working properly); and, fundamentally, they allow profits to be earned today on future developments and projects. The fact that Goethe did not yet recognize all of this in his lifetime may be forgiven. Nonetheless, it is consistent with his basic attitude toward the sciences: Here, too, Goethe had sometimes sound, though frequently less well-founded, reservations about established sciences. This was reflected in his advocacy of the Theory of Colors, scientific holism, and the primacy of sensory observation. No doubt, Goethe went his own way. Still, his path (including in economics) was often much more forward-looking than that of his contemporary literary colleagues.

## Conclusion

From a theoretical point of view, the idea of the honest businessman (or rather the honest businessperson), has not become totally obsolete. However, in a globalized economy, structural measures like Corporate Social Responsibility, incentive schemes and compliance programs must be seen as the continuation of this ideal on a structural level.

From a historical and literary point of view, not many German writers have focused on economics and business as literary subjects. And most of these have been dealing with pre-modern models of economic activity. Only some have portrayed modern versions of honest businessmen and their activities, virtues and values. It remains to be seen whether literature will continue to do so in the future or whether it will change its view towards a more realistic and contemporary way.

## References

Chun, S. (2012), *Major Aspects of Chinese Religion and Philosophy: Dao of Inner Saint and Outer King.* Heidelberg/New York: Springer.
Homann, K.; Lütge, C. (2004/2013), *Einführung in die Wirtschaftsethik*, 3rd ed., Münster: LIT.
IHK für München und Oberbayern (ed.) (2012): *Den Ehrbaren Kaufmann leben: Mit Tradition zur Innovation*, joint publication with Christoph Lütge.
Luetge, C. (2012), Economic Ethics, in: *Encyclopedia of Applied Ethics*, Vol. 2, Oxford: Elsevier, 13-19.

Luetge, C. (ed.) (2013): *Handbook of the Philosophical Foundations of Business Ethics*, 3 vols., Heidelberg/New York: Springer.

Luetge, C. (2014): *Ethik des Wettbewerbs: Über Konkurrenz und Moral*, München: Beck.

Luetge, C. (2015), *Order Ethics vs. Moral Surplus: What Holds a Society Together?*, Lexington, Lanham, Md.

Luetge, C., Armbrüster, T., and Müller, J. (2016): Order Ethics: Bridging the Gap Between Contractarianism and Business Ethics", *Journal of Business Ethics* 136 (4), 687-697.

Luetge, C.; Strosetzki, C. (eds.) (2017), *The Honest Businessperson: Between Modesty and Risk*, Heidelberg: Springer.

Mann, T. (1901/1998), *Buddenbrooks*, New York: Vintage Classics.

Mann, T. (1943/2004): *Joseph und seine Brüder. Der vierte Roman: Joseph, der Ernährer*, Frankfurt: Fischer (in English: *Joseph the Provider*).

Miyazaki, I. (1981): *China's Examination Hell: The Civil Service Examinations of Imperial China*, New Haven: Yale University Press, New Haven.

Rucellai, G. (1772), *Ricordanze*, Padua.

Shibusawa, E. (1916), *Rongo to soroban*. Tokio: Toado Shobo ("The Analects and the Abacus").

Shimazu, I. (2017), The Most Successful and Moralistic Merchant at the Dawn of Japanese Capitalism: Shibusawa and his Confucianism, forthcoming in: Luetge/Strosetzki 2017.

Weber, M. (1905/2005), *The Protestant Ethic and the Spirit of Capitalism*, translated by T. Parsons with an introduction by A. Giddens, London: Routledge Classics (Original: Weber, M., Die protestantische Ethik und der Geist des Kapitalismus, Archiv für Sozialwissenschaften und Sozialpolitik, vol. 20, 1-54, 1905 and vol. 21, 1-110, 1905).

## The Author

**Christoph Luetge**, Full Professor and Chair of Business Ethics, Technical University of Munich

# What Justice? Things as They Are

Íñigo Álvarez Gálvez

## Abstract

Godwin's *An Enquiry concerning political justice* was published in 1793; and one year later, the novel *Caleb Williams, or Things As They Are*. It is sometimes said that the second is, somehow, an attempt to put his *Enquiry* in other words and to convey his thoughts about justice, law or politics to a wider audience. Be as it may, in *Caleb Williams* we can find out important ideas about those topics (specifically about justice and law) and we can link those ideas to his political philosophy (developed in the *Enquiry*). Godwin shows in *Caleb Williams* how things are; how justice and law are made by and for the ruling class. And behind these ideas we can guess those others that are not expressed in the novel (i. e. what law should be in a fair world, or how things should be if they were not as they are).

Godwin was a supporter of anarchism (according to Kropotkin, the first to formulate the political doctrine *in toto*), and being so, we can be quite sure that a great amount of ideas not expressed in *Caleb Williams* have to do with this political theory. But he can also be considered as a supporter of utilitarianism, so that we can hold that the novel is, in the same way, a defense of this moral doctrine.

## Keywords

Justice; Law; Utilitarianism; Anarchism

## Introduction

The novel *Caleb Williams or Things as They Are* was first published in 1794. William Godwin, the author, was not a novelist; and the novel was never regarded as a masterpiece of literature (although it wouldn't deserve to be thrown to a bonfire, as a friend of Godwin's said when he read part of it). The merit of the novel is not literary but, I would say, philosophical. Godwin was, at that time, a well-known philosopher (his *Political Justice* was published in

1793), so we may think that he approached his literary work from a philosophical standpoint and we may also think that there's a philosophical background spreading across the novel. Anyway, that doesn't mean that the novel is just a literary translation of a philosophical essay (although Godwin said it was). It is not. It's indeed a novel, but a novel written by a philosopher; the same philosopher who wrote, as I have said, *An Enquiry Concerning Political Justice and its influence on General Virtue and Happiness*. Thus, we would say that the novel, of course, matches the essay (as we will see, in this essay William Godwin defends an anarchist and a utilitarian approach to ethics and politics).

It's been said that Godwin was not an anarchist nor an utilitarian[1]. I don't think this discussion deserves more than one minute. I think it's clear that Godwin is a supporter of anarchism and of utilitarianism. Anyway, whether we call him an anarchist or an utilitarian is not what matters. The point is that Godwin said what he said and that those ideas mean what they mean, and nothing else. Let's see by way of example some quotes. About anarchism he says: "It were earnestly to be desired that each man was wise enough to govern himself without the intervention of any compulsory restraint; and, since government even in its best state is an evil, the object principally to be aimed at is, that we should have as little of it as the general peace of human society will permit" (Godwin, 1793: 185-186). Or this one: "That government therefore is the best, which in no one instance interferes with the exercise of private judgment without absolute necessity" (Godwin, 1793: 193). In *Patterns of Anarchy*, Krimerman and Perry (1966: 185) say that Godwin presents in his *Political Justice*, "an epistemological basis for anarchism", and I think they are right. That's what we can see in Godwin's essay. And about utilitarianism, he says, for example: "If justice have any meaning, it is just that I should contribute every thing in my power to the benefit of the whole" (Godwin, 1793: 81). Or this: "…let us next enquire into the degree in which we are obliged to consult the good of others. And here I say that it is just that I should do all the good in my power […] But how much I am bound to do for the general weal, that is, for the benefit of the individuals of whom the whole is composed? Every thing in my power" (Godwin, 1793: 86-87). Or: "But all approbation or preference is relative to utility or general good" (Godwin, 1793: 309). I know it is not just a replica of Bentham's theory. So what? Does Bentham monopolize the truth about utilitarianism? Because if he doesn't, why can't we think that Godwin's theory is a utilitarian theory (as utilitarian as Bentham's is). There is utilitarianism beyond Bentham. And Godwin is a good example of this. Godwin links, ties together, moral good (or justice), happiness (general happiness) and pleasure. And that's the essence of utilitarianism[2].

In short, what matters is that we can link the philosophical ideas from *Caleb Williams* to *Political Justice*. Thus, having previously read *Political Justice* we can guess what the author had in mind when he wrote *Caleb Williams*, and we can see through the novel the philosophical background that's implicit in the adventures that Godwin describes. And,

---

1   See, for example, García Moriyón (1985) and Lamb (2009).
2   See Bentham (1996). The same can be said about Mill (1991). He is, of course, an utilitarian, despite the fact his Utilitarianism is, in some respects, far from Bentham's ideas.

likewise, having previously read *Caleb Williams*, we will be able to understand better the philosophical ideas of *Political Justice*, since we know the social background that's behind it, since we know how the social reality is constructed; I mean, since we know the world Godwin is writing about. Having said that, I think we can present the ideas of the novel as a good sample (a literary sample) of Godwin's philosophical theory.

There are two things, about the composition of the book, I want to point out. First, we need to know that the novel was written backwards (Godwin himself said so in the preface to the book in 1832). He wrote firstly the third part, and then the second and the first parts were written just to support the third. Thus, we may think that this part contains the main ideas of the novel. In accordance with this, we can say that the first intention of Godwin was to introduce a frightened, distressed young man; a poor boy chased by a powerful man; a prey of the social system. Those ideas of fear, anguish, harassment, unavoidable evil, insurmountable obstacles, etcetera, are (I think) the key to the interpretation of the novel. Godwin wanted to convey a feeling of permanent fear, of helplessness. As we know, the title of the novel is: *Caleb Williams or Things as They Are*. And we may ask: Are things like that? Is there no solution for social injustice? If that's the message Godwin wants to present, we can see here a contrast between the novel and the philosophical essay. Because in the essay Godwin criticizes the social system, but he also foresees a bright future in which Truth and Justice will shine. However in *Caleb Williams* there's a tragic view of reality. There's nothing we can do but give our hopes up.

The second thing I want to point out (connected with the first) is that Godwin wrote two endings for the novel. In the first, Caleb Williams ends up suing his chaser, Mr. Falkland, but nobody pays attention to him, nobody believes in him, and he is again humiliated, put to shame, mocked, insulted and sent to prison. Once again, the strength of wealth, the power of the rich, and in fact, their tyranny, their falseness, their hypocrisy, overcome the simple truth. The conclusion we can draw is that truth cannot survive by itself in the realm of falsehood and injustice. To put it in a nutshell: There's no hope for Caleb Williams. However, this is not the ending that was published. In the novel we know, Caleb Williams sues Mr. Falkland; and he (Falkland), shattered, ashamed of himself, realizing that that's the end of him, confesses his crimes. Williams, apparently, overcomes his pursuer. But, is it really a victory? Not at all. Suddenly, he is fully aware that he has used the judicial system for punishing a fellow creature and he blames himself for doing so.

This second ending, as Bode puts it (Bode, 1990: 103), has nothing to do with Falkland's personality, with the development of the book, and with the political ideas of the previous chapters, first of all, the idea that justice and truth cannot succeed in the society where Williams lives. Why this change? Did Godwin want to tell us that justice can succeed even in this society? Did he want to tell us that changes are possible, despite institutional corruption? We know that Godwin rejected violence and defended the power of reason and the power of the word in the struggle for truth and justice. Let's read some quotes: "Force has already appeared to be an odious weapon; and, if the use of it be to be regretted in the hands of government, it does not changed its nature though wielded by a band of patriots" (Godwin, 1793: 195). Or: "The best security for an advantageous issue is free and unrestricted discussion. In that field truth must always prove the successful champion" (Godwin, 1793: 202). Or this one: "There are two principles therefore which the man who desires the regeneration of his species ought ever to bear in mind, to regard the improvement of every hour as essential in the discovery and dissemination of truth…" (Godwin, 1793: 204). Did he want to tell us that this is the path? I don't think so. We can see it is possible to use the judicial system to succeed, but is it advisable? The price is too high; Caleb Williams blames himself for acting like everybody else, for acting like one of them; Is that the victory we are looking for? And, what's worse, now the chaser becomes the prey; Caleb Wiliams is, apparently, the winner; How can we match this idea with the feelings of fear and anguish that Godwin wanted to convey?

But there might be another subtle interpretation. In the first ending we reach a dead end. Apparently. The message is: Truth and Justice will never succeed in this system of corruption. But, despite this, we may think that Godwin could be mistaken; we may think there's still hope. And we may think that although there's little probability of victory, we can succeed. In the second ending the message is worse (and perhaps sharper): Don't get your hopes up. You deceive yourself if you think there could be a solution. There's not. Even if you succeed, you lose. Because the problem is the system. So if you want Truth and Justice to win you have to break the system. Godwin shows us how things are. What justice are we looking for, then? Are we looking for justice inside the system? It doesn't exist. That's not Justice; that's not Truth. To sum up: We have to smash the system and start again from the beginning. That, I think, is the main message of the novel.

## 1    The Plot of the Novel

Caleb Williams, a poor and orphan boy, becomes the secretary of a powerful, rich, noble, kind, honest, honorable and handsome man, Mr. Falkland. Due to his position he learns about the story of his master and Mr. Tyrrel, a powerful and rich man, but also wicked and dishonest. One day these two men had a terrible argument and Tyrrel knocked down Falkland. That very night Tyrrel was found dead. Falkland was initially charged with murder, but he pleaded non guilty and in the end the culprits were caught (Mr. Hawkins and his son). That's the story Caleb Williams learnt about. Godwin shows us a social system that produces men like Tyrrel, but also men like Falkland. And he shows us a judicial system in motion that works perfectly well. We may think that Justice and Truth shine upon this society, and despite all the Tyrrels and everything, all is well that ends well: Tyrrell dead, the Hawkinses in prison and Falkland, the honest, honorable, kind and noble man, finally wins. But is that the whole truth and nothing but the truth? Caleb Williams is not sure about his master's veracity. One day, all of a sudden, he comes across the terrible secret, hidden in a chest, and he is caught red-handed. Now he knows the truth and his master knows that he knows it. Falkland confesses his crime: He is the real murderer of Mr. Tyrrel. Williams promises him that he will keep the secret. Days go by, and Caleb Williams feels more and more uneasy. Falkland keeps a close watch on him. One day he finally runs away.

And that's the beginning of his unfortunate life, because from that day on he becomes a victim of tyranny and oppression. There's no hiding place for a poor boy like him, with no money, no family and no friends. He is now the prey of Mr. Falkland.

Williams is chased, detained, and sent to prison charged with robbing some jewels from his master. Nobody believes him. Falkland, the honest and noble man, uses the social and judicial system in his favour. In prison, Williams realizes that in this society Justice and Truth means the justice and the truth of the rich, and he falls apart. Now he can see things as they are: "These are the engines that tyranny sits down in cold and serious meditation to invent. This is the empire that man exercises over man. Thus is a being, formed to expiate, to act, to smile, and enjoy, restricted and benumbed [...] This is society. This is the object, the distribution of justice, which is the end of human reason. For this sages have toiled, and midnight oil have been wasted. This!" (Godwin, 2014: 136-137). What's left? Williams is plainly clear: "My resentment was not restricted to my prosecutor, but extended itself to the whole machine of society. I could never believe that all this was the fair result of institutions inseparable from the general good [...] Cruel, inexorable policy of human affairs, that condemns a man to torture like this" (Godwin, 2014: 138). That's what it is. Thomas, another character from the novel, ends up admitting it too: "Zounds, how I have been deceived! They told me what a fine thing was to be an Englishman, and about liberty and property, and all that there; and I find it is all a flam. Lord, what fools we be! Things are done under our very noses, and we know nothing of the matter" (Godwin, 2014: 151). Williams has to run for his life; his chaser gives him no rest. As days go by, his fear, anguish, and grief, increase. Mr. Falkland, that is to say, the system, is against him. There's no room for Justice and Truth in this system. He says: "Those very laws which, by a perception of their iniquity, drove me to what I am, preclude my return [...] They leave no room for amendment, and seem to have a brutal delight in confounding the demerits of offenders [...] What can I do?" (Godwin, 2014: 167). There's nothing he can do but give up the struggle. There's no room for him in the system. What can he do? He tries to live outside the system, like a tramp, like a homeless person, like a beggar. "This is the form –he acknowledges- in which tyranny and injustice oblige me to seek for refuge: but better, a thousand times better is it, that to incur contempt with the dregs of mankind, than trust to the tender mercies of our superiors" (Godwin, 2014: 171). His protest is understandable: "I cursed the whole system of human existence. I said, 'Here I am, an outcast, destined to perish with hunger and cold. All men desert me. All men hate me. I am driven with mortal threats from the sources of comfort and existence. Accursed world! that hates without a cause, that overwhelms innocence with calamities which ought to be spared even to guilt! Accursed world! dead to every manly sympathy; with eyes of horn, and hearts of steel!" (Godwin, 2014: 183). Or later: "I was ignorant of the power which the institutions of society give to one man over others; I had fallen unwarily into the hands of a person who held it as his fondest wish to oppress and destroy me" (Godwin, 2014: 186). What then? What can he do in this situation? He is the loser. When he realizes that there's nothing left to do he plans to take his life. Now he knows the real truth; he knows how things are. Prostrated with grief, he acknowledges: "And this at last was the justice of mankind!" (Godwin, 2014: 200). "Why should I repeat the loathsome tale of all that was endured by me, and is endured by every man who is unhappy enough to fall under the government of these consecrated ministers of national jurisprudence? […] But the law has neither eyes, nor ears, nor bowels of humanity; and it turns into marble the hearts of all those that are nursed in its principles […] There is no man that is ignorant, that to humble yourself at the feet of the law is a bootless task; in her courts there is no room for amendment and reformation" (Godwin, 2014: 201). The game is over, for him. Society has condemned him. The brutal, merciless, false, dishonest society gave him a social death sentence. 'What justice?' you ask. This is the justice we can expect from society. Caleb's testimony is tragic: "Was the odious and atrocious falsehood that had been invented against me, to follow me wherever I went, to strip me of character, to deprive me of sympathy and good-will of mankind, to wrest me from the very bread by which life must be sustained? […] I had seen too much of the reign of triumphant falsehood" (Godwin, 2014: 218). And later: "Such is the state of mankind, that innocence, when involved in circumstances of suspicion, can scarcely ever make out a demonstration of its purity; and guilt can often make us feel an insurmountable reluctance to the pronouncing it guilt" (Godwin, 2014: 223).

Caleb Williams is a victim of this unfair and false society, but so is Falkland. He is, in fact, a virtuous man corrupted by society. Thus, Williams and Falkland are both victims of the same perverted system. We know the ending: Falkland confesses his crime; and Williams blames himself for punishing that man, for using the same system he was rejecting upon a victim of that very system. Just by chance he was the prey and Falkland was the chaser; but he could have been Falkland or Tyrrel and Falkland could have been Williams.

So, if things are as Williams puts them, is there anything we can do? Williams sets his heart in the future: "Posterity –he says- might be induced to do me justice; and seeing in my example what sort of evils are entailed upon mankind by society as it is at present constituted, might be inclined to turn their attention upon the fountain from which such bitter waters have been accustomed to flow" (Godwin, 2014: 219). And later, with naïvety: "It is not to be endured that falsehood and tyranny should reign for ever" (Godwin, 2014: 227). And we may ask: Is it not?

## 2      What Justice?

In this novel William Godwin shows the world as it is, things as they are. But he also believes in a better world. We have said it before: We are living in a perverted system where there's no room for justice and truth. This society produces men like Tyrrel and Falkland. Both use the same system to succeed in life. We may say that Falkland is not Tyrrel. Be as it may. But in the end, aren't they very similar? Both Tyrrel and Falkland want social recognition, success, social power. And both of them play their cards as well as they can. They use different methods, but neither of them do anything but what the system allows them to do. Are they vicious? Are they bad people? Aren't they in accordance with the system?

Where are we to put the blame on, then? Where's social evil? In Falkland? In Tyrrel? Or in the system that allows Falkland or Tyrrel to be as they are?

We were saying that *Caleb Williams* is not just a literary translation of *Political Justice*. Nevertheless, it is true that there's a philosophical background we cannot ignore. In the novel, Godwin tries to convey the feelings of fear and anguish of Caleb Williams. We know now that the source of those feelings is not just Falkland but the whole system. The novel is, in fact, a fierce criticism of the social system. Let's hear Godwin, the novelist, through Caleb Williams: "Turn me a prey to the wild beasts of the desert, so I be never again the victim of man, dressed in the gore-dripping robes of authority! Suffer me at least to call life, and the pursuits of life my own! Let me hold it at the mercy of the elements, of the hunger of beasts, or the revenge of barbarians, but not of the cold-blooded prudence of monopolists and kings!" (Godwin, 2014: 155). Or later: "This is the form in which tyranny and injustice oblige me to seek for refuge: but better, a thousand times better is it, thus to incur contempt with the dregs of mankind, than trust to the tender mercies of our superiors!" (Godwin, 2014: 171). Or: "Madam, madam! if would be imposible for you to hold this language, if you had not always lived in this obscure retreat, if you had ever been conversant with the passions and institutions of men" (Godwin, 2014: 216). Or, finally: "Such is the state of mankind, that innocence, when involved in circumstances of suspicion, can scarcely ever make out a demonstration of its purity; and guilt can often make us feel an insurmountable reluctance to the pronouncing it guilt" (Godwin, 2014: 223).

And that is what *Political Justice* is too. Let's now hear Godwin, the philosopher: "A system of government, that should lend no sanction to ides of fanaticism and hypocrisy, would presently accustom its subjects to think justly upon topics of moral worth and importance. [...]. But government [...] gives substance and permanence to our errors. It reverses the genuine propensities of mind, and, instead of suffering us to look forward, teaches us to look backward for perfection. It prompts us to seek the public welfare, not in innovation and improvement, but in a timid reverence for the decisions of our ancestors, as if it were the nature of mind always to degenerate, and never to advance" (Godwin, 1793: 31-32). Or later: "First then, legislation is in almost every country grossly the favourer of the rich against the poor [...] Secondly, the administration of law is not les iniquitous than the spirit in which it is framed. [...] Thirdly, the inequality of conditions usually maintained by political institution, is calculated greatly to enhance the imagined excellence of wealth" (Godwin, 1793: 39-41).

Thus, there's an obvious link between both works. To put it in a nutshell: In both works we can see the same message: The social system is the problem; the social system is the evil. So, if this is not what it should be, what should it be?

An obvious answer is: Something different. A different system based on different principles; based on the principles of truth, liberty and justice. The main ideas of Godwin's argument are the following:

1. First: We should fight for truth and justice not with the sword but with the word. He says: "When a great majority of any society are persuaded to secure any benefit to themselves, there's no need of tumult or violence to effect it", says Godwin (Godwin, 1793: 64).

2.  Second: We should know that there's only one truth and one justice. However, that doesn't mean that we can discover the truth once and for all. There's no such thing. Truth and justice depend on facts and circumstances of each case; nevertheless in each case there's only one correct answer. In his words: "Is justice then in its own nature precarious or immutable?" –he wonders. "Surely immutable" (Godwin, 1793: 150); or this one: "Truth is in reality single and uniform" (Godwin, 1793: 181).

3.  Third: Since we are rational animals (and we share a common nature: "We have the same senses, the same inlets of pleasure and pain, the same faculty to reason, to judge and to infer", says Godwin (1793: 182)) we should develop our reason in the search for truth and justice. We should improve our reflective thinking in order to find the truth. We should reject dogmas and authority and develop our free thought. There's only one truth, and there's only one proper search tool: free reason. "To a rational being –he says- there can be but one rule of conduct, justice, and one mode of ascertain that rule, the exercise of his understanding" (Godwin, 1793: 120).

4.  Fourth: This is a constant search, and in this search we can, of course, make mistakes. We have a limited intelligence; and that's why we need to discuss and share our ideas with other people. In the same way that we can say there's only one truth and one search tool, we can say there's only one path: free discussion. In Godwin's words: "The only substantial method for the propagation of truth is discussion, so that the errors of one man may be detected by the acuteness and severe disquisition of his neighbours" (Godwin: 1793: 186). Strangely enough, in Godwin's view all these ideas of freedom (free thought, free discussion, free reason) are linked with the defense of determinism. "None of these principles seems to be of greater importance than that which affirms that all actions are necessary", says Godwin (1793: 284). Or: "He who affirms that all actions are necessary, means, that if we form a just and complete view of all the circumstances in which a living or intelligent being is placed, we shall find that he could not in any moment of his existence have acted otherwise than he had acted [...] Where all is constant and invariable, and the events that arise uniformly flow from the circumstances in which they originate, there can be no liberty" (Godwin, 1793: 285). Thus, all of us are part of this material world. We are human beings, but as long as we are also material objects we are not free from laws of causality. And if this is the case, it's obvious that there's no room for free will. Nevertheless, it looks like Godwin is not aware of this conclusion, or at least, that he is not concern about it. He just points out that "happiness and wisdom will be objects worthy to be desired, misery and error worthy to be disliked. If therefore by virtue we mean that principle which asserts the preference of the former over the later, its reality will remain undiminished by the doctrine of necessity" (Godwin, 1793: 307-308).

5.  Fifth: Truth and Justice have to do with our happiness. As I have said before, Godwin defends a utilitarian theory. Let's remember him: "But all approbation or preference is relative to utility or general good" (Godwin, 1793: 309). Or, some pages before: "Justice, as it was defined in a preceding chapter, is coincident with utility [...] The nature of happiness and misery, pleasure and pain, is independent of all positive institution: that

is, it is immutably true that whatever tends to procure a balance of the former is to be desired, and whatever tends to procure a balance of the later is to be rejected" Godwin, 1793: 121). Or this one: In other words, morality requires that we should be attentive only to the tendency which belongs to any action by the necessary and universal laws of existence" (Godwin, 1793:123). Or this: "If justice have any meaning, it is just that I should contribute every thing in my power to the benefit of the whole" (Godwin 1793: 81). Or this other one: "But how much am I bound to do for the general weal, that is, for the benefit of the individuals of whom the whole is composed? Every thing in my power" (Godwin, 1793: 87). I think that it's obvious that Godwin is a supporter of utilitarianism, since he likens moral good to happiness and pleasure. He is not Bentham but he is still a utilitarian thinker.

6. Sixth: The happiness Godwin is talking about is made from different kinds of pleasures. There are lower pleasures and upper pleasures, and the latter are preferable to the former. "Among pleasures some are more exquisite, more unalloyed and less precarious tan others. It is just that there should be preferred" (Godwin, 1793: 106). And afterwards: "However many are the kinds of pleasure of which we are susceptible, the truly prudent man will sacrifice the inferior to the more exquisite [...] I shall derive infinitely more pleasure from simplicity, frugality and truth, than from luxury, empire and fame" (Godwin, 1793: 833-834).

7. Seventh: Justice (and when he says 'justice' he means 'utility') is the first and last moral criterion. Whatever other considerations you may have in mind have no value; and when he says 'whatever other considerations' he means rights (right to life, to personal integrity, to property, etcetera), promises, gratitude or family. We have only one duty: the duty to promote the greatest good, the greatest happiness. In other terms, we have only one task in our life: Justice. And if we want justice to shine in this world, we mustn't pay attention to valueless circumstances such as our own feelings or rights. Justice has nothing to do with all that. Godwin is clear: "Justice it appears therefore ought to be done, whether we have promised it or not" (Godwin, 1793: 151). Or, talking about property: "Justice obliges him to regard this property as a trust, and calls upon him maturely to consider in what manner it may best employed for the increase of liberty, knowledge and virtue. He has no right to dispose of a shilling of it at the will of his caprice" (Godwin, 1793: 88). Or this other one: "Duty is a term the use of which seems to be to describe the mode in which any being may best be employed for the general good (Godwin, 1793: 101). Or: "From hence it inevitably follows that men have no rights. By right, as the word is employed in this subject, has always been understood discretion, that is, a full and complete power of either doing a thing or omitting it, without the person's becoming liable to animadversion or censure from another, that is, in other words, without his incurring any degree of turpitude or guilt. Now in this sense I affirm that man has no rights, no discretionary power whatever" (Godwin, 1793: 111). Or: "Duty is a term the use of which seems to be to describe the mode in which any being may best employed for the general good" (Godwin, 1793: 101). Or this one: "But does all this imply that men have a right to act any thing but virtue, or

to utter any thing but truth? Certainly not. It implies indeed that there are points with which society has no right to interfere, not that discretion and caprice are more free, or duty less strict upon these points, than upon any others with which human action is conversant" (Godwin, 1793: 119). This is Godwin's utilitarian doctrine.

8. Eighth: If we want these utilitarian ideas to be put into practice we need to build a proper social system, based on the principle of liberty. Godwin says: "There is nothing that more eminently contributes to intellectual energy, than for every man to be habituated to follow without alarm the train of his speculations, and to utter without fear the conclusions that have suggested themselves to him" (Godwin, 1793: 119). Or, speaking about government: "It is only by giving a free scope to these excursions [of human mind], that science, philosophy and morals have arrived at there present degree of perfection, or are capable of going on to that still greater perfection, in comparison of which all that has been already done will perhaps appear childish" (Godwin, 1793: 118).

9. Ninth: It is obvious that our current system, based on authoritarianism, dogmas, and punishment, has never improved human beings. Laws are like iron girdles for free thought and individual responsibility. Punishment itself is just the application of injustice and it is only useful for maintaining people in moral stupidity. In his own words: "Countries, exposed to the perpetual interference of decrees instead of arguments, exhibit within their boundaries the mere phantoms of men" (Godwin, 1793: 127). "There can be no doubt, that the proper way of conveying to my understanding a truth of which I am ignorant, or of impressing upon me a firmer persuasion of a truth with which I am acquainted, is by an appeal to my reason [...] Punishment inevitably excites in the sufferer, and ought to excite, a sense of injustice [...] Punishment is a specious name, but is in reality nothing more than force put upon one being by another who happens to be stronger" (Godwin, 1793: 132).

So, the answer to the question 'What system?' is, to begin with, a system in which law and punishment don't exist. But, we may think that the result of this experiment would be worse than everything that we know. Law and punishment may not be moral goods in themselves, but without them there will be no boundaries for evil. What will be of society without the government? For Godwin, this is a groundless fear. Firstly, he is not talking about social chaos. There's a big difference between social chaos and the absence of government. In his words: "...it is incumbent upon us to remark that anarchy as it is usually understood, and a well conceived form of society without government, are exceedingly different from each other" (Godwin, 1793: 734). And secondly, when he rejects government he rejects authoritarianism and domination of some people upon others. If we all share a common nature, there's no room for domination of one human being upon another. As Godwin puts it: "It has already appeared that there is no criterion perspicuously designating any other man or set of men to preside over the rest" (Godwin, 1793: 158)[3].

---

3    There are numerous quotes about it. Let's see a couple of them: "No truth can be more simple, at the same time that no truth has been more darkened by the glosses of interested individuals,

This doesn't mean that it is not advisable to constitute a group of public administrators in order to efficiently conduct public affairs (as a matter of fact, every social member must be part of this group at a given time). Godwin is clear: "...as government is a trans-action in the name and for the benefit of the whole, every member of the community ought to have some share in its administration" (Godwin, 1793: 158). The following idea is a fundamental one: Our society consists of all of us (our society means all of us on the whole). There's nothing like 'the society' beyond the union of all its members. If this is so, therefore it is obvious that the affairs that society is interested in are the affairs that all of us are interested in. So all of us are an important part of the public deliberation devoted to those affairs. This is something very different than to be, for example, a subject of the king, for in this case you are not subject to anyone but your-self. And this is, of course, the path of moral dignity and responsibility. When you acknowledge yourself as a subject of the king you abandon your own moral dignity and put your responsibility in the hands of others, and you become "the most mischevous of all animals" (Godwin, 1793: 174). "Ceasing to examine every proposition that comes before him for the direction of his conduct, he is no longer the capable subject of moral instruction" (Godwin, 1793: 174).

10. And Tenth: To sum up: Godwin thinks that the new world is in our hands; and he is confident about it: "Shew to mankind by a few examples the advantages of political discussion undebauched by political enmity and vehemence, and the beauty of the spectacle will soon render the example contagious. Every man will commune with his neighbor. Every man will be eager to tell and to hear what the interest of all requires them to know [...] Knowledge will be accessible to all. Wisdom will be the inheritance of man, from which none will be excluded but by their own heedlessness and prod-igality. If these ideas cannot completely be realized, till the inequality of conditions and the tyranny of government are rendered somewhat less oppressive, this affords no reason against the setting afloat so generous a system" (Godwin, 1793: 214-215)[4].

And he urges us to abolish every government: "...government is an evil, an usurpation upon the private judgment and individual conscience of mankind" (Godwin, 1793: 380).

And he encourages us to abolish all the social institutions which are the dens of false-hood, privilege, domination, slavery, and injustice. He encourages us to abolish law and punishment, and to fight for truth and justice. Amongst moral beings there's no need

---

tan that one man can in no case be bound to yield obedience to any other manor set of men upon earth" (Godwin, 1793: 169). Or, speaking about monarchy: "Was ever a name so fraught with degradation and meanness as this of subjects? I am, it seems, by the very place of my birth become a subject. Of what, or whom? Can an honest man consider himself as the subject of any thing but the laws of justice? Can he acknowledge a superior, or hold himself bound to submit his judgment to the will of another, no less liable than himself to prejudice and error?" (Godwin, 1793: 450-451).

4    "There is not in reality –he says later- the smallest room for scepticism respecting the omnipo-tence of truth" (Godwin, 1793: 452).

for punishment: "Render the plain dictates of justice level to every capacity; remove the necessity of implicit faith; and the whole species will become reasonable and virtuous. It will then be sufficient for juries to recommend a certain mode of adjusting controversies, without assuming the prerogative of dictating that adjustment [...] Will there be many vices to correct and much obstinacy to conquer?" (Godwin, 1793: 577-578). This is the path of progress: "This is one of the most memorable stages of human improvement. With what delight must every well informed friend of mankind look forward to the auspicious period, the dissolution of political government, of that brute engine, which has been the only perennial cause of the vices of mankind, and which, as has abundantly appeared in the progress of the present work, has mischiefs of various sorts incorporated with its substance, and no otherwise to be removed than by its utter annihilation!" (Godwin, 1793: 578-579).

We don't find all these ideas in the novel. What we find there are the feelings of anguish and fear of a poor boy who is a poor victim of the system. But what we can guess beyond that is a cry for justice, a cry for truth, and that means, as we see in the philosophical work, a cry for utilitarian anarchism.

## References

BENTHAM, Jeremy (1996): *An Introduction to the Principles of Morals and Legislation*, Oxford, Clarendon Press, 1996.

BODE, Christoph (1990): "Godwin's *Caleb Williams* and the Fiction of 'Things as they are'", en Günther Ahrends y Hans-Jürgen Diller (eds.), *English Romantic Prose*, Die Blaue Eule, Essen, 1990, pgs. 95-115.

GARCÍA MORIYÓN, Félix (1985): *Del socialismo utópico al anarquismo*, Cincel, Madrid, 1985.

GODWIN, William (1793): *Enquiry Concerning Political Justice*, London, G.G.J. and J. Robinson, 1793.

GODWIN, William (2009): *Caleb Williams*, Oxford University Press, Nueva York, 2009 [on line: www.gutenberg.org/files/11323/11323-h/11323-h.htm (nov. 2014)].

KRIMERMAN, Leonard I. y PERRY, Lewis (1966): *Patterns of Anarchy*, Anchor Books, Nueva York, 1966.

LAMB, Robert (2009): "Was William Godwin a Utilitarian?", *Journal of the History of Ideas*, vol. 70, núm. 1, 2009, pgs. 119-141.

MILL, John Stuart (1991): *On Liberty and Other Essays*, Oxford, Oxford University Press, 1991.

## The Author

Íñigo Álvarez Gálvez, PhD., University of Chile, Faculty of Philosophy and Humanities, Chile

# From Brave New World to Island:
# Huxley's Tales of Alternatives To Law?*

José Manuel Aroso Linhares

**Abstract**

This paper aims to explore the so-called *Alternativendebatte* (Kurt Seelman) -- and in particular the problem of *alternatives to law* (Castanheira Neves) -- by developing a deliberate exercise in *law in literature*. As this problem concerns the institutionalization of plausible social orders in which law (as an *autonomous,* civilizationally specific *order of validity*) remains absent, two major novels by Aldous Huxley (the first published in 1931 and the second more than thirty years later!) are revisited: the aim is in fact to *confront* the (very well-known) overlap between a totalitarian *order of necessity* and a rational *order of possibility* (if not *social engineering*) which characterizes the global society (the "world State") represented in *Brave New World* (1931) with the (less well-known) experience of *continuum* between ethics, morality, science, philosophy, mysticism and shared narratives which distinguishes the utopian experience of (eastern) Pala fictionalized in *Island* (1962). The intention is not, however, to pursue a purely intellectual exercise (more or less arbitrarily conceived) — far less to reconstitute in detail the historical-cultural contexts which inspired both novels — but instead to examine whether the counterpoint deliberately constructed by Huxley in these two masterworks offers a specific contribution to the contemporary discussion on law (and law's cultural project), namely when considering the emergence of an alternative of *pure ethics* and the challenge of *inter-civilizational debates* (if not, in global terms, the need to distinguish between alternatives to law *in* the Western-European canon and alternatives to law *beyond* this canon).

---

\*   This essay was written as an integral part of the activities of a research group ["O Direito e o Tempo" (Law and Time)/ Instituto Jurídico da Faculdade de Direito da Universidade de Coimbra (Portugal)—http://www.ij.fd.uc.pt/index_en.html] and concerns a specific strategic program [the project "Desafios Sociais, Incerteza e Direito"—"Social Challenges, Uncertainty and Law" (UID/DIR/04643/2013)]. The opportunity to present the corresponding working paper in Washington [IVR 27th World Congress / Law, Rationality and Emotions (Georgetown University 27 July/1 August 2015) / Special Workshop n° 2, "The Idea of Justice in Literature" (27 July) ] was due to the possibilities generously created by two different institutions: Fundação Luso-Americana para o Desenvolvimento—FLAD (http://www.flad.pt/), which subsidized the traveling, and Fundação para a Ciência e a Tecnologia– FCT (http://www.fct.pt/), which (in the context of the referred project) covered the registration fee and specific accommodation costs.

© Springer Fachmedien Wiesbaden GmbH, part of Springer Nature 2018          79
H. Kabashima et al. (Hrsg.), *The Idea of Justice in Literature*,
Wirtschaftsethik in der globalisierten Welt,
https://doi.org/10.1007/978-3-658-21996-3_8

### Keywords

alternatives to law; law in literature; Aldous Huxley; social engineering; inter-civilizational debates; utopia

Is it possible to discover in the counterpoint deliberately constructed by Huxley in *Brave
New World* (1931) and *Island* (1962) — a more complex (and less unequivocal!) counterpoint
than it seems at first sight — a significant contribution to the contemporary discussion on
law (and law's *cultural project*), mainly through the so-called *Alternativendebatte* (Kurt
Seelmann, Castanheira Neves)? This is the question I will endeavour to answer in the essay which follows. Accordingly, the path to be taken involves three indispensable (almost
*natural*) steps: the first to clarify, as briefly as possible, the meaning or meanings of the
so-called *debate on the alternatives to law* [1], the second to revisit the *dystopian/utopian*
social orders fictionalized by Huxley from the perspective of this debate (and its categories
and defining possibilities) — confronting the fable of a (future) "world State" (set in London
in the "year of stability, A. F. [After Ford] 632"[1]) with the narrative of the last (ten) days of
the hundred-year old Pala *civilization*[2] (taking place in the sixties, in a "forbidden"[3] small
island somewhere in Southeast Asia)[4]— **[2.]**, and the third to synthesise the *outcomes* of
the previous interpretation (which also involves exploring the possibilities and limits of a
deliberate *law and literature* exercise) **[3]**.

---

1   Corresponding to 2540 A.D.! See Huxley, Brave New World (1932), London, Vintage Classics
    (Penguin Random House), 2007, chapter 1, p. 2.

2   "The work of a hundred years destroyed in a single night…" (Huxley, Island, London, Granada,
    cit. in a 1981 reprint, chapter 15, p. 335).

3   Ibidem, chapter 1, p. 12.

4   A more detailed exploration of Huxley's fictional universe would involve supplementing the
    experience of Brave New World with the narrative of Ape and Essence (1948), also set in a
    dystopian future (100 years after the catastrophic events of a devastating third World War,
    named "the Thing"). This paper (which concentrates on the two major novels) also restricts the
    exploration of Huxley's essays to the indispensable Brave New World Revisited (1958), although
    in order to arrive at the utopian Island, at least three other essays could have been used: The
    Doors of Perception (1954), Heaven and Hell (1956) and Moksha: Writings on Psychedelics and
    the Visionary Experience (1977).

# 1

The expression *Alternativendebate* was coined by Kurt Seelmann and corresponds to an ambitious comprehensive approach, combining and integrating different possible problems concerning the loss of *naturalness (obviousness)* or *self-evidence* of law and legal thinking *(Recht ist nicht selbsterverständlich)* in a *key* thematic core [5]. As the intention is to learn (albeit "tentatively"[6]) about law's *identity* (and its typical *Erscheinungsformen)* whilst considering practices and institutional situations which are *located* (or which successful critical reflection *locates)* beyond the limits or frontiers of law *(durch Untersuchung von dem gelingt, was jenseits der Grenze liegt[7])*[8], the signs and resources that can be combined (involving every past and present reflective trend which somehow "questions" law's response itself[9]) seem as heterogeneous as they are inexhaustible, ranging from the persistent *traces* of a plural (sophistic, Augustinian and Franciscan) *pre-modern* critical legacy —successively (and contrastingly) invoking an irreducible relativistic ("egocentric") anthropocentrism[10] and the ("eccentric") celebration of a theologically reasoned *communitas* (highlighting the non-juridical principles of grace and love)[11] — to the Hegelian and Marxist reconstitution of law's *isolation* (considering its specific *Zustand* from the perspective of other possible human *forms of interaction)*[12], as well as (in the present context) from an effective ("concrete") search for alternatives *in law (Alternativen im Recht)* — regarding different *(ethnologically* based or procedurally conceived) *ways* of *alternative (not jurisdictional) dispute resolution (traditional palaver, negotiation, mediation, arbitration)*[13] — to a more diffuse evocation of alternatives *to law (Alternativen zum Recht)* — the latter advocating the general expansion of "family" and "friendship" to *Gemeinschaftstypen,* as well as celebrating "spontaneity" and "flexible openness" regarding "social development perspectives"... whilst avoiding converting this critical potential into "positively formulated utopias"[14]! Is

---

5    Seelmann, Rechtsphilosophie, 3. überarbeitete und erweiterte Auflage, München, Beck, 2004, pp. 5 ff. ("Die Alternativendebatte oder: Recht ist nicht selbstverständlich"), 14-21 ("Heute eröterete Gründe für die Suche nach Alternativen") 92 ff ("Die Problematik der Alternativen und die Leistungen des Rechts").

6    "Die "Alternativendebatte" eröffnet so in (sehr vorläufiges) Verständnis davon, was "Recht" ausmacht..." (Ibidem, p. 6).

7    Ibidem, pp. 5-6.

8    Ibidem, 70-91 (§3. "Recht und seine Abgrenzung zu ähnlichen Phänomenen")

9    "Es gibt auch immer wieder eine Kritik am Recht in dem Sinne , das das Recht als solches in Frage gestellt wird... " (Ibidem, p.6).

10   Ibidem, pp. 7-8 ("Rechtskritik in der Antike").

11   Ibidem, pp. 8-12 ("Aspekte der Rechtskritik des Mittelalters von Augustinus bis zur Reformation").

12   Ibidem, pp. 12-14 ("Rechtskritik in der Neuzeit").

13   Ibidem, pp. 22-26.

14   Ibidem, p. 22.

there a plausible context that can integrate all these different problems and their many intersecting and overlapping elements? According to Seelmann, the key to measuring the common impact of these combined factors can be found in the reconstitution of the "grounds" or "reasons" that justify the contemporary pursuit of alternatives. Rather than the usual reasons for alternatives *in law* (which cite the inefficiently absorbed costs and the formalism of jurisdictional processes[15]), we should, in fact, consider those regarding alternatives *to law*, including the damage inflicted on "spontaneous ethical-communitarian relations" by the *interruptions* of the "impartial third" (if not the global disturbance of the *communitas* experience due to legal *societas* imperatives)[16], the reductive abstract simplification imposed on the complexity of real social relations and conflicts[17], the threats to freedom justified by law's interference[18] and, *last but not least*, the weight of a certain "indeterminacy thesis", confirming the general difficulty (if not impossibility *tout court*) of distinguishing law from *economics* and *politics* (if not *political morality*)[19]. Yet, notwithstanding the pertinence of Seelmann's diagnosis, the integrative purpose does not succeed without quite drastically sacrificing the comprehensive potential. However, the difficulty lies less in the way in which arguments concerning *abstraction, formalism* and *violence* are reproduced in this context (without exploring other alternatives or triggering the indispensable *contradictory*) than in the a-critical insistence on an objectivist-cognitivist *agenda*[20], which preserves the leading question "what is law?" *(was Recht eigentlich ist[21])* and with it the need to crystallise the tissue of reasons and outcomes in a plausible (even though multifarious) *concept of law (als Normsystem, als soziale Ordnung, als bestimmte koärent Form einer menschlichen Interaktion)[22]*.

Without rejecting the partial contributions offered by this analysis, I nevertheless aim to focus on another *discourse of alternatives* — exclusively and unequivocally conceived

---

15   Ibidem, p. 15, 21 ("Ineffizienz und Formalismus"), 95-97 ("Recht, dogmatik und Formalism")

16   Ibidem, pp. 15-17 ("Störung für Gemeinschaften"), 92-93 ("Recht, Gemeinschaft und Freiheit").

17   Ibidem, pp. 17-18 ("Abstraktheit"), 93-95 ("Recht, Abstraktion und Freiheit").

18   Ibidem, pp.18-19 ("Freiheitsbedrohung").

19   Ibidem, pp. 19-20 ("Unbestimmtheit"), 97-99 ("Recht und Unbestimmtheit")

20   This cognitivism has evidently nothing to do with the meta-ethical debate (cognitivism versus non-cognitivism) regarding the possibility/impossibility of treating practical propositions as true or false (and including the states of mind in question). The aforementioned legally relevant cognitivism has rather to do with the implicit or explicit persistence of a theoretical subject/object structure, treating law as a possible datum. It is thus practically synonymous with objectivism as the formulations clearly show: whereas cognitivism considers the subject/object structure by focusing on the perspective-subject, objectivism privileges the presupposition of the datum. See, in this sense, Castanheira Neves, Teoria do Direito. Lições proferidas no ano lectivo de 1998/1999, Coimbra, polic., 1999, pp. 59 ff. (also pp. 32 ff. in a currently available A4 version).

21   Seelmann, Rechtsphilosophie, cit., p. 5.

22   See mainly pp. 27 ff. (§2. "Aspekte des Rechtsbegriffs"), 70 ff. (§3. "Recht und seine Abgrenzung zu ähnlichen Phänomenen"), 228 ff. (§ 13. "Autonomie des Rechts").

of as *alternatives to law* — which, mobilizing Castanheira Neves' proposal[23], I will explore as a *leading perspective* whilst revisiting Huxley's narratives. This decision is partly due to its thematic focus, but mainly the illuminating *radicalness* of the problem it identifies — a problem which is constructed precisely from the reflective impetus of a *Heideggerian*-like question ("why Law (…) in the *human world* (…) rather than Law's absence?"[24]). Both this focus and radicalness — coherently developed in counterpoint with a complex diagnosis of law and legal philosophy's contemporary crisis (evidently a crisis of our own European civilization and its successive paradigms) — culminate in an eloquent problematization of Law's universality and even in an explicit questioning (and refutation) of the aphorism *ubi societas, ibi jus* ("our situation allows us to doubt the necessary subsistence of this aphorism"[25]). According to Castanheira Neves, this problematization urges us to recognise that law's autonomous response (fully invented in the jurisprudential *Isolierung* accomplished in Roman *civitas* and then pursued and transformed in successive cycles) is not a

23    The problem of alternatives to law has been developed by Castanheira Neves under this heading since the beginning of the eighties. See mainly O problema actual do direito. Um curso de filosofia do direito, policop., first version, Coimbra-Lisbon, 1982-1983, seventh and eighth lessons ( "O por-quê do direito" /"As alternativas ao direito"), "O direito como alternativa humana. Notas de reflexão sobre o problema actual do direito" (1988), in Digesta, vol. 1º, Coimbra, Coimbra Editora, 1995, pp. 286 ff., "Coordenadas de uma reflexão sobre o problema universal do direito — ou as condições da emergência do direito como direito", in Digesta, vol. 3º, Coimbra, Coimbra Editora, 2008., pp. 9 ff., A crise actual da filosofia do direito, Coimbra, Coimbra Editora, 2003, pp.140-147 (V). See also "O princípio da legalidade criminal", Digesta, vol 1º, cit., pp. 413419, Metodologia Jurídica. Problemas fundamentais, Coimbra, Coimbra Editora, 1993, pp. 231-234, "Pessoa, direito e responsabilidade", Digesta, vol.3º, cit., pp. 154-155, "O direito hoje e com que sentido? O problema actual da autonomia do direito", ibidem, pp. 62 ff., "Uma reflexão filosófica sobre o direito — "o deserto está a crescer..." ou a recuperação da filosofia do direito?", ibidem, pp.94-96, "O problema da universalidade do direito ou o direito hoje, na diferença e no encontro humano-dialogante das culturas", ibidem, pp.118-121, "O direito interrogado pelo tempo presente na perspectiva do futuro", in Avelãs Nunes / Miranda Coutinho (ed.), O direito e o futuro. O futuro do direito, Coimbra, Almedina, 2008, pp.59-63, "Pensar o direito num tempo de perplexidade", in João Lopes Alves et al., Liber Amicorum de José de Sousa e Brito em comemoração do 70º aniversário. Estudos de Direito e Filosofia, Coimbra, Almedina, 2009, pp.11-15.

24    "Coordenadas de uma reflexão sobre o problema universal do direito — ou as condições da emergência do direito como direito", cit., pp. 9-11. In terms of the urgent renewal of the central problem of law's autonomy (finally freed from its formalist resonances), this radical why-question (o "por-quê" do direito) constitutes only the first step, which should be followed by (if not constitutively intertwined with) a specific reconstitution of law's tasks or functions in its different historical cycles (o "para-quê" do direito) and by an inevitable autonomous discussion of juridically specific self-transcendental and self-disposable foundations (o "quê" do direito): A crise actual da filosofia do direito, cit., pp. 145-147; "Uma reflexão filosófica sobre o direito — "o deserto está a crescer..." ou a recuperação da filosofia do direito?",cit., pp. 94-100; "Pensar o direito num tempo de perplexidade", cit., pp. 16-18

25    "O direito como alternativa humana. Notas de reflexão sobre o problema actual do direito", cit., p. 286.

*necessary* answer, but only *one* culturally *plausible* and civilizationally moulded (and, as such, also continuously renewed) response[26] among *other* possible responses to the *universal* (anthropologically necessary) problem of the institutionalization of a *social order*. This acknowledgement corresponds, in fact, to an essential reconstitution of the conditions under which law emerges. Three conditions are explored here: (a) the *worldly-social condition*, identifying an objective relational (inter-subjective) performative *space* as an ensemble of (positive and negative) *apportionment*-relationships; (b) the *anthropological-existential condition*, considering the incompleteness and openness of the human species and the corresponding invention of a cultural and institutional second nature, which remain components of an irreducible dialectics between subjective autonomy and communitarian integration; (c) the *ethical* or *ethical-juridical condition* (the decisive one), acknowledging the invention of a specific kind of *intersubjectivity* (between *relativized*, *comparable* and *limited* spheres of *autonomy* and *responsibility* and the corresponding *masks* of subjects-*persons*) and which — whilst justifying an autonomous experience of *personhood* (based on a constitutive equilibrium between *suum* and *commune*, freedom-equality and *formally* and materially limited responsibility) — is considered a specific "axiological acquisition" but also —assuming the *methodological priority* of *controversy* — as a specific *internal* way of conceiving and experiencing *humanitas* and *phronêsis*[27]. The possibility of suppressing the latter (*not necessary*) condition — precisely the one which gives law its identity as an autonomous *order-ordinans of validity* — opens up the path to institutionalising an answer to the first two (*necessary*) conditions which, whilst frustrating specific intentions and specific ways of creating communitarian meaning (obviously those corresponding to the claims of the *ethical-juridical* condition), should be definitively inscribed in (or rationalized as components of) *alternative orders*. Which orders are these? Castanheira Neves considers three basic types (all accentuating contemporary "real trends"): the *order of necessity* justified by pure power, the *order of possibility* rationalised by techno-science, and the *order of finality* supported by politics[28]. This is certainly a perfunctory description of the so-called *why question* and its implications, although it will suffice to enable us to take *its specific challenges* as a starting point for examining Huxley's narratives...

---

26   Significantly inscribed in the deployment of what may be called the Idea of Europe (or the heritage of European civilization): see mainly "O problema da universalidade do direito ou o direito hoje, na diferença e no encontro humano-dialogante das culturas", cit, 101-116.

27   The most relevant development of the three conditions is proposed in "Coordenadas de uma reflexão sobre o problema universal do direito — ou as condições da emergência do direito como direito", cit., passim. See also the recent synthesis proposed in "Pensar o direito num tempo de perplexidade", cit. 11-15 (III.1)

28   The most comprehensive development of these alternative types is proposed in "O direito como alternativa humana. Notas de reflexão sobre o problema actual do direito", cit., pp. 287-310

# 2

What does it mean to treat *Brave New World* and *Island* as exemplary tales of the *absence of law* (a certain *law*)? It inevitably involves focusing on their *narrated worlds* (the worlds which their *imaginative variations* productively depict or create) as if they offered immediately plausible experiences of *social orders* and, even more directly[29], as if they could be *tested* as authentic responses to our main problem of collective life, revisited — as a kind of elementary core (albeit with a sharp awareness of the human animal's unfinished or incomplete condition[30]) — as a *necessary (not naturally solved)* problem of *sharing* (not only natural resources and instrumental *artifacts* but also symbolic cultural meanings, all different dimensions of a limited and scarce *world[31]*). The insistence on this obvious filter now seems indispensable, on the one hand in order to justify a deliberate disregard for the relevant narrative dimensions in both novels and, on the other hand, to understand why the judgment on the *absence of law* (as the absence of a certain *order of validity*) here presupposes (when it is not completely absorbed by) an identification of the corresponding *alternative type* (*order of necessity, order of possibility, order of finality*), in the certainty that this exercise in identification appears easy in relation to *Brave New World* [**2.1.**], but is no longer so obvious when revisiting (the significantly less well-known) *Island* [**2.2**]. Will these conjectural elements survive (and prove their mettle) until the reflective exercise has run its course?

## 2.1

When confronted with the exceptional *mimetic* force of *Brave New World*'s "plot" and its "split or cleft reference", which immerses us (with a prodigious "productive imagination") in the "reality" of an authentic "world of action" (inseparable from our specific condition as *historical beings*)[32], the reflective reconstitution developed in *Brave New World Revisited* (1958) almost always seems dispensable, if not unproductive or redundant. Regarding our specific problem of identifying *alternative types*, the focus of this essay[33] is, nevertheless,

---

29 From the perspective of the second alternative discourse (due to Castanheira Neves).

30 This is the core meaning of the abovementioned necessary "anthropological-existential" condition (a condition to which only culture, as a kind of second nature, may respond).

31 With the core meaning of worldly-social condition.

32 To use the categories proposed by Ricoeur: "La fonction narrative" (1979), cited in the English translation "The Narrative function", in Hermeneutics and the human sciences (ed. by John Thompson), Paris/Cambridge, Maison des Sciences de l'Homme/Cambridge University Press, 1982, pp. 274 ff.

33 Here Huxley considers the Western world in the fifties, in counterpoint with the "nightmare of the future" he had fictionalized twenty five years earlier: "In 1931, when Brave New World was being written, I was convinced that there was still plenty of time. The completely organized society, the scientific caste system, the abolition of free will by methodical conditioning, the servitude made acceptable by regular doses of chemically induced happiness, the orthodoxies drummed

significantly rewarding, precisely on account of the explicit comparison Huxley develops between the *social orders* depicted in his major novel and George Orwell's *1984* (written in 1948): "George Orwell's *1984* was a magnified projection into the future of a present that contained Stalinism and an immediate past that had witnessed the flowering of Nazism. *Brave New World* was written before the rise of Hitler to supreme power in Germany and when the Russian tyrant had not yet got into his stride. In 1931 systematic terrorism was not the obsessive contemporary fact which it had become in 1948, and the future dictatorship of my imaginary world was a good deal less brutal than the future dictatorship so brilliantly portrayed by Orwell…"[34]. Whereas the repressive world of "superstate Oceania" — with its permanent state of war, its telescreens, its *Newspeak* (making "all other modes of thought impossible"), its "oligarchical collectivism" and its enforced love of Big Brother (justified by *Ingsoc*, i.e. English Socialism) — corresponds exemplarily to the unmasked *totalitarianism* which identifies the first type of *alternatives to law* — i.e. the *order of necessity* of *pure power* (a self-subsistent, self-intoxicating power, converted into itself as irresistible object[35]) — the brave new civilized "world society" — with its permanent state of peace and its (near!) perfect stability (and pursuit of stability)[36], its worship of scientific progress ("progress is lovely…"[37])[38], "genetic standardization" and "predestination" (with the corresponding "caste system")[39], its extreme specialization[40], its sexual

---

in by nightly courses of sleep-teaching -- these things were coming all right, but not in my time, not even in the time of my grandchildren. (…)Twenty-seven years later, in this third quarter of the twentieth century A.D., and long before the end of the first century A.F., I feel a good deal less optimistic than I did when I was writing Brave New World. The prophecies made in 1931 are coming true much sooner than I thought they would.(…) In the West, it is true, individual men and women still enjoy a large measure of freedom. But even in those countries that have a tradition of democratic government, this freedom and even the desire for this freedom seem to be on the wane…" (Brave New world revisited, London, Vintage, 2004, pp. 3-4).

34   Ibidem, p. 4.

35   It is enough to recall O'Brien's well-known conclusions: "The object of persecution is persecution. The object of torture is torture. The object of power is power." (Orwell, 1984, part III, chapter III)

36   "The World State›s motto" is in fact "Community, Identity, Stability": "'Stability,' said the Controller, 'stability. No civilization without social stability. No social stability without individual stability' (…)" [Huxley, Brave New World, cit., chapters I and III, pp.1, 36]

37   Ibidem, Chapter VI – 3, p. 86.

38   And yet, we should not forget the troubling confession of Mustafá Mond concerning the need to stop the progress and subversive nature of real science: ibidem, Chapter XVI, pp. 197-202. "[W]e have our stability to think of. We don't want to change. Every change is a menace to stability. That's another reason why we're so chary of applying new inventions. Every discovery in pure science is potentially subversive; even science must sometimes be treated as a possible enemy. Yes, even science… (…).Science is dangerous; we have to keep it most carefully chained and muzzled. " (Ibidem, p. 198).

39   Ibidem, Chapter I, pp. 2 ff.

40   "'There's so much one doesn't know; it wasn't my business to know. I mean, when a child asks you how a helicopter works or who made the world-well, what are you to answer if you're a

liberty or virtuous promiscuity ("everyone belongs to everyone else!")[41], its "systematic reinforcement of desirable behavior"[42] and, *last but not least*, its *living in the present* as the utilitarian celebration of a *child-like* immediate happiness[43] (also a chemically induced happiness[44]) — combines the *dictatorial institutionalization* exclusive to the first of the three *alternative types* with the intentions and resources associated with *social engineering* which characterize the second — i.e. the *order of possibility* of science ("'In the end,' said Mustapha Mond, 'the Controllers realized that force was no good.' (...) 'Such are the advantages of a really scientific education'[45] /'Liberalism', of course, was dead of anthrax, but all the same you couldn't do things by force."[46]). The outcomes of this overlapping *power /science (necessity/possibility)* become immediately evident when confronted with the claims of the absent *ethic-juridical condition* (and the corresponding form or mode of *intersubjectivity*). This happens exemplarily with the process of *methodical neo-pavlovian (post-natal) conditioning* ("All conditioning aims at that: making people like their inescapable social destiny..."[47]), which is pursued under the direction of State Conditioning and Adult Re-conditioning Centres (and through the expertise of the College of Emotional Engineering) as an indispensable device (a "slow", but "infinitely sure method") for abolishing "free

---

Beta and have always worked in the Fertilizing Room? What are you to answer?' (...) Linda never seemed to know. The old men of the pueblo had much more definite answers..." (Ibidem, Chapter VII and VIII, pp. 105, 113).

41   "Lenina shook her head. "Somehow," she mused, "I hadn't been feeling very keen on promiscuity lately. There are times when one doesn't. Haven't you found that too, Fanny?" Fanny nodded her sympathy and understanding. "But one's got to make the effort," she said, sententiously, "one's got to play the game. After all, every one belongs to everyone else."..." (Ibidem, Chapter III, pp. 36-37).

42   "The society described in 1984 is a society controlled almost exclusively by punishment and the fear of punishment. In the imaginary world of my own fable, punishment is infrequent and generally mild. The nearly perfect control exercised by the government is achieved by systematic reinforcement of desirable behavior, by many kinds of nearly non-violent manipulation, both physical and psychological, and by genetic standardization..." (Brave New World Revisited, cit., p. 7).

43   "'Never put off till to-morrow the fun you can have to-day'. (...) Alphas are so conditioned that they do not have to be infantile in their emotional behaviour. But that is all the more reason for their making a special effort to conform. It is their duty to be infantile, even against their inclination." (Brave New World, cit., Chapter V, pp.84-85).

44   "The world's stable now. People are happy; they get what they want, and they never want what they can't get. They're well off; they're safe; they're never ill; they're not afraid of death; they're blissfully ignorant of passion and old age; they're plagued with no mothers or fathers; they've got no wives, or children, or lovers to feel strongly about; they're so conditioned that they practically can't help behaving as they ought to behave. And if anything should go wrong, there's soma..." (Ibidem, Chapter XVI, pp. 193-194).

45   Ibidem, Chapter III, pp. 43, 44.

46   Ibidem, Chapter III, p. 41.

47   Ibidem, Chapter I, p. 12.

will" (using "sleep-teaching, or hypnopaedia", as an instrument for "moral education"[48]) and thus (almost!) precluding every rational and emotional individual construction of *selfhood (ipse)*, as well as the correlative opportunity to found a truly communitarian responsibility or responsive identity *(idem)*. We should not forget that self-consciousness ("self-consciousness intensified to the pitch of agony"[49]), i. e. the "knowledge" that he is an "individual"[50], is precisely the problem that makes Bernard Marx utterly miserable, as well as the cause of his social failure[51]! This deliberate, subtle refusal of the dialectics of *suum /commune* is achieved *on the one hand* through the rejection of a democratic "open society"[52] (this *openness*, justified by the model of the *community of scientists*, is in fact a fundamental presupposition of a typical order of possibility[53]!) and, *on the other hand*, through an eloquent effect to *bridge* collective moral convictions (hypnopaedic *proverbs!*) and scientific or scientific-technological empirical-explicative statements or corroborated conjectures — a *bridging* effect whose sense and implacable unilateral dynamics is obviously assimilated from *social engineering* models and thus allow for (in the words of Hans Albert) infallible judgements on *explicability, realisability* and *congruence*[54]. The *principle*

---

48   "'These early experiments,' the D.H.C. was saying, 'were on the wrong track. They thought that hypnopaedia could be made an instrument of intellectual education ...' (...)'Whereas, if they'd only started on moral education,' said the Director, leading the way towards the door. The students followed him, desperately scribbling as they walked and all the way up in the lift. 'Moral education, which ought never, in any circumstances, to be rational.'" (Ibidem, Chapter II, pp. 20, 21).

49   Ibidem, Chapter V, p. 74.

50   "What Bernard Marx and Helmoltz Watson shared was the knowledge that they were individuals..." (Ibidem, Chapter IV, p.58).

51   "Odd, odd, odd, was Lenina's verdict on Bernard Marx!" (Ibidem, Chapter VI, p. 75)

52   One of the elements of this refusal of openness is precisely the hypnopaedic construction of undisputable axiomatic statements: "The students nodded, emphatically agreeing with a statement which upwards of sixty-two thousand repetitions in the dark had made them accept, not merely as true, but as axiomatic, self-evident, utterly indisputable..." [Ibidem, Chapter III, p.34] See also the exemplary allusion to the need to overcome liberalism and democracy: "'Sleep teaching was actually prohibited in England. There was something called liberalism. Parliament, if you know what that was, passed a law against it. The records survive. Speeches about liberty of the subject. Liberty to be inefficient and miserable. Freedom to be a round peg in a square hole.' (...) 'Or the Caste System. Constantly proposed, constantly rejected. There was something called democracy. As though men were more than physico-chemically equal.' ..." [Ibidem, Chapter III, pp. 39, 40).

53   Obviously, in the well-known Popperian sense of "open society".

54   Hans Albert provides us with the opportunity to distinguish three "bridging" steps and the corresponding tests (of contextualisation and experimentation), all made intelligible in the light of three plausible sets of precepts or postulates, aptly termed Brücken-Prinzipien (ein Brücken-Prinzip (...) [als] eine Maxime zur Überbrückung der Distanz zwischen Soll-Sätzen und Sachaussagen und damit zwischen Ethik und Wissenschaft (...), deren Function darin besteht, eine wissenschaftliche Kritik an normative Aussagen zu ermöglichen)[Albert, Traktat über kritische Vernunft (1968), 3., erweiterte Auflage, Tübingen, Mohr Siebeck, 1975, p. 76.]. (a) The first of these principles (the principle of explicability) confronts us with the need to submit

*of congruence* is of particular interest in considering Huxley's fable. The main acquisitions

---

normative criteria (more or less explicitly reduced to an ensemble of programmed goals and selected resources) to an immediate test of efficacy, as if the connection between all the pre-determined components — treated (in the self-sufficiency of this globally assumed anticipation) as a simple means-ends problem (a problem of instrumental rationalisation) — should be directly (implacably) exposed (submitted) to nomological knowledge and the available set of (corroborated) hypotheses of regularity (conceived of as universally valid "tentative" conjectures), so that it may be asked whether the informative content which these conjectures provide (as long as they continue to prove their " mettle" or "fitness to survive" critical refutation) globally (and objectively) confirms the anticipated connection (and the propensity that sustains it) [Traktat über kritische Vernunft, cit., pp. 32-37, 183-184, Traktat über rationale Praxis, Tübingen, Mohr Siebeck, 1978, pp. 7 ff., 36 ff., 150-155.]. (b) The second step, guided by the complementary realisability principle (Realisierbarkeit), adds a specific problem of performance (or efficiency) to the previous global explicative connection (justified as a problem of efficacy), undoubtedly because the pre-determined strategy is now deliberately confronted with the anticipation of its situated (tactical) execution, i. e. with the rational (maximising) choice that should privilege one of the probable effects or outcomes that this execution is apparently able to produce, if not directly with the corresponding alternative of decision (picked from an ensemble of concurrent, all instrumentally plausible, alternatives!). This involves asking whether this globally (scientifically) possible connection of resources is finally realisable (will produce consequent outcomes) in that specific particular ground (conceived of as a temporal and spatial unrepeatable cluster of conditioning factors) [Albert, Traktat über kritische Vernunft, pp. 75 ff., 175-176, 205-206, Traktat über rationale Praxis, pp. 85-86, 131-132, 150-155 (23.), 171-172.]. (c) The third postulate is aptly called the principle of congruence (Kongruenz) [Traktat über kritische Vernunft, cit., pp. 77-79, 93 ff., Traktat über rationale Praxis, cit., 171- 176, 182-186, "Erkenntnis und Recht. Die Jurisprudenz im Lichte des Kritizismus", in Albert/ Luhmann/ Maihofer/ Winberger (Hg.), Rechtstheorie als Grundlagenwissenschaft der Rechtswissenschaft, Jahrbuch für Rechtssoziologie und Rechtstheorie, Band II, Düsseldorf, Bertelsmann Universitätsverlag, 1972, pp. 80 ff., 94-96 ("Sozialphilosophie, Rechtskritik und Rechtspolitik")] The rationalising possibility is now directly the cognitive Aufklärung that science or scientific practice — finally treated as an authentic world view (Weltbild/ Weltauffassung) or as an autonomous way of life (producing a human world of "problems", "tentative theories" and "criticism" or "error elimination") — should (must!) impose on normative choices (its material solutions and its conceptual formulations): on the one hand negatively, excluding options that clash with the present nomological knowledge [Albert, "Erkenntnis und Recht. Die Jurisprudenz im Lichte des Kritizismus", cit., p. 95], i. e. rejecting value systems (or value-orientated practices, but also linguistic resources) that are culturally incompatible with the value of "objective truth" or with the value of its continuous "growth" [Popper, Objective Knowledge. An Evolutionary Approach (1972), Oxford, Clarendon Press, 1979, pp. 257 ff. ("Some Remarks about Problems and the Growth of Knowledge")]; on the other hand positively, discussing the different outcomes or the different "performance characteristics" (Leistungsmerkmäle) that correspond to alternative projects of a social order — outcomes or characteristics such as "stability" and "flexibility" (vershiedene Grade von Stabilität oder Flexibilität), and also "social certainty" and "freedom" (vershiedenen Arten von Freiheit), which may help us to grant specific "citizen interests", if not to directly recognise (and avoid) different manifestations of "social evil" (such as "power", "arbitrariness", "exploitation", "poverty") [Albert, Rechtswissenshaft als Realwissenschaft. Die Recht als Sozialtatsache und die Aufgabe der Jurisprudenz, Baden-Baden, Nomos, 1993, p. 25].

or civilizational conquests which distinguish the *new* world are, in fact, presented to us (as well to the successively amazed and horrified John the Savage) as instant and evident manifestations of the cognitive *Aufklärung* that *science* or *scientific practice* in general (and life sciences in particular[55], albeit as tamed applied sciences!) have persistently and unilaterally imposed on moral education and normative-prescriptive choices: precisely the (cumulatively *explicable, realisable...* and *congruent!*) choices — to give only a few examples! — which have eradicated viviparous reproduction, natural birth, family life, marriage, monogamy, romantic love, Christianity and religion[56] (and with them "obscene" words such as *mother, father[57], brother, sister, husband, wife, home, lover, soul*), together with the (scientifically *possible, efficient, enlightened*) *choices* which have suppressed suffering, fear of death, sexual repression and history teaching — whilst cutting off every relevant link to the past and excluding any possibility of sense to cultural heritage[58], as well as banning every book before A.F. 150[59] (including, obviously, the dangerous Shakespeare). *The people who govern the Brave New World may not be sane (in what may be called the absolute sense of the word); but they are not madmen, and their aim is not anarchy but social stability. It is in order to achieve stability that they carry out, by scientific means, the ultimate, personal, really revolutionary revolution[60].*

---

55   "The theme of Brave New World is not the advancement of science as such; it is the advancement of science as it affects human individuals. The triumphs of physics, chemistry and engineering are tacitly taken for granted. The only scientific advances to be specifically described are those involving the application to human beings of the results of future research in biology, physiology and psychology. It is only by means of the sciences of life that the quality of life can be radically changed. The sciences of matter can be applied in such a way that they will destroy life or make the living of it impossibly complex and uncomfortable; but, unless used as instruments by the biologists and psychologists, they can do nothing to modify the natural forms and expressions of life itself..." [Huxley, Foreword to Brave New World (1946), available in the cit. edition of Brave New World , pp. xliv-xlv].

56   "'Take Ectogenesis. Pfitzner and Kawaguchi had got the whole technique worked out. But would the Governments look at it? No. There was something called Christianity. Women were forced to go on being viviparous.'" (Brave New World, cit., Chapter III, p. 39).

57   " "[F]ather" was not so much obscene as-with its connotation of something at one remove from the loathsomeness and moral obliquity of child-bearing-merely gross, a scatological rather than a pornographic impropriety..." (Ibidem, Chapter X, pp. 131-132).

58   "'You all remember,' said the Controller, in his strong deep voice, 'you all remember, I suppose, that beautiful and inspired saying of Our Ford's: History is bunk. History,' he repeated slowly, 'is bunk.' (...) He waved his hand; and it was as though, with an invisible feather whisk, he had brushed away a little dust. (...) Whisk, the cathedrals; whisk, whisk, King Lear and the Thoughts of Pascal. Whisk, Passion; whisk, Requiem; whisk, Symphony; whisk ..." (Ibidem, Chapter III, p.29).

59   "... 'Accompanied by a campaign against the Past; by the closing of museums, the blowing up of historical monuments (luckily most of them had already been destroyed during the Nine Years' War); by the suppression of all books published before A.F. 150.'" (Ibidem, Chapter III, pp. 43-44).

60   Huxley, Foreword to Brave New World, cit., p. xlv.

## 2.2

Let us leave the World State (and 632 A.F.!) recalling the infrequent and relatively mild (visible negative) sanctions that sustain its enlightened order: *externally*, the "gas bombs" which "tame" the "savages" living in the Reservations — responding to (and preventing) any possible "tricks"[61]—, and *internally*, in addition to the expected "good soma vaporizations", the possibility of being *packed off* to Adult Re-conditioning Centres[62] and, regarding Alphas — as was almost the case with Mustapha Mond as a young man and happens (in front of our eyes) with the fainthearted and selfish Bernard Marx and the generous and sensitive Helmholz Watson (due to their *resistance to community* ), — the alternative of *being sent to an island* — not really such a painful exile (less a "punishment" than a "reward"!), since they will have the opportunity (as Mond himself recognizes) to study the dangerous *pure science* or dedicate themselves to subversive artistic creation (the results of which will not, however, be presented to the public!), in contact with "the most interesting set of men and women to be found anywhere in the world" ("All the people who, for one reason or another, have got too self-consciously individual to fit into community-life, [a]ll the people who aren't satisfied with orthodoxy, who've got independent ideas of their own, [e]veryone, in a word, who's anyone…")[63].[64]

Let us return to our contemporaneity (around fifty years ago) and, certainly not by chance, also to an island — a fictional place in Southwest Asia which, unlike the nearby (menacing) Rendang, escaped the presence of the Portuguese[65]! — in order to characterize the social order in Pala. Let us also begin, still in the sidelines, with the negative sanctions and corresponding manifestations of an apparent legal order. Nothing seems better than surprising a piece of dialogue between Will Farnaby (the English journalist

---

61  Brave New World, cit., Chapter VI, p. 91.

62  As happened to a leading black character in the movie "Three weeks in a helicopter": Ibidem, Chapter XI, pp. 146-147.

63  Ibidem, Chapter XVI, pp. 199-200.

64  "'It's lucky,' [Mustapha Mond] added, after a pause, 'that there are such a lot of islands in the world. I don't know what we should do without them. Put you all in the lethal chamber, I suppose…'" (Ibidem, Chapter XVI, p. 201).

65  "[Pala] had the luck, first of all, never to have been anyone's colony. Rendang has a magnificent harbor. That brought them an Arab invasion in the Middle Ages. We have no harbor, so the Arabs left us alone. (…) Well, to return to Rendang. After the Arabs it got the Portuguese. We didn't. No harbor, no Portuguese. Therefore no Catholic minority, no blasphemous nonsense about its being God's will that people should breed themselves into subhuman misery, no organized resistance to birth control. And that isn't our only blessing: After a hundred and twenty years of the Portuguese, Ceylon and Rendang got the Dutch. And after the Dutch came the English. We escaped both those infestations. No Dutch, no English, and therefore no planters, no coolie labor, no cash crops for export, no systematic exhaustion of our soil. Also no whisky, no Calvinism, no syphilis, no foreign administrators. We were left to go our own way and take responsibility for our own affairs."…" (Huxley, Island, London, Granada, cit. in a 1981 reprint, chapter VI, pp. 94-95).

or pseudo-journalist who here plays the role of the *man from the Outside*) and Dr. Robert MacPhail (the grandson of the Scottish physician Andrew MacPhail who, together with the Old Raja Muragan, was one of the two *founding fathers* of Pala):

> *"Law," Will echoed. "I was just going to ask you about law. Are you absolutely swordless and punishmentless? Or do you still need judges and policemen?"*
>
> *"We still need them," said Dr. Robert. "But we don't need nearly so many of them as you do. In the first place, thanks to preventive medicine and preventive education, we don't commit many crimes. And in the second place, most of the few crimes that are committed are dealt with by the criminal's MAC [Mutual Adoption Club]. Group therapy within a community that has assumed group responsibility for the delinquent. And in difficult cases the group therapy is supplemented by medical treatment and a course of moksha-medicine experiences, directed by somebody with an exceptional degree of insight."*
>
> *"So where do the judges come in?"*
>
> *"The judge listens to the evidence, decides whether the accused person is innocent or guilty, and if he's guilty, remands him to his MAC and, where it seems advisable, to the local panel of medical and mycomystical experts. At stated intervals the experts and the MAC report back to the judge. When the reports are satisfactory, the case is closed."*
>
> *"And if they're never satisfactory?"*
>
> *"In the long run," said Dr. Robert, "they always are"... .[66]*

This piece is particularly eloquent with regard to the inevitable troubling parallelism that any reader will immediately establish with *Brave New World*. Even though they are not all recognizable in the extract above, some of the main instrumental resources for social institutionalization appear to be quite similar. These include education in the form of conditioning celebrating the present ("pure Pavlov!"[67]), the defence of *free love* (and the naturalness of all kinds of love-making)[68], the acceptation of death[69] and the use of hypnotism and moksha medicine — "the reality revealer, the truth-and-beauty pill"[70] (a kind of equivalent to soma!)—together with an "emphasis on sciences of life"[71], the goal of raising the I.Q. (making artificial insemination a significant factor)[72], the exploration of bridges between

---

66   Huxley, Island, cit., chapter IX, pp. 182-183.

67   Ibidem, chapter XII, p. 222.

68   Ibidem, chapter VI, p. 85.

69   Ibidem, chapter XI, p. 280.

70   Ibidem, chapter VIII, p. 159.

71   Ibidem, chapter XIII, p. 246.

72   "Most married couples feel that it is more moral to take a shot having a child of superior quality than to run the risk of slavishly reproducing whatever quirks and defects may happen to run in the husband's family. Pious fathers now feel happy at the thought that they're giving their wife's children a chance of creating a better destiny for themselves and their posterity.' 'A better destiny?' 'Because they carry the germ plasm of a better stock. having a child of superior quality

science and ethics[73], and a certain overlapping of malthusianism[74] and utilitarianism (with the reinvention of the principle of greatest happiness[75]), not forgetting that the Palanese order consecrates an escape from the immediate family (ensured by the use of the so-called MAC[76])[77] and even a scientifically (biologically) based social functionalization (sometimes using pills to control different types of personality![78]), the latter featuring as soft *succedanea* for the World Society's *eradication of the family* and the *caste system* (respectively).

However, the similarities are less relevant than they may appear, not only because all these resources and choices are now pursued within the *environment* of an immaculate "open society" ("Pala is a constitutional monarchy!"[79]) — which lets every citizen see for himself "what the Outside is"[80] — but also because they are mobilized in the context (and from the perspective) of a communitarian *ethos* which radically converts them, distinguishing the social order they institutionalize from the typical answers which we have considered above, not only answers which would correspond to the order of the *possibility* of science, but also those involving the experience of *inter-subjectivity* attributed to law's cultural project and its specific order of validity. Condensing a very complex but no less coherent intertwinement of perspectives[81], it may be said that the integrating horizon experienced in Palanese culture (since the reform of the *founding father*, which began in the middle of the 19th century!) corresponds to a kind of *practical continuum*, the components of which are the Western practice of science and democracy and Eastern pantheism — the latter assuming a Buddhist

---

than to run the risk of slavishly reproducing whatever quirks and defects may happen to run in the husband's family'..." (Ibidem, chapter XI, p. 220).

73   Ibidem, chapter XIII, p. 247-248.

74   Ibidem, chapter VI, p. 96.

75   Ibidem, chapter XI, p. 216.

76   "'Whenever the parental Home Sweet Home becomes too unbearable, the child is allowed, is actively encouraged—and the whole weight of public opinion is behind the encouragement—to migrate to one of its other homes. (...) We all belong (...) to an MAC—a Mutual Adoption Club. Every MAC consists of anything from fifteen to twenty-five assorted couples. (...) [E]verybody in the club adopts everyone else. Besides our own blood relations, we all have our quota of deputy mothers, deputy fathers, deputy aunts and uncles, deputy brothers and sisters, deputy babies and toddlers and teen-agers'..." (Ibidem, chapter VII, p. 104)

77   "In our part of the world 'Mother' is strictly the name of a function. When the function has been duly fulfilled, the title lapses; the ex-child and the woman who used to be called 'Mother' establish a new kind of relationship. If they get on well together, they continue to see a lot of one another. If they don't, they drift apart..." (Ibidem, chapter VII, pp.102-103).

78   Ibidem, chapter IX, pp. 175 ff.

79   Ibidem, chapter V, p. 48.

80   Ibidem, chapter VI, p. 92.

81   To do justice to this multifarious unity, it would be essential to comment in detail on the excerpts from Old Raja's Notes on What's What, and on What It Might be Reasonable to Do about What's What, which are recreated (from Will Farnaby's reading) in the novel!

legacy "shot through and through with Tantra"[82], as well as the specification due to Mahayana philosophy[83] (and relevant contributions ranging from Taoism's "passive resistance"[84] to Panchatantra fables[85])[86]. The political-social propose, involving a successful ongoing process of "bridge-building" (between science and ethics, metaphysics and Buddhist wisdom[87])[88] — the latter creating new fields of knowledge such as neuro-theology[89], autology, metachemistry, mycomysticism, thanatology[90] — corresponds, in fact, to the aspiration of constructing a "fully human society" ("a society fit for fully" or "full-blown" human beings") which would combine the "best of both worlds"[91] (the "Oriental and the European, the ancient and the modern"[92]). This aim is pursued by establishing an ensemble of social arrangements and conditioning ("Pavlov purely for a good purpose"!"[93]) — ranging from the yoga of love-making (*maithuna*)[94] to the "hybridization of micro-cultures" (ensured by the open and changing MACs)[95],

---

82   Ibidem, chapter VI, p.86.

83   Ibidem, chapter VI, pp. 86, 94

84   "'What can you do about Colonel Dipa?' Will asked. 'Except for passive resistance, nothing. We have no army and no powerful friends. The Colonel has both...'" (Ibidem, chapter VIII, p. 127)

85   See the analogies with animals regarding child physique and temperament: ibidem, chapter XIII, pp. 240 ff.

86   "[P]ure experimental science at one end of the spectrum and pure experimental mysticism at the other. Direct experience on every level and then clear, rational statements about those experiences..." (Ibidem, chapter VIII, p. 131).

87   This no longer unilateral bridge-building (as social engineering inevitably is): see chapter XIII, pp. 239 ff., 248 ff. ("the science of relationship in conjunction with the ethics of relationship").

88   "The new conscious Wisdom—the kind of Wisdom that was prophetically glimpsed in Zen and Taoism and Tantra—is biological theory realized in living practice, is Darwinism raised to the level of compassion and spiritual insight." (Ibidem, chapter XII, p. 227).

89   Ibidem, chapter VII, pp. 109-110.

90   Ibidem, chapter XIII, p. 258.

91   Ibidem, chapter XIII, p. 258.

92   Ibidem, chapter VIII, pp. 150-151.

93   Ibidem, chapter XII, p. 222.

94   "When you do maithuna, profane love is sacred love..." (Ibidem, chapter VI, p. 88). "Awareness transfigures it, turns love-making into the yoga of love-making. (...) And that's the whole point of maithuna. It's not the special technique that turns love-making into yoga; it's the kind of awareness that the technique makes possible. Awareness of one's sensations and awareness of the not-sensation in every sensation..." (Ibidem, chapter IX, p. 175).

95   "'Take twenty sexually satisfied couples and their offspring; add science, intuition and humor in equal quantities; steep in Tantrik Buddhism and simmer indefinitely in an open pan in the open air over a brisk flame of affection...' (...) "And what comes out of your open pan?' (...) 'An entirely different kind of family. Not exclusive, like your families, and not predestined, not compulsory. An inclusive, unpredestined and voluntary family.' 'Do people stay in the same adoption club all their lives?' 'Of course not. Grown-up children don't adopt their own parents or their own brothers and sisters. They go out and adopt another set of elders, a different group of peers and juniors...'" (Ibidem, chapter VII, pp. 104-105).

from the "yoga of everyday living"[96] to the "yoga of death"[97] and from the skill of "distorting" time[98] to the experience of eternity as pure unconcerned contemplation[99] (the two latter due to *meditation* and *moksha-medicine*!) — in the (corroborated!) conviction that these practices (combined with the legacy of Pala's "primitive village communism"[100]) are indispensable in reformulating the relationship between God and man ("God would have to be thought of as immanent and man would have to be thought of as potentially self-transcendent"[101]) but also in order to ensure self- knowledge as a Good Being ("knowing who in fact we are")[102]. Only the possibility of accessing the "world of Suchness, of Mind, of the Clear Light"[103] (and the "gifts of luminous bliss and knowledgeless understanding"[104]), whilst simultaneously considering the "mystery of the other person"[105], paves the way for building an *order-ordinans* of friendliness, love, trust and *compassion (Karuna)*, as an order which, through awareness ("complete and constant awareness") — the mynah birds[106] persistently repeat "attention" ("attention to attention"[107])! — is able to transform "concrete materialism" (as the "raw stuff of a fully human life") into "concrete spirituality"[108], which (following "Buddhism and modern science") "thinks of the world" not in "terms" of "pebbles" and "substantial things" (as the "philosophers of the West" do), but in terms of "tunes and processes", i. e. in "terms of music"[109]!

A less succinct exploration of Pala's order and its resourceful (albeit frequently questionable) solutions would certainly constitute a fairly rewarding reflective exercise. However, for present purposes, the previous (simply allusive) reconstitution of this order as an effective *practical continuum* — in which no component (from science to ethics, traditional narratives to religion, or political morality to concrete spirituality) plays (or claims to play) an effectively autonomous role *(nothing short of everything will really do[110])* — must suffice,

---

96   Ibidem, chapter IX, pp. 174-175.

97   Ibidem, chapter XIV, pp. 299 ff. (Lakshmi's death).

98   Ibidem, chapter XIII, pp. 239 ff.

99   "Pure contemplation, unconcerned, beyond contingency, outside the context of moral judgements…" (Ibidem, chapter XV, p. 313)

100  Ibidem, chapter IX, p. 175 chapter VII, p.103

101  Ibidem, chapter XIII, p. 259. See also chapter VIII, pp. 134 ff.

102  Ibidem, chapter V, p. 43 (II),

103  Ibidem, chapter X, p. 198. See also the fundamental (last) chapter XV, pp. 308-336.

104  Ibidem, chapter XV, pp. 332-333.

105  Ibidem, chapter VI, p. 90.

106  These birds (their inhuman voices) are the beautiful succedanea of Brave New World's anonymous hypnopeadic voices!

107  Ibidem, chapter III, p. 23.

108  Ibidem, chapter IX, pp.174-175.

109  Ibidem, chapter XI, pp. 200-201.

110  "Science is not enough, religion is not enough, art is not enough, politics and economics are not enough, nor is love, nor is duty, nor is action however disinterested, nor, however sublime,

since it enables us to understand how the idea-image of *full blown humanity* which inspires this *continuum* dispenses with law — not only law's autonomous participation (strictly speaking, every component appears and is experienced here as constitutively inseparable!) but also law's participation *tout court* (as a plausible *sense-giving* dimension). It is as if legal institutionalization (deprived of its specific aspirational elements and its own inter-subjective experience) is reduced to a purely instrumental enacting and prescribing device, confined here to an almost residual (*substitute* or ancillary) intervention. Isn't the order-*ordinans* in question an institutionalization of compassion-Karuna (or does it not claim to be so)? And isn't Karuna simultaneously Love and Light ("heaven on earth"[111])? The comparable (inter-subjectively *relativized*) *homo humanus* of law (with its masks of correlative rights and duties, its *patterns of comparability* and its *artefacts*) is certainly unable to compete with this understanding of *humanitas* (as incomparable and infinite *fullness* attained by practicing the "art of living"). And yet, what kind of *alternative to law* are we presented with here? None of the abovementioned three types seem capable of corresponding to its challenges (either autonomously or in combination) ...

## 3

In addition to the opportunity to revisit two radiant (even though differently succeeded) literary masterpieces — one opportunity which, needing no external rationale, justifies itself by exposing us, with exceptional force, to the contrasting "potentialities" of our own world —, the outline sketched above, considering Huxley's *narrated worlds* from the perspective of the problem of *alternatives to law*, highlights some peculiar paths *of its own* (inseparable from its specific intersection as an exercise in *law in literature*), which I would synthesise as two main thematic possibilities. What follows is simply the allusive *signalling* of these possibilities, each undoubtedly meriting individual consideration (although this cannot be developed here).

## 3.1

The first of these possibilities concerns the issue of resources-*means* (the means which are instrumentally and pragmatically-strategically mobilized in the institutionalization of the different orders). Do these resources have a purely instrumental quality, i. e. are they protected by a plausible claim to neutrality or indifference regarding the contingent variety of ends and values that they can be used to achieve — so that different teleological arrangements and different axiological claims may confer radically different configurations

---

is contemplation, Nothing short of everything will really do..." (Ibidem, chapter IX, p. 154).
111  Ibidem, chapter XV, p. 327

on the same tool and produce unmistakably distinct effects? The possibility of repeating this question — as well as the opportunity to create a reflective path in which a negative answer (attributing a relatively autonomous intelligibility to *means* and *devices*, although not necessarily a substantive identity) may operate as leading conjecture! — is, in fact, one of the evident *outcomes* of this exercise in *law in literature*. The best way to accentuate it is undoubtedly to return to the structuring resources-*means* which the future (dictatorial) World Society and the contemporary (democratic) Palanese experience have in common... and in particular to the example of *methodical conditioning*. This example, in fact, suffices to raise the problem of knowing whether a *Pavlovian* model *for "stability" and "happiness"* (imposed in a closed, non-democratic order) and a *Pavlovian* model *for "friendliness"*, *"trust" and "compassion"* (presupposing the democratic and epistemic possibilities of an "open society") do *live* in absolutely separate worlds, rigorously *cut off from each other, producing distinct effects* and meriting different evaluations — as would seem to be the case when we hear Vijaya Bhattacharya (Dr. MacPhail's assistant and one of Will Farnaby's guides to the island) invoking "Pavlov purely for good purpose"[112] — or whether, on the contrary, they give rise to some (potentially dangerous) common outcomes which may, in *the medium and long term, silently* and *insidiously* undermine (and even destroy) this *openness*. Moreover, the question raised by this observation does not confine us to Huxley's fictional worlds (and an exploration of their troubling parallels), but leads us to ask whether the intensification of *social engineering* models in our Western democracies (on its unavoidable path towards institutionalizing plausible *orders of possibility*, reducing *praxis* to *technē*) does contain uncontrollable *dehumanizing* effects which progressively dispense with democracy. In order to explore this question, we do not even have to leave Huxley, as this premonitory and striking passage from *Brave New Word Revisited* reveals:

> The constitutions will not be abrogated and the good laws will remain on the statute book; but these liberal forms will merely serve to mask and adorn a profoundly illiberal substance. (...) [B]y means of ever more effective methods of mind-manipulation, the democracies will change their nature; the quaint old forms —elections, parliaments, Supreme Courts and all the rest — will remain. The underlying substance will be a new kind of non-violent totalitarianism. All the traditional names, all the hallowed slogans will remain exactly what they were in the good old days. Democracy and freedom will be the theme of every broadcast and editorial -— but democracy and freedom in a strictly Pickwickian sense. Meanwhile the ruling oligarchy and its highly trained elite of soldiers, policemen, thought-manufacturers and mind-manipulators will quietly run the show as they see fit. (...)"Free as a bird," we say, and envy the winged creatures for their power of unrestricted movement in all the three dimensions. But, alas, we forget the dodo. Any bird that has learned how to grub up a good living without being compelled to use its wings will soon renounce the privilege of flight and remain forever grounded. Something analogous is true of human beings"[113].

---

112  See supra, note 93.
113  Brave New World Revisited, cit., pp. 145-146, 152..

## 3.2

The second of these possibilities exclusively concerns *Island*'s world and the previously mentioned difficulty of identifying the kind of *alternative* constructed by its *order of Karuna* — i. e. the difficulties in determining the meaning which its (not only instrumental, but also residual) treatment of law assumes. Two stages or steps seem plausible here, both of which consider the opportunity to provide contemporary legal theory with new *non-negligible opportunities for mapping*.

### 3.2.1

The first stage is developed exclusively from the perspective of the Western canon and directly explores the family resemblances which bring Pala's answer closer to the practical world(s) referred to (i. e. reconstituted and defended) in certain significant strands of contemporary legal thinking. I allude here mainly to the so-called *humanistic approaches* (or "humanistic" interdisciplinary projects)[114], i. e. those which resist legal formalism and legal pragmatism and mobilise the "sources of *external* knowledge" which "the humanities", as such, provide[115]. In exploring different paths (and assuming different legacies), these approaches do, in fact, converge in the defence of *narrative* (as an explicit or implicit archetypal form of practice), as well as in a reinvention of practical thinking which (reappraising the concern with "the ultimate and the particular"[116]) brings *phronêsis* and *poiesis* together (through the specific mediation of *aesthesis*, if not through the potentialities of a certain "perception" or "sense-perception" analogy), and which (frequently following the claims of unconditional alterity and infinite compassion) justifies a holistic ethical commitment — a commitment in which *energeia* and *kinesis*, *praxis* and *poiesis*, but also

---

114  A focus on communitarian theories of Justice (and a certain "instrumental" submission of law to the particularism of mores and positive dominant morality) would also enable us to discuss an alternative of pure ethics without, however, offering any relevant contribution to the discussion of Pala's world (and its distinctiveness in relation to other possible worlds).

115  These humanistic approaches may be recognized not only as immediate (productive) offshoots of the linguistic literary turn (and the Law and Literature Movement) but also as elements in other complementary (sometimes supposedly alternative) trends such as narrative critical jurisprudences, law as musical and dramatic performance, legal iconology, law and film, law and emotions and law and culture movements. I have attempted to reconstruct the common ground where all these possibilities converge in "Law in/as Literature as a- "Law in/as Literature as an Alternative Humanistic Discourse: the Unavoidable Resistance to Legal Scientific Pragmatism or The Fertile Promise of a Communitas Without Law?", in M. Paola Mittica (ed.), Law and Literature. A Discussion on Purposes and Method. Proceedings of the Special WS on Law and Literature held at 24th IVR World Conference in Beijing [pp. VII +145], published online in September 2010, pp. 22-42, available at http://www.lawandliterature.org/area/documenti/Law%20and%20Literature%20%20IVR%20WS%20Proceedings%202010.pdf., and also in B. Wojciechowski, P. Juchacz, K. M. Cern (eds.), Legal Rules, Moral Norms and Democratic Principles, Peter Lang, Frankfurt am Main, 2013, pp. 257-282.

116  Aristotle, Nicomachean Ethics, VI, 9, 1142a 25

êthos (ἦθος) and éthos (ἔθος), *ethos* and *pathos,* seem to be definitively reconciled and merged. A consideration of these family resemblances, highlighting the role of compassion and incomparability, if not infinite responsibility (as well as the promises of an *art of living* which also involves an *aesthetics of existence[117]*), may in fact lead us to the possibility of adding a *fourth* alternative to the abovementioned *three* types (no less present as a trend in contemporary reflection and no less incompatible with the autonomy of law). It would therefore be feasible to consider the *alternative of pure ethics*, thus covering every social-political institutionalization (or every philosophical-cultural "politicization" project) which, faced with the challenge of a specific sensitivity to otherness and difference, would defend the need to invent another *homo humanus* — i. e. to develop a *quest for the humanitas* or *dignitas of man* which could be said to be pursued beyond the *limits of humanism* (or the already known *forms* of humanism, including the *juridical*)[118].

### 3.2.2

Despite highlighting some of its main components, does this addition of a fourth *alternative to law* provide a compelling characterization of Pala's project (a successful understanding of its specific practical-cultural *meaning*)? I would say that it does not. We need only return to the narrative of the *founding moment* — resulting from the generous ambitions of Dr. Andrew MacPhail and the Old Raja ("the Calvinist-turned-atheist and the pious Mahyana Buddhist (...) [,] what a strangely assorted pair!"[119])— to conclude that this tale of the absence of law is only productively highlighted from the perspective of the *alternative debate* when the issue of inter-cultural dialogue is introduced, explicitly pursued without the a-problematic presupposition of a trans-civilizational meta-discourse. This, in effect, means engaging with the opportunity to distinguish law's cultural answer (and its order of validity) not only *from* the (four) conceivable alternative answers *in* the Western canon

---

117  "Palanese superiority does not lie in symbolic expression but in an art which, though higher and far more valuable than all the rest, can yet be practiced by everyone—the art of adequately experiencing, the art of becoming more intimately acquainted with all the worlds that, as human beings, we find ourselves inhabiting. Palanese culture is not to be judged as (for lack of any better criterion) we judge other cultures. It is not to be judged by the accomplishments of a few gifted manipulators of artistic or philosophical symbols. No, it is to be judged by what all the members of the community, the ordinary as well as the extraordinary, can and do experience in every contingency and at each successive intersection of time and eternity..." (Huxley, Island, chapter XI, pp. 201-202.

118  I have partially considered this issue in a sequence of dialogues with Levinas and Derrida: see "Autotranscendentalidade, desconstrução e responsabilidade infinita. Os enigmas de Force de loi" (2004), in Figueiredo Dias, Gomes Canotilho, Faria Costa (ed.), Ars iudicandi. Estudos em homenagem ao Prof. Doutor António Castanheira Neves, I, cit., pp., pp. 551 ff., "O dito do direito e o dizer da justiça. Diálogos com Levinas e Derrida" (2006), in Themis—Revista da Faculdade de Direito da Universidade Nova de Lisboa, VIII, no. 14, 2007, pp. 5 ff., "Dekonstruktion als philosophische (gegenphilosophische) Reflexion über das Recht. Betrachtungen zu Derrida" (Maio 2005), Archiv für Rechts- und Sozialphilosophie (ARSP), Band 93 / 2007, Heft 1, pp. 39 ff.

119  Huxley, Island, chapter VIII, p. 150.

— exploring experiences of power and of rationalizing *autonomous* (scientific, ideological and ethical) intentions which are (as well as in law) decisive factors in a certain *Idea of Europe* — but also *from* the cultural challenges that other practices, from *alien* civilizational horizons, present when they respond to the problem of social institutionalisation (and social order), i. e. when they conceive of this *life in common* problem (and plausible solution) by referring to a practical *continnum* — a kind of horizon-*ethos* in which communitarian morality, religious (and mystical) practices, shared narratives, concepts *of good life*, self-understanding *exempla* (understanding without knowledge!) and other social canons are experienced as constitutively inseparable and *law* is not a specific *identifiable* (separable) voice (determined by an explicit claim to autonomy) but only a (relatively effective and subsidiary) regulative or coercive projection of the content of this *continnum*. The consideration of this last alternative (or spectrum of alternatives), with the *continuum* it consecrates (and the place it attributes to legally relevant practices), certainly provides us with a precious clue to reconstituting the Palanese *order of compassion*, in particular since this special political program (invented by a Scottish doctor and a Palanese king in the mid 19th century and designed to last only a hundred years!) —as a *project* for reconciling the Oriental and the European, ancient traditions and contemporary science — seems to have forgotten law as an autonomous way of producing communitarian meanings, admitting, at most, to diluting its practices within the institutional environment of democratic *openness*... — at most, that is to say, on the very rare reflective occasions which provide for a non-instrumental treatment of these practices!

## The Author

José Manuel Aroso Linhares is an Associate Professor (with Habilitation-*Agregação*) of Legal Theory, Philosophy of Law and Introduction to Law at the Faculty of Law, University of Coimbra (Portugal). He coordinates the research group "Law and Time" (Instituto Jurídico da Faculdade de Direito da Universidade de Coimbra). His current research interests include the theory of evidence, narrative rationality, intercultural dialogue, judge-made law, law as an autonomous practical-cultural project, inclusive positivism, law and literature. He is the Vice-President of *Associação Portuguesa de Teoria do Direito, Filosofia do Direito e Filosofia Social*, Portuguese Section of the IVR. He is an author of several monographs and essays.

# Kafka und Schwejk
## Karikatur des modernen Rechtssystems und Gefühl der Ungerechtigkeit

Jan Wintr[1]

**Zusammenfassung**

Die Romane *Der Prozess* und *Das Schloss* von Franz Kafka und *Die Abenteuer des braven Soldaten Schwejk* von Jaroslav Hašek wurden in der gleichen Zeit und in der gleichen Stadt geschrieben und werden oft verglichen. Unter anderem thematisieren alle die Position des Einzelnen gegenüber dem modernen Rechtssystem.

Die Figuren in den Romanen sind Adressaten zahlreicher Befehle, deren Sinn und Zweck oft unklar ist oder gar fehlt. Schwejk vermutet regelmäßig einen anderen Zweck der Befehle und wendet sie so komischerweise gegen ihren eigenen Zweck. Kafkas Helden sind machtlos angesichts ungreifbarer Befehle und werden Opfer des Systems. Beide Werke sind ambivalent. Das moderne Rechtssystem ist einerseits auf unpersönliche allgemeine Normen angewiesen, andererseits steht es jedoch in Gefahr, den Einzelnen zu unterdrücken oder sogar zu vernichten.

Es geht nicht nur um das Überleben und das Verständnis, sondern auch um das Gefühl der Gerechtigkeit oder der Ungerechtigkeit. Der Mensch möchte den Sinn und Zweck der Normen verstehen. Hat der Leser ein Gefühl der Ungerechtigkeit bei der Lektüre von Kafkas Romanen, beruht dieses Gefühl nicht auf einer Ungleichbehandlung von Gleichen. Vielmehr sehen wir als ungerecht, dass der Mensch bloßes Objekt eines unsinnigen und unbegründeten „Rechts" ist.

Auch Hašeks Roman bietet viel Stoff zum Nachdenken über die Gerechtigkeit. Schwejk beschreibt mit Ironie und Sarkasmus mehrere strafrechtliche Fälle, wo oft das Strafmaß überschritten oder unterschritten war, und macht sich lustig über das Streben anderer nach der Gerechtigkeit. Es wäre nützlich auch da zu analysieren, woraus genau in diesen Geschichten das Gefühl der Ungerechtigkeit entsteht und ob das ähnlich zur Ungerechtigkeit der Kafkas literarischen Welt ist.

Kafkas und Hašeks Werke zeigen manche wesentlichen Probleme des modernen Rechtssystems in seiner kritischen Phase zur Zeit des Ersten Weltkrieges.

---

1    The article was supported by Charles University in Prague research project PROGRES Q04, "Law in the Changing World".

© Springer Fachmedien Wiesbaden GmbH, part of Springer Nature 2018
H. Kabashima et al. (Hrsg.), *The Idea of Justice in Literature*,
Wirtschaftsethik in der globalisierten Welt,
https://doi.org/10.1007/978-3-658-21996-3_9

**Schlüsselbegriffe**

Gesetz und Literatur; Franz Kafka; Jaroslav Hašek; Justiz; Zweck des Gesetzes

# 1    Einführung

Die Romane *Der Prozess* und *Das Schloss* von Franz Kafka und *Die Abenteuer des braven Soldaten Schwejk*[2] von Jaroslav Hašek wurden in der gleichen Zeit und in der gleichen Stadt[3] geschrieben und werden oft verglichen.[4] Unter anderem thematisieren alle diese Romane die Position des Einzelnen gegenüber das moderne Rechtssystem.

Die Figuren in den Romanen sind Adressaten zahlreicher Befehle, deren Sinn und Zweck oft unklar ist oder gar fehlt. Es wird oft gesagt, dass Schwejk mit einem absurden Textualismus reagiert; dass er nach dem Wortlaut des Befehls gegen jeden möglichen Zweck handelt.[5] Es ist jedoch anders. Schwejk vermutet eher einen anderen Zweck der Befehle und wendet sie so komischerweise gegen ihren eigenen Zweck an.[6]

Kafkas Helden sind machtlos angesichts ungreifbarer Befehle und werden Opfer des Systems. Beide Werke sind ambivalent. Das moderne Rechtssystem ist einerseits auf un-

---

2    Orig. Osudy dobrého vojáka Švejka za světové války; unten gekürzt als "Schwejk".

3    Beide sind 1883 in Prag geboren und lebten überwiegend in dieser Stadt. Hašek starb 1923, Kafka ein Jahr später. Die Abenteuer des braven Soldaten Schwejk schrieb Hašek 1921–1923 (auf Tschechisch, die erste und klassische Übersetzung ins Deutsch von Grete Reiner wurde 1926 veröffentlicht) und ließ sie unvollendet, die Figur Schwejk erschien in seinen Erzählungen jedoch bereits 1912. Kafka schrieb Den Prozess 1914–1915 (auf Deutsch, veröffentlicht 1925) und Das Schloss 1922 (auf Deutsch, veröffentlicht 1926), auch dieser Roman blieb unvollendet.

4    Siehe z. B. KOSÍK, Karel: Kdo je Švejk: Hašek a Kafka neboli groteskní svět, in: Z dějin českého myšlení o literatuře 3 (1958-1969). Praha: Ústav pro českou literaturu AV ČR, 2003, S. 103-112.

5    Zum Textualismus, Intentionalismus und Purposivismus mit dem Beispiel des Schwejks siehe SOBEK, Tomáš: Úmysl zákonodárce a skutečné právo, in: Gerloch, A. / Tryzna, J. / Wintr, J. (eds.): Metodologie interpretace práva a právní jistota, Plzeň 2012, s. 79–80.

6    In einem der besten Beispiele sollte Schwejk für Offiziere den zweiten Teil eines Romans besorgen. Das Buch diente zur Entschlüsselung der geheimen Kommunikation. Schwejk war jedoch der Meinung, dass die Offiziere zuerst den ersten Teil des Romans lesen möchten: „So hab ich mir gedacht, daß alle besoffen sind, weil, wenn man ein Buch von Anfang lesen soll, so einen Roman, was ich gebracht hab, von den ›Sünden der Väter‹, denn ich kann auch Deutsch, so muß man mitn I. Teil anfangen, weil wir keine Juden sind und nicht von rückwärts lesen. Drum hab ich Sie auch per Telefon gefragt, Herr Oberlajtnant, wie Sie ausn Kasino zurückgekommen sind, und hab Ihnen das von den Büchern gemeldet, obs vielleicht jetzt beim Militär umgekehrt is und ob man nicht die Bücher in verkehrter Reihenfolge liest, zuerst den Zweiten und dann den Ersten Teil. Und Sie ham mir gesagt, daß ich ein besoffenes Rindvieh bin, wenn ich nicht mal weiß, daß im Vaterunser zuerst steht: ›Vater unser‹ und dann erst ›Amen‹." HAŠEK, Jaroslav: Die Abenteuer des braven Soldaten Schwejk, Bd. 2, 36. Aufl., Reinbek bei Hamburg 2001, S. 72–73.

persönliche allgemeine Normen angewiesen, andererseits steht jedoch es in Gefahr, den Einzelnen zu unterdrücken oder sogar zu vernichten.

Kafkas und Hašeks Werke zeigen manche wesentlichen Probleme des modernen Rechtssystems in seiner kritischen Phase zur Zeit des Ersten Weltkrieges. Die Romane von Franz Kafka sind voll von Rechtsthemen, im *Prozess* spielt das Gerichtsverfahren eine zentrale Rolle, im *Schloss* bilden die Beziehungen des K. zur Verwaltung einen wesentlichen Rahmen. Auch Josef Schwejk wurde bereits am Anfang wegen verbaler Delikte festgenommen und wanderte dann durch verschiedene Instanzen. Am Ende des Romans steht Schwejk wieder vor einem Militärgericht.

Der Humor beider Autoren bezieht sich oft gerade auf die Rechtsthemen. Mit der Art und Weise dieses Humors fangen wir an.

## 2     Das Recht als Groteske

*Die Abenteuer des braven Soldaten Schwejk* wird oft als ein humoristischer Roman charakterisiert. Nicht selten werden jedoch auch Kafkas Werke als Grotesken interpretiert.[7] Jiří Přibáň, tschechischer Professor der Rechtsphilosophie und Rechtssoziologie in Cardiff, zeigt, wie die Rechtsformen in Kafkas Romanen zum Humor beitragen. In der Rechtswelt des *Prozesses* und des *Schlosses* ist nämlich groteskerweise alles umgekehrt. Das Verfahren findet am Sonntag statt, nicht am Alltag. Die Gerichtsgebäude ist kein repräsentatives Haus im Stadtzentrum, sondern ein Miethaus am Rande der Stadt; die Gerichtsräume sind im Dachboden.[8] Im Schloss empfangen die Beamten den K. regelmäßig im Bett, zuerst der Vorsteher, dann der Sekretär Bürgel, ebenso wie der Rechtsanwalt im *Prozess*.

Die Gerichtsakten im *Prozess* sind geheim, mindestens sagte der Rechtsanwalt es Josef K. so:

*„K. möge doch nicht außer acht lassen, daß das Verfahren nicht öffentlich sei, es kann, wenn das Gericht es für nötig hält, öffentlich werden, das Gesetz aber schreibt Öffentlichkeit nicht vor. Infolgedessen sind auch die Schriften des Gerichts, vor allem die Anklageschrift, dem Angeklagten und seiner Verteidigung unzugänglich, man weiß daher im allgemeinen nicht oder wenigstens nicht genau, wogegen sich die erste Eingabe zu richten hat, sie kann daher eigentlich nur zufälligerweise etwas enthalten, was für die Sache von Bedeutung ist. Wirklich zutreffende und beweisführende Eingaben kann man erst später ausarbeiten, wenn im Laufe der Einvernahmen des Angeklagten die einzelnen Anklagepunkte und ihre Begründung deutlicher hervortreten oder erraten werden können. Unter diesen*

---

7     Siehe z. B. JAMEK, Václav : Muž, který se nikdy nesmál, in: Souvislosti 1-2/2003, oder KUN-DERA, Milan: Kastrující stín svatého Garty, Praha 2006.

8     PŘIBÁŇ, Jiří: Toto není „právo", toto není „literatura": O Kafkově Procesu, literárních obrazech a interpretaci práva, in: Bobek, M.; Šimíček, V. (eds.): Jiné právo literární, Praha 2011, S. 101–103.

*Verhältnissen ist natürlich die Verteidigung in einer sehr ungünstigen und schwierigen Lage. Aber auch das ist beabsichtigt. Die Verteidigung ist nämlich durch das Gesetz nicht eigentlich gestattet, sondern nur geduldet, und selbst darüber, ob aus der betreffenden Gesetzesstelle wenigstens Duldung herausgelesen werden soll, besteht Streit. Es gibt daher strenggenommen gar keine vom Gericht anerkannten Advokaten, alle, die vor diesem Gericht als Advokaten auftreten, sind im Grunde nur Winkeladvokaten. Das wirkt natürlich auf den ganzen Stand sehr entwürdigend ein, und wenn K. nächstens einmal in die Gerichtskanzleien gehen werde, könne er sich ja, um auch das einmal gesehen zu haben, das Advokatenzimmer ansehen. Er werde vor der Gesellschaft, die dort beisammen sei, vermutlich erschrecken. Schon die ihnen zugewiesene enge, niedrige Kammer zeige die Verachtung, die das Gericht für diese Leute hat. Licht bekommt die Kammer nur durch eine kleine Luke, die so hochgelegen ist, daß man, wenn man hinausschauen will, wo einem übrigens der Rauch eines knapp davor gelegenen Kamins in die Nase fährt und das Gesicht schwärzt, erst einen Kollegen suchen muß, der einen auf den Rücken nimmt. Im Fußboden dieser Kammer – um nur noch ein Beispiel für diese Zustände anzuführen – ist nun schon seit mehr als einem Jahr ein Loch, nicht so groß, daß ein Mensch durchfallen könnte, aber groß genug, daß man mit einem Bein ganz einsinkt.*"[9]

Das ist eine Parodie auf das Rechtsstaatsprinzip, im Widerspruch zum bekannten Satz im ersten Kapitel: „*K. lebte doch in einem Rechtsstaat, überall herrschte Friede, alle Gesetze bestanden aufrecht…*"[10]

Kafka macht sich lustig über die Rechtsformen an vielen Stellen seiner Romane, woraus ich noch die Szene beim Vorsteher im Schloss auswählte. Der Vorsteher schilderte dem K. die Geschichte seiner Einberufung zum Landvermesser, beschrieb die Genialität eines Beamten Sordini und sprach seine Bewunderung über die Arbeit der Behörden aus:

„*Und nun komme ich auf eine besondere Eigenschaft unseres behördlichen Apparates zu sprechen. Entsprechend seiner Präzision ist er auch äußerst empfindlich. Wenn eine Angelegenheit sehr lange erwogen worden ist, kann es, auch ohne daß die Erwägungen schon beendet wären, geschehen, daß plötzlich blitzartig an einer unvorhersehbaren und auch später nicht mehr auffindbaren Stelle eine Erledigung hervorkommt, welche die Angelegenheit, wenn auch meistens sehr richtig, so doch immerhin willkürlich abschließt. Es ist, als hätte der behördliche Apparat die Spannung, die jahrelange Aufreizung durch die gleiche, vielleicht an sich geringfügige Angelegenheit nicht mehr ertragen und aus sich selbst heraus, ohne Mithilfe der Beamten, die Entscheidung getroffen. Natürlich ist kein Wunder geschehen, und gewiß hat irgendein Beamter die Erledigung geschrieben oder eine ungeschriebene Entscheidung getroffen, jedenfalls aber kann, wenigstens von uns aus, von hier aus, ja selbst vom Amt aus nicht festgestellt werden, welcher Beamte in diesem Fall entschieden hat, und aus welchen Gründen. Erst die Kontrollämter stellen das viel später fest; wir aber erfahren es nicht mehr, es würde übrigens dann auch*

---

9    KAFKA, Franz: Gesammelte Werke, Köln 2013, S. 594–595.
10    Ibidem, S. 507.

*kaum jemanden noch interessieren. Nun sind, wie gesagt, gerade diese Entscheidungen meistens vortrefflich, störend ist an ihnen nur, daß man, wie es gewöhnlich die Sache mit sich bringt, von diesen Entscheidungen zu spät erfährt und daher inzwischen über längst entschiedene Angelegenheiten noch immer leidenschaftlich berät."*[11]

Dieser Anthropomorphismus der Verwaltung wirkt absurd. Kafkas Figuren sind wie besessen vom Recht und haben vor dem Recht einen übertriebenen Respekt, woraus die Komik (und auch die Tragik) der Romane entstehen. Dagegen hat Hašeks Schwejk keinen Respekt vor dem Recht. Man kann in diesem humoristischen Roman zwei typische Konstellationen beobachten – entweder (a) macht sich Hašek lustig über die Rechtsnormen sowie ihre Anwendungen, oder (b) kommentieren seine Figuren zynisch die Bereitschaft anderer, dem Recht zu gehorchen.

In der ersten Situation (a) übertreibt man die Richtigkeitsvermutung der Rechtsakte:

*„Ein Geheimtelegramm von Ihrer Division. Der Kommandant Ihrer Brigade ist verrückt geworden. Man hat ihn nach Wien geschickt, nachdem er von der Brigade einige Dutzend ähnlicher Telegramme nach allen Seiten abschickte. In Budapest werden Sie sicher ein neues Telegramm vorfinden. Alle seine Telegramme müssen natürlich annulliert werden, aber wir haben in dieser Richtung noch keinen Wink erhalten. Ich habe, wie ich sage, nur den Befehl von der Division, daß unchiffrierte Telegramme nicht in Erwägung gezogen werden sollen. Einhändigen muß ich sie, weil ich in dieser Hinsicht von meinen Instanzen keine Antwort erhalten habe. Durch meine Instanzen habe ich mich beim Armeekommando informiert, und es ist eine Untersuchung eingeleitet worden."*[12]

Schwejk und sein Kumpel als Arrestanten sprechen einen Korporal an, der im Arrestantenwaggon einen betrunkenen Feldkurat übrig hatte und ihn melden gehen wollte:

*„Sie sind Eskortekommandant. Sie dürfen sich nicht von uns entfernen. Und nach der Vorschrift dürfen Sie auch niemanden von der begleitenden Wache herauslassen, um Meldung zu erstatten, solange Sie keinen Ersatz haben. Sie sehn, es ist eine harte Nuß. Mit einem Schuß ein Zeichen geben, daß jemand hereinkommen soll, geht auch nicht. Es ist hier nichts geschehen. Anderseits besteht wieder die Vorschrift, daß sich außer den Arrestanten und der sie begleitenden Eskorte im Arrestantenwaggon keine fremde Person befinden darf. Unbefugten ist der Eintritt streng verboten. Die Spuren Ihrer Übertretung zu verwischen und den Oberfeldkuraten während der Fahrt auf unauffällige Art aus dem Zug zu werfen, geht auch nicht, weil Zeugen zugegen sind, die gesehen haben,*

---

11  Ibidem, S. 747–748.
12  HAŠEK, Jaroslav: Die Abenteuer des braven Soldaten Schwejk, Bd. 2, 36. Aufl., Reinbek bei Hamburg 2001, S. 85.

*daß Sie ihn in den Waggon gelassen haben, wohin er nicht gehört. Das bedeutet sichere*
*Degradation, Herr Korporal."*[13]

Auch anderswo macht sich Hašek lustig über die Rechtslücken:

*„Einmal bin ich Ihnen, Herr Feldkurat, im Arrest in Budweis beim Regiment gesessen,*
*und man hat einen Kadettstellvertreter zu mir gebracht. So ein Kadettstellvertreter, das*
*war was Ähnliches wie Feldkurat, nicht Schwein und nicht Maus, hat die Soldaten ange-*
*brüllt wie ein Offizier, und wenn was geschehn is, so hat man ihn zwischen die gemeine*
*Mannschaft gesperrt. Das waren Ihnen, Herr Feldkurat, solche Bastarde, daß man sie*
*in der Unteroffiziersküche nicht in die Menage aufgenommen hat, auf die Menage für*
*die Mannschaft ham sie keinen Anspruch gehabt, da waren sie höher, und die Offiziers-*
*menage hat ihnen wieder nicht gebührt. Wir ham ihrer damals fünf dort gehabt, und am*
*Anfang ham sie Ihnen in der Kantine lauter Käsl gefressen, weil sie nirgendwo Menage*
*gekriegt ham, bis dort einmal der Oberlajtnant Wurm auf sie gekommen is und es ihnen*
*verboten hat, weil sichs herich nicht mit der Ehre eines Kadettstellvertreters verträgt, in*
*die Mannschaftskantine zu gehn. Aber was ham sie machen solln, in die Offizierskantine*
*hat man sie nicht gelassen. So sind sie in der Luft gehangen und ham in einigen Tagen so*
*einen Leidensweg durchgemacht, daß einer von ihnen in die Maltsch gesprungen is und*
*einer vom Regiment gegangen is und nach zwei Monaten in die Kaserne geschrieben hat,*
*daß er in Marokko Kriegsminister is. Es waren ihrer vier, weil man den aus der Maltsch*
*lebendig herausgezogen hat, er hat nämlich in der Aufregung, wie er hineingesprungen*
*is, vergessen, daß er schwimmen kann und die Freischwimmerprüfung mit Auszeichnung*
*abgelegt hat. Man hat ihn ins Krankenhaus geschafft und dort hat man sich wieder keinen*
*Rat mit ihm gewußt, ob man ihn mit einer Offiziersdecke oder mit einer gewöhnlichen*
*für die Mannschaft zudecken soll. So hat man also einen Weg gefunden und hat ihm*
*überhaupt keine Decke gegeben und hat ihn nur in ein nasses Leintuch eingewickelt, so*
*daß er in einer halben Stunde gebeten hat, man soll ihn zurücklassen in die Kaserne,*
*und das war grad der, was man noch ganz naß zu mir eingesperrt hat. Er is ungefähr*
*vier Tage dort gesessen, und es hat ihm sehr gefallen, weil er dort Menage bekommen*
*hat, zwar Arrestantenmenage, aber doch Menage, er hats sicher gehabt, wie man sagt.*
*Am fünften Tag hat man sich ihn geholt, und er is dann nach einer halben Stunde um*
*die Mütze zurückgekommen und hat Ihnen vor Freude geweint. Er sagt mir: „Endlich is*
*eine Entscheidung über uns gekommen. Von heut an wern wir Kadettstellvertreter auf*
*der Hauptwache zwischen den Offizieren eingesperrt wern, auf die Menage wern wir uns*
*in der Offiziersküche zuzahlen, und bis sich die Offiziere angegessen ham, so bekommen*
*wir zu essen, schlafen wern wir mit der Mannschaft, und Kaffee wern wir auch von der*
*Mannschaftsküche kriegen, und Tabak fassen wir auch mit der Mannschaft."*[14]

---

13   HAŠEK, Jaroslav: Die Abenteuer des braven Soldaten Schwejk, Bd. 1, 36. Aufl., Reinbek bei
      Hamburg 2001, S. 294.
14   HAŠEK, Jaroslav: Die Abenteuer des braven Soldaten Schwejk, Bd. 2, 36. Aufl., Reinbek bei
      Hamburg 2001, S. 275–276.

Das ist jedoch schon eine Art vom Galgenhumor. Die Rechtslage der Kadettstellvertreter erinnert an die Staatenlosen in der ersten Hälfte des 20. Jahrhunderts, deren äußerst heikle Situation Hannah Arendt beschrieb.[15]

Wo Kafkas Figuren von der Absurdität des realen Rechts innerlich erschüttert sind, dort beobachten Hašeks Figuren oder Hašek selbst die Rechtsnormen und kommentieren sie zynisch von außen. Der Zynismus steigt in der zweiten typischen Situation (b), wo direkt die rechtmäßig handelnden Personen verspottet sind, wie z. B. ein ehrlicher Finder:

> *„Bei uns in Budweis beim Regiment war ein Soldat, so ein gutmütiges Rindvieh, der hat mal 600 Kronen auf der Gasse gefunden und hat sie auf der Polizei abgegeben, und in den Zeitungen hat man von ihm als ehrlichem Finder geschrieben, und er hat einen Schkandal davon gehabt. Niemand wollte mit ihm reden, jeder hat gesagt: ›Du Trottel, du, was hast du da für eine Dummheit gemacht. Das muß dich bis in den Tod verdrießen, wenn du noch bißl Ehr im Leib hast.‹ Er hat ein Mädl gehabt, und die hat aufgehört, mit ihm zu reden. Wie er auf Urlaub nach Haus gekommen is, ham ihn die Kameraden bei der Musik deswegen ausm Wirtshaus herausgeworfen. Er hat angefangen zu kränkeln, hat sichs in den Kopf genommen, und zum Schluß hat er sich vom Zug überfahren lassen.“[16]*

Schwejk sprach auch den Unterschied zwischen Normativität und Faktizität an:

> *„Bei Kulaschno sah man unten in einem Flüßchen einen vom Eisenbahndamm gestürzten, zertrümmerten Rot-Kreuz-Zug... Diese Erscheinung erweckte auch die Aufmerksamkeit der Mitreisenden Schwejks. Am meisten regte sich Koch Jurajda auf: „Darf man denn auf Waggons vom Roten Kreuz schießen?"*
>
> *„Man darf nicht, aber man kann", sagte Schwejk. „Es war jedenfalls ein guter Schuß, und jeder redet sich dann aus, daß es in der Nacht war und daß das Rote Kreuz nicht zu sehn gewesen is. Es gibt überhaupt viel Sachen auf der Welt, was man nicht machen darf, aber machen kann. Hauptsache is, daß jeder probiert, obs ihm gelingt, und wenn ers nicht darf, ob ers kann. Bei den Kaisermanövern in Pisek is so ein Befehl gekommen, daß man die Soldaten am Marsch nicht krummschließen darf. Aber unser Hauptmann is drauf gekommen, daß mans darf, weil so ein Befehl schrecklich is, denn jeder hat leicht begreifen können, daß ein krummgeschlossener Soldat nicht marschieren kann. Er hat also den Befehl eigentlich nicht umgangen, hat einfach und vernünftig die krummgeschlossenen Soldaten in die Trainwagen werfen lassen, und man is mit ihnen weitermarschiert.""[17]*

---

15  ARENDT, Hannah: Elemente und Ursprünge totaler Herrschaft. Antisemitismus, Imperialismus, totale Herrschaft, 12. Aufl., München-Zürich 2008, II. Teil, IX. Kapitel.

16  HAŠEK, Jaroslav: Die Abenteuer des braven Soldaten Schwejk Bd. 1, 36. Aufl., Reinbek bei Hamburg 2001, S. 129–130.

17  HAŠEK, Jaroslav: Die Abenteuer des braven Soldaten Schwejk Bd. 2, 36. Aufl., Reinbek bei Hamburg 2001, S. 193.

Am Ende des Romans steht Schwejk vor dem Militärgericht als Deserteur, weil er sich freiwillig die russische Uniform anzog (buchstäblich). Der vorsitzende Offizier wollte ihn sofort hinrichten, die anderen waren jedoch dagegen und *„schloß sich schließlich doch der Meinung des Hauptmanns an, daß dieser Mensch erst nach der längeren Prozedur gehängt werden müsse, die man so lieblich „Rechtsweg" nennt."*[18] Wenn es sichergestellt wurde, dass Schwejk nur verloren gegangen war, *„gab der General unzähligemal durch fürchterliche Flüche sein Mißfallen darüber kund, daß er Schwejk nicht auf eigenes Risiko ohne jede Untersuchung sofort hatte hängen lassen. Der Major opponierte und sprach etwas davon, daß Recht und Gerechtigkeit einander die Hände reichen; er sprach in glänzenden Perioden über gerechte Urteile im allgemeinen, über Justizmorde und alles mögliche, was ihm der Augenblick auf die Zunge brachte, denn er hatte nach dem verflossenen Abend einen unbeschreiblichen Kater, der einer Auslösung bedurfte."*[19]

Damit kommen wir schon nah zum Thema Gerechtigkeit. Auf diese zynische Weise betrachtet Schwejk viele Rechtsfälle, wo das Ergebnis im krassen Widerspruch mit der Gerechtigkeit steht.

## 3      Das moderne Rechtssystem und Gefühl der Ungerechtigkeit

Der Mensch möchte den Sinn und Zweck der Normen verstehen. Hat der Leser Gefühl der Ungerechtigkeit bei der Lektüre von Kafkas Romane, beruht dieses Gefühl nicht auf einer Ungleichbehandlung von Gleichen. Vielmehr sehen wir als ungerecht, dass der Mensch bloßes Objekt eines unsinnigen und unbegründeten „Rechts" ist.

Auch Hašeks Roman bietet viel Stoff zum Nachdenken über die Gerechtigkeit. Schwejk beschreibt mit Ironie und Sarkasmus mehrere strafrechtliche Fälle, wo oft das Strafmaß überschritten oder unterschritten war, und macht sich lustig über das Streben anderer nach der Gerechtigkeit. Es wäre nützlich auch da zu analysieren, woraus genau in diesen Geschichten das Gefühl der Ungerechtigkeit entsteht und ob das ähnlich zur Ungerechtigkeit der literarischen Welt Kafkas ist.

Fangen wir mit Schwejk an. Die berühmte Szene zeigt Schwejk nach seiner Verhaftung. Im Gefängnis sitzt er mit anderen Häftlingen, die alle der Zustimmung mit dem Attentat in Sarajewo verdächtig sind. Schwejk tröstet seine Gefährten: *„Jesus Christus war auch unschuldig, und sie ham ihn auch gekreuzigt. Nirgendwo is jemals jemandem etwas an einem unschuldigen Menschen gelegen gewesen."*[20]

Dazu erzählt er recht absurde Fälle, wie:

---

18   Ibidem, S. 259.

19   Ibidem, S. 290.

20   HAŠEK, Jaroslav: Die Abenteuer des braven Soldaten Schwejk Bd. 1, 36. Aufl., Reinbek bei Hamburg 2001, S. 22.

*„Und wieviel unschuldige Leute sind schon verurteilt worn. Und nicht nur beim Militär, sondern auch von den Gerichten. Einmal is, ich erinner mich noch gut, eine Frau verurteilt worn, weil sie ihre neugeborenen Zwillinge erwürgt hat. Obgleich sie steif und fest geschworen hat, daß sie die Zwillinge nicht hat erwürgen können, weil sie nur ein Mäderl zur Welt gebracht hat und es ihr gelungen war, es ganz schmerzlos zu erwürgen, is sie trotzdem wegen Doppelmord verurteilt worn."*[21]

Die Verurteilung des Wirts Palivec kommentierte Schwejk so:

*„Das hab ich mir nicht gedacht", sagte er, „daß sie einen unschuldigen Menschen zu zehn Jahren verurteilen wern. Daß sie einen unschuldigen Menschen zu fünf Jahren verurteilt ham, das hab ich schon gehört, aber zehn, das is bißl viel."*[22]

Manchmal stammt die Ungerechtigkeit aus einem bösartigen Formalismus:

*„In der Karolinentaler Kaserne war ein gewisser Lajtnant Hausner, und der hat auch einen Burschen gehabt und hat ihn auch geohrfeigt und mitn Füßen gestoßen. Einmal war der Bursch so abgeohrfeigt, daß er davon blöd geworden is und sich zum Rapport gemeldet hat, und beim Rapport hat er gemeldet, daß er geohrfeigt worn is, weil er sich das alles verwechselt hat, und sein Herr hat auch wirklich nachgewiesen, daß er lügt, daß er ihn an dem Tag nicht abgeohrfeigt, sondern nur mitn Füßen gestoßn hat, so hat man den lieben Jungen wegen falscher Beschuldigung auf drei Wochen eingesperrt."*[23]

Das Recht ist in den *Abenteuern des braven Soldaten Schwejk* gewissermaßen realitätsnah geschildert. Die Rechtsnormen selbst kann man gut begreifen, manchmal werden sie zwar zu rigid, manchmal fehlerhaft oder missbräuchlich angewendet. Dazu zeigt Jaroslav Hašek eine gewisse Herabwürdigung gegenüber dem Recht und der Rechtsmäßigkeit, was mit seiner anarchistischen und später kommunistischen politischen Orientation verbunden sein kann.

Das wahrscheinlich zynischste Zitat ist dieser Kommentar Schwejks zum Attentat von Sarajewo:

*„Wenn ich mir das so überleg, ein Onkel Seiner Majestät des Kaisers, und sie erschießen ihn! Das is ja ein Schkandal, die ganzen Zeitungen sind voll damit. Bei uns in Budweis hat man vor Jahren auf dem Markt bei irgendeinem kleinen Streit einen Viehhändler erstochen, einen gewissen Bratislav Ludwig, der hatte einen Sohn namens Bohuslav, und wenn der seine Schweine verkaufen kam, wollte niemand was von ihm kaufen, und jeder*

---

21  Ibidem.

22  Ibidem, S. 49.

23  HAŠEK, Jaroslav: Die Abenteuer des braven Soldaten Schwejk Bd. 2, 36. Aufl., Reinbek bei Hamburg 2001, S. 188.

*hat gesagt: ›Das ist der Sohn von diesem Erstochenen. Das wird gewiß auch ein feiner
Lump sein.‹ Er hat in Krummau von der Brücke in die Moldau springen müssen, und
man hat ihn wieder zu Bewußtsein bringen müssen, und man hat aus ihm das Wasser
herauspumpen müssen, und er hat in den Armen des Arztes seinen Geist aufgeben müssen,
wie der ihm irgendeine Injektion gemacht hat."*[24]

Die Absurdität dieses Gedankenganges erinnert an Situationen, in denen sich Figuren der
Kafkas Romane befinden. Nach Jiří Přibáň ist Kafkas *Prozess* kein Symbol der Verlorenheit
und Entfremdung des Menschen in der modernen Welt. Der Roman sagt nichts über das
Wesen und die Arbeitsweise der Bürokratie und des Rechtsverfahrens. Vielmehr benutzt
die literarische Imagination die scheinbar technische juristische Sprache und karikiert
die allgemein gültigen sozialen Erwartungen an Rechtsnormen und Rechtsverfahren.[25]
Ich stimme Jiří Přibáň zu.

Der Leser kann jedoch trotzdem die Ungerechtigkeit fühlen, wenn er beobachtet,
wie machtlos Josef K. dem unsinnigen und unbegründeten Verfahren gegenüber steht.
Tragisch wirkt die dauerhafte Bemühung des Josef K. den Sinn (und auch den Inhalt) der
Rechtsnormen zu begreifen.

Einen solchen Versuch das Verfahren zu begreifen stellt die Rede von Josef K. vor dem
Gericht:

„*Es ist kein Zweifel, daß hinter allen Äußerungen dieses Gerichtes, in meinem Fall also
hinter der Verhaftung und der heutigen Untersuchung, eine große Organisation sich
befindet. Eine Organisation, die nicht nur bestechliche Wächter, läppische Aufseher und
Untersuchungsrichter, die günstigsten Falles bescheiden sind, beschäftigt, sondern die
weiterhin jedenfalls eine Richterschaft hohen und höchsten Grades unterhält, mit dem
zahllosen, unumgänglichen Gefolge von Dienern, Schreibern, Gendarmen und andern
Hilfskräften, vielleicht sogar Henkern, ich scheue vor dem Wort nicht zurück. Und der
Sinn dieser großen Organisation, meine Herren? Er besteht darin, daß unschuldige
Personen verhaftet werden und gegen sie ein sinnloses und meistens, wie in meinem
Fall, ergebnisloses Verfahren eingeleitet wird. Wie ließe sich bei dieser Sinnlosigkeit des
Ganzen die schlimmste Korruption der Beamtenschaft vermeiden? Das ist unmöglich,
das brächte auch der höchste Richter nicht einmal für sich selbst zustande. Darum suchen
die Wächter den Verhafteten die Kleider vom Leib zu stehlen, darum brechen Aufseher
in fremde Wohnungen ein, darum sollen Unschuldige, statt verhört, lieber vor ganzen
Versammlungen entwürdigt werden. Die Wächter haben nur von Depots erzählt, in die
man das Eigentum der Verhafteten bringt, ich wollte einmal diese Depotplätze sehen,*

---

24  HAŠEK, Jaroslav: Die Abenteuer des braven Soldaten Schwejk Bd. 1, 36. Aufl., Reinbek bei
    Hamburg 2001, S. 14–15.
25  PŘIBÁŇ, Jiří: Toto není „právo", toto není „literatura": O Kafkově Procesu, literárních obrazech
    a interpretaci práva, in: Bobek, M.; Šimíček, V. (eds.): Jiné právo literární, Praha 2011, S. 102.

*in denen das mühsam erarbeitete Vermögen der Verhafteten fault, soweit es nicht von diebischen Depotbeamten gestohlen ist."*[26]

Vergeblich. Auch diese Versuche, irgendeinen Sinn zu finden, scheitern. Es geht nicht um einen Justizirrtum oder Rechtsmissbrauch, es ist eher der absolute Mangel des Sinns und Zwecks der Normen und des Verfahrens. Das Gesetz ist zwar immer angesprochen, es fehlt jedoch nicht nur der Gesetzeszweck (τέλος), sondern auch eine elementare Bestimmtheit des Gesetzes als Grundlage für die Rechtssicherheit, für den Zweck des Rechts selbst. Die Tragödie des K. liegt darin, dass er für seine Bereitschaft, das Recht zu gehorchen, gar nichts bekommt. Man unterwirft sich dem Recht, um mindestens eine elementare Sicherheit für sich zu schaffen, aber hier ist seine Lage desto unsicherer, je mehr sich Josef K. bemüht.

Die Methoden des langjährig angeklagten Kaufmanns Block, wie sich im Verfahren zu orientieren, sind noch hoffnungsloser. Beim Rechtsanwalt erzählte er dem Josef K.:

*„Sie scheinen die Leute dort noch nicht zu kennen und werden es vielleicht unrichtig auffassen. Sie müssen bedenken, daß in diesem Verfahren immer wieder viele Dinge zur Sprache kommen, für die der Verstand nicht mehr ausreicht, man ist einfach zu müde und abgelenkt für vieles, und zum Ersatz verlegt man sich auf den Aberglauben. Ich rede von den anderen, bin aber selbst gar nicht besser. Ein solcher Aberglaube ist es zum Beispiel, daß viele aus dem Gesicht des Angeklagten, insbesondere aus der Zeichnung der Lippen, den Ausgang des Prozesses erkennen wollen. Diese Leute also haben behauptet, Sie würden, nach Ihren Lippen zu schließen, gewiß und bald verurteilt werden. Ich wiederhole, es ist ein lächerlicher Aberglaube und in den meisten Fällen durch die Tatsachen auch vollständig widerlegt, aber wenn man in jener Gesellschaft lebt, ist es schwer, sich solchen Meinungen zu entziehen. Denken Sie nur, wie stark dieser Aberglaube wirken kann. Sie haben doch einen dort angesprochen, nicht? Er konnte Ihnen aber kaum antworten. Es gibt natürlich viele Gründe, um dort verwirrt zu sein, aber einer davon war auch der Anblick Ihrer Lippen. Er hat später erzählt, er hätte auf Ihren Lippen auch das Zeichen seiner eigenen Verurteilung zu sehen geglaubt."*[27]

Das Versuch, aus der Zeichnung der Lippen, den Ausgang des Prozesses zu erkennen, erinnert an die kriminalanthropologischen Theorien von Cesare Lombroso,[28] die man auch als Teil der Rechtsgeschichte einordnen muss. Eine solche Pervertierung des Rechts

---

26   KAFKA, Franz: Gesammelte Werke, Köln 2013, S. 540.

27   Ibidem, S. 642–643.

28   Siehe LOMBROSO, Cesare: L'uomo delinquente. In rapporto all'antropologia, alla giurisprudenza ed alle discipline carcerarie, Turin 1876. Lombrosos Werk ist auch im Schwejk erwähnt: „Als er die Aufschrift erblickte, daß das Spucken auf den Gängen verboten sei, bat er den Polizisten, ihm zu erlauben, in den Spucknapf zu spucken, und strahlend in seiner Einfalt betrat er die Kanzlei mit den Worten: „Winsch einen guten Abend, meine Herren, allen miteinand." Statt einer Antwort puffte ihn jemand in die Rippen und stellte ihn vor den Tisch, hinter dem ein Herr mit einem kühlen Beamtengesicht von so tierischer Grausamkeit saß, als wäre er gerade

und der Auffassung des Rechts in der Bevölkerung ist immer möglich und die Garantien des Rechtsstaates müssen ausgebaut werden, um dies zu vermeiden.

Hašek und Kafka zeigen in ihren Romanen manche Risiken, die mit dem modernen Rechtssystem verbunden sind – Justizirrtümer, Rechtsmissbrauch, exzessiver Formalismus, aber manchmal auch das Gefühl der Sinnlosigkeit des ganzen Rechtssystems. Das Rechtssystem dient der Sicherheit des freien und würdigen Lebens des Menschen in der Gesellschaft, die oben genannten Risiken sind jedoch immer präsent.

## Der Autor

**Jan Wintr**, Associate Professor, Department of Legal Theory and Legal Doctrines, Faculty of Law, Charles University in Prague, Czech Republic. E-mail: wintr@prf.cuni.cz. This paper will be presented at the special workshop titled The Idea of Justice in Literature at XXVII World Congress of the International Association for the Philosophy of Law and Social Philosophy (IVR) in Washington, D.C., 2015.

---

aus Lombrosos Buch „Verbrechertypen" herausgefallen." HAŠEK, Jaroslav: Die Abenteuer des braven Soldaten Schwejk Bd. 1, 36. Aufl., Reinbek bei Hamburg 2001, S. 23–24.

III

# The Idea of Justice in Poetry and Essays

# Romanticism and Political Violence

Hiroshi Kabashima

**Abstract**

Political violence is what we hear about perpetually these days. It appears sometimes in the form of individual acts of radicalized terrorists like as suicide bombing, hostage taking, and assassination, and also in the form of organized killing like as civil war incited by the so-called Islamic State and the Ukraine separatist militants. It is commonly featured by the mindset of agents who are fighting not only on the material level, but rather on the intellectual one, that is what S. Huntington called "clash of civilizations".

In the history of ideas in general, the war has been perceived not only as a political means, but rather as a sort of intellectual battle between different cultural groups. To take a historical instance of this issue, my report will discuss the intellectual dimension of the World War II between the Axis Powers of Germany and Japan and the Allied Powers of West-European-American nations.

The German philosopher, H. Plessner, pointed out that the German hostility against the Western nations was already expressed in the literature movement of romanticism, indeed in its simplified dichotomy of intuition versus reason, passion versus calculation, miracle versus necessity, loyalty versus freedom, and authority versus democracy. Also in Japan interestingly, the literary romanticism arose in the early 20th century under the German influence. Y. Yasuda, one of the most representative among the Japanese romanticists, tried to crystallize in his essays and poetry the pure beauty appearing from the Japanese cultural tradition, in contrast to the European civilization of pragmatism and utilitarianism. He inclined therefore to support the Japanese aggression against the Allied Powers in 1941, in connection with the intellectual fight of the Eastern against the Western.

Those questions would be asked in my report: Is it necessary and inevitable for the ideal in the literature to be realized by means of the political violence? Can we meaningfully distinguish between the aesthetic in the literature and the validity in the politics? Can we even identify the raison d'etre of literature, independent of politics?

© Springer Fachmedien Wiesbaden GmbH, part of Springer Nature 2018      115
H. Kabashima et al. (Hrsg.), *The Idea of Justice in Literature*,
Wirtschaftsethik in der globalisierten Welt,
https://doi.org/10.1007/978-3-658-21996-3_10

**Keywords**

Helmuth Plessner; Totalianism; Facism; Yojuro Yasuda

# 1     Preface

## 1.1    Current Problems

We daily hear about political violence reported by the international media. Politically motivated violence takes different forms indeed. Sometimes it appears as an individual act of radicalized terrorists like as suicide bombing, hostage taking, and assassination, and sometimes as an organized killing of irregular non-governmental units like as the so-called Islamic State and also the Pro-Russian separatist militants in the Ukraine conflict. Despite various appearance forms, political violence is mostly connected with political ideology, that is the mindset of a certain identity group within a domestic, a transnational, or also an international society. Agents of the political violence are ready to use force not just in the purpose of the group-based material satisfaction, but rather for the sake of the spiritual fulfillment in terms of their religious, ethnic, or cultural beliefs and ideas.

This is the phenomenon that Samuel Huntington called "the clash of civilizations"[1] already in 1993. Whereas the First and the Second World War as well as the Cold War can commonly be characterized as hegemony struggle, Huntington identified the new type of wars as "fault line wars",[2] which occur on the borderline between different ethnic, religious, and cultural groups, such as seen in the dissolution process of the former Yugoslavia since 1989. This kind of regional conflicts is not merely a struggle for the territorial dominance, but rather for the mental control over the population in terms of their identity and sense of belonging. It hence takes a long time to resolve it, because the fighting parties don't share any common sense and common value to reach a compromise, but sometimes they hate each other so deeply to conclude with genocide.[3]

This Huntington's concept could be applied to our current situation of the political violence. In Western societies, there are certain amounts of ethnic and religious minorities,

---

1    Huntington, Samuel P.: The clash of civilizations and the remaking of world order, London: Simon & Schuster, 2002, p. 13.

2    Huntignton, S., op.cit. FN1, p. 252 ff.

3    Genocide has gradually been recognized as an international crime since Nuremberg Military Tribunals established in 1945, ITCY (International Criminal Tribunal for the former Yugoslavia) in 1993, and then ICTR (International Criminal Tribunal for Rwanda) in 1994, and currently stipulated by the Article 6 of The Rome Statute of the International Criminal Court adopted in 1998, which has established permanently ICC in The Hague since 2002. See about this above all, May, Larry: Crimes against humanity, a normative account, New York: Cambridge UP, 2005, p. 157 ff.

though exceptional ones, in their acute sensitivity of discrimination and alienation, so as to commit such indiscriminate terrors like as, for example, Boston Marathon bombings and the murder of the British soldier Lee Rigby in 2013, Jewish Museum of Belgium shooting and Sydney Lindt Cafe hostage crisis in 2014, Paris' Charlie Hebdo shooting followed by Dammartin-en-Goële hostage crisis, Copenhagen terror attack and November Paris attacks in 2015. These terror acts seem, at least in one aspect, to be related with the larger dimension of "clash of civilizations", namely the conflict between the Islamic and the Western civilization. The terrorists might conduct their terror acts more or less in connection with the global scale of religious conflicts, which the so-called Islamic State is fighting in the Middle East against the Counter-ISIL Coalition led by the US military, being similar to what Huntington called fault line conflicts.

## 1.2    Setting the Explanatory Framework

Here would be no room for further entering into details of current international relations, because our common concern is the idea of justice appearing in the literature. I mentioned these current circumstances because I would like to develop my own idea about the mental structure of the society as shown in the table below, supported by the Huntington's idea combined with the general approach of "history of ideas", namely "Geistesgeschichte" in the German terminology.[4]

Mental structure of a society could be divided into four sections:

- Political Elites, who seek for power, related to hierarchy, hegemony, and so on;
- Economical Elites, who seek for money, related to profit, market share, price making, and so on;
- Intellectuals, who seek for truth and creation, related to literature, science, art, culture, and so on;
- People, who seek for life and happiness related to family, community, religion, consumption, and so on.

I want to show with this illustration that a society consists of these four functional groups of political elites, economical elites, intellectuals, and people, which altogether form a political unit, usually in the form of sovereign state, but sometimes also in the form of irregular political grouping. When a certain number of political units have a close relationship with each other based on their common sense and ethnic, cultural, and/or religious similarity, they build up a more comprehensive unit in the form of civilization. Even though there is of course a wide variety of how to think and how to behave, the majority of the people in a civilization share minimum contents of sense of value, world-view, and ethnic, cultural,

---

4    Art. "Geistesgeschichte", in: Brockhaus Enzyklopädie in 24 Bde, 8. Bd., 19. völlig neu bearb. Aufl., Mannheim: Brockhaus, 1989, S. 234.

and/or religious identity, which determine their political tendency. So far as the people in one civilization have a different mindset from those in another one, political relations between different civilizations can easily get unstable, as Huntington saw this between the dominating Western-Christian and the Islamic, the Russian-Orthodox, as well as potentially the Chinese civilization. Fault line wars are a bold appearance of unstable relations, which sometimes endure hardly to resolve, when conflicting parties become too radical and fanatic, due to different mindsets, to reach a compromise with a reasonable solution.

Coming from this framework, namely the mental structure of a society and the clash of civilizations, I would like in the next two sections to investigate historical examples. There are, surely in the world history, some cases of war fought more radically and fanatically than the fault line wars in our current situation. One of the most extreme examples is the World War II, which I would characterize as "the total war",[5] because it ended up with the unconditional surrender we have never heard of before and after. In view of our theme of justice and literature, it is remarkable that some prominent writers at that time in Germany as well as in Japan perceived the World War II as an intellectual battle, even though, in the reality, it was merely the totalitarian aggression and the indiscriminate mass killing. This is the reason why we would below take a brief look at the literary movement of romanticism, which had a strong influence on the sprit at the time before the World War II especially in Germany and Japan. The purpose of this consideration would be, consequently, to examine intellectual characteristics and problems of the political violence in general.

## 2    German Romanticism and Nazism

### 2.1    Character of Nazism

National Socialism could be seen as being distinguished in its extreme politics of nationalism, racism, and inhumanity more than any other political regime however unlimited.[6] Hannah Arendt made her determined effort, in "The origins of totalitarianism"[7] published in 1951, to identify what Nazism was in essence in relation to a more widespread phenomenon of totalitarianism, based on her own experiences as a Jew who was oppressed and exiled from Germany to the United States. She picked up, in her book, those three elements of Nazism. The first characteristic of Nazism was the indiscriminate violence inflicted to

---

5    This word was originally used by the German general Erich Ludendorff in terms of the World War I, see his: Der totale Krieg, München: Ludendorffs Verlag, 1937 (c1935). I would like to use this word also to characterize the World War II.

6    Cf. Art. "National Socialism", in: The new encyclopaedia britannica, vol. 8, 15. ed. Chicago: Encyclopaedia Britannica Inc. 1993, p. 550 f.

7    Arendt, Hannah: The origins of totalitarianism, introduction by Samantha Power, New York: Schocken Books, 2004 (originally published in 1951).

anyone indifferently as expressing its political energy as such without any goal. The second essential of Nazism was the secret police named Gestapo to utilize the indiscriminate violence for itself. The last and third element was the concentration camps in order to annihilate anyone regarded as an enemy of the Germans viz. the Aryans.[8] Contrary to these elements, the antisemitism and the imperialistic racism were not specific to the German Nazism, as she suggested,[9] for example, that the antisemitism appeared obviously in France when the Dreyfus affair went on between 1894 and 1906, and the racism prevailed in the colonial policy of England in the late 19th century when Cecil Rhodes took the economic and political power in Southern Africa.

Keeping Arendt's analysis in mind in terms of what Nazism was in its political essence, it would be necessary to further examine the intellectual background from which the ideology of Nazism grew. It is the book "Die verspätete Nation (The belated nation)", written by Helmuth Plessner, that devoted a full length to investigate the romanticist components of Nazism in terms of the Norse or Aryan mythology and the blood and soil chauvinism, that was the roots of the Third Reich's ideology having demagogic effects.[10]

## 2.2    Romanticism Against Enlightenment

The central question to be asked in Plessner's concerns was: In what meaning and to what extend the inhuman ideology of Nazism emerged from the intellectual background of romanticism that originated as an intellectual movement in the end of the 18th and continued to grow during the 19th century?

According to Plessner, German romanticism was characterized by its emotional tendency, namely, the twisted combination of heaviness and darkness, greatness and vehemence, inwardness and dreaminess, and unpredictable wildness and pedantry.[11] Having these emotional characters, German nation produced a number of great poets, composers and philosophers. The reason why this spiritual inclination was named romanticism was because the romanticist intellectuals regarded not only the Roman Empire in the ancient age, but also the Holy Roman Empire of the German Nation in the middle ages as their ideal, especially in connection with the cultural integrity of the German folk. In this context, it would be easy to understand why the romanticism included the tendency towards the historical authority and the legacy of feudal relations and the avoidance from the modern enlightened mindset of liberty and freedom, equality and rationality.[12]

---

8    Cf. Arendt, H., op. cit. FN 7, p. 507 ff. (vol. 3, ch. 3).

9    Cf. Arendt, H., op. cit. FN 7, p. 117 ff. (vol. 1, ch. 4).

10   Cf. Plessner, Helmuth: Die verspätete Nation. Über die Verführbarkeit bürgerlichen Geistes, 5. Aufl., Frankfurt am Main: Suhrkamp 1994, S. 10. This book was originally written in Groningen, where Plessner was exiled to, and published in Swizerland in 1935.

11   Cf. Plessner, H., op. cit. FN 10, S. 25.

12   Cf. Plessner, H., op. cit. FN 10, S. 14 ff.

In addition, the Napoleonic Wars between 1803 and 1815 were decisive for the German spirit to turn away from the ideal of the French Revolution in terms of human rights and democracy. While Napoleon held up the motto of "liberty, equality, fraternity" in the fight against the monarchical Anti-France Coalition, the Napoleonic Wars meant for the German people merely the aggression of the French military into their fatherland, which led to the collapse of the integrity of the Holy Roman Empire, divided it into Prussia and Confederation of the Rhine, and resulted enormous victims and casualties. In this counter-revolutionary milieu, the German philosopher, Johann Gottlieb Fichte (1762-1814), published "Reden an die deutsche Nation (Addresses to the German Nation)"[13] in Berlin under the Napoleon's occupation in 1808, so as to evoke the German nationalism and romanticism based on its tradition, language, and literature.

To take a detour to our general concern about justice and literature, it would be also interesting to compare the German nationalism against Napoleon with the Russian one as expressed by the great novelist, Lev Tolstoy (1828-1910), in his epic work "War and Peace" published between 1805 and 1813. From the experience of "the Patriotic War of 1812", there arose an anti-enlightened and nationalistic tendency prevailing in the Russian spirit throughout the 19th century, which brought about the revolutionary nihilism like as seen in the motive demonstrated by another great novelist, Fyodor Dostoyevsky (1821-1881).[14] It seems to me, therefore, not contingent that the Stalin's Soviet Russia appeared as another outstanding example of the totalitarian regime than the Hitler's Nazism, so as that H. Arendt analyzed the common character of both as inhuman apparatus.[15] Anyway, there would here be no room to enter into further details on comparing the German and the Russian nationalism and totalitarianism.

## 2.3    Resentment and Protest of the Belated Nation

To return back to the Plessner's discussion, the romanticist tendency of the German intellectuals was not a single factor from which the Nazi ideology nurtured its roots. According to Plessner, it was decisive, politically seen, that the German nation delayed establishing its own nation state, and remained still a cultural nation without political entity, until Bismark founded the German Empire in 1871, which was constituted in the old type of absolute monarchy. The Second Reich was, in other words, governed by the Bismark's bureaucrats who acquired the technical and mechanical expertise without having any

---

13    Fichte, Johann Gottlieb: Reden an die deutsche Nation, hrsg. von Fritz Medicus mit einer Einleitung von Alwin Diemer, Hamburg : Felix Meiner 1955; see also, Plessner, H., op. cit. FN 10, S. 52 ff.

14    Cf. Berdyaev, Nikolai: Die russische Idee: Grundprobleme des russischen Denkens im 19. Jahrhundert und zu Beginn des 20. Jahrhundert, eingeleitet, übersetzt und erläutert von Dietrich Kegler, Sankt Augustin: Richarz, 1983, S. 140.

15    Cf. Arendt, H., op. cit. FN 7, p. 450 ff. (vol. 3 ch. 2).

moral compass, so as to be seen as Plessner described: "The civil society [of Germany, H.K.] affirms the state as securing economic progress and national unity in its bureaucratic and military function, that is, as pure power, because it lacks of a specific political idea."[16] To the contrary, Western nations, especially England, France, Holland, and the United States, established their own nation state through the 17th and the 18th century, equipped with the new moral philosophy based on those humanist principles as liberty, freedom, civilization, international solidarity, democracy, citizenship, reason, free consensus, rule of law, and so on, that is the idea of enlightenment.[17]

According to Plessner, further, the German Protestantism, above all Lutheran Evangelicalism, deterred the German people from having their own political awareness, because they were integrated into the state-church system (Landeskirche), in which the secular lord (Landesherr) had the power to decide what religious creed his commoner should adopt. Therefore, the Protestant authority of the state-church could not reach the inner sphere of the people, but controlled only their outer life, indeed in a similar way as the territorial lord did, because both of the state-church and the secular lordship worked as a technical and mechanical bureaucracy in the same way. In these circumstances, people felt alienated from the religious life of the church, though they still held a strong desire for a rich spirituality in the sense of self, so as to seek for the mental fulfillment by adopting the secular creed of romanticism, which functioned as an equivalent religion.[18] This romanticist attitude was what Plessner called the "secular piety in the world" (innerweltliche Weltfrömmigkeit) and also the "secularized Protestantism" (säkularisierter Protestantismus).[19] In this way, the German romanticism raised the secularized protest even less against the religious authority of the Catholic church rather than against the secular creed of humanism, which the Western nations held up in the bourgeois revolution.

While the German nation lodged a romanticist protest against the Western humanism, the industrial revolution made rapid progress also in Germany through the 19th century. The capitalism expanded in the economic system, in which the manufacturing process became more and more divided into fragments, so as that the increasing number of urban workers felt thrown into senselessness of their life, that is nihilism. It was those three giants who tried to resolve this absurdity and alianation perceived by modern human beings.[20] Karl Marx, firstly, thought that the revolutionary criticism could liberate proletariats from their self-deceiving illusion and awake the class consciousness so as to perceive real social relations within the prevailing capitalistm.[21] Søren Kierkegaard, secondly, found out a final resort for the desperate self-awareness to make an existential decision to submit himself to

---

16 Plessner, H., op. cit. FN 10, S. 91. The original German text is translated into English by H.K.
17 Cf. Plessner, H., op. cit. FN 10, S. 63, 91.
18 Cf. Plessner, H., op. cit. FN 10, S. 65 ff., esp. S. 69.
19 Plessner, H., op. cit. FN 10, S. 41.
20 Cf. Plessner, H., op. cit. FN 10, S. 167 ff.
21 Cf. Marx, Karl: Deutsche Ideologie, (1845/46) MEW3 S. 19 ff.; Das Kapital, (1890) MEW23, S. 21 ff.

God's will in genuine faith.[22] Friedrich Nietzsche, thirdly, required to be a "super-human" (Übermensch), who was able to carry out the "re-valuation of all values (Umwerthung aller Werthe)"[23] to create a new set of values in place of an old type of slave moral.

These three philosophers expressed the protest, in each of their own ways, against the modern society featured by the functional bureaucracy and the efficient capitalism. Though their criticism was not directed against the humanism as such, their moral attitude was rather negative toward the idea of enlightenment, especially because the combination of individualism and liberalism brought about egoism. It seemed to them contradictory that the enlightenment stood once for humanism, whereas the enlightened modern society treated humans inhumanely as if these were mere objects. Regrettably, this criticism of the great philosophers was afterwards abused by Nazism so as to exterminate every value of the enlightenment and to justify the inhuman policy. At this point, we could see how the anti-enlightened tendency of the romanticism built up the early phase on the way to the Nazi ideology with its irrational, crazy, brutal, and inhuman mindset.

## 3    Japanese Romanticism and Militarism

### 3.1    German Influence to the Japanese Romanticism

In view of the theme of idea of justice in literature, the next question might be whether it would be possible to find out any connection between literature movement and political ideology in another culture than in Germany. In asking this question, it would be interesting to trace the developing process of the Japanese romanticism in the early 20th century under the influence of the German romanticism, so as to compare, at least in the spiritual level, the anti-enlightened and irrational mindset of the Japanese militarism with that of the German Nazism. In this section, therefore, I would like to take a brief look at one of the most prominent critics in Japan in the time before and during the World War II viz. the Pacific War, Yojuro YASUDA, who himself was representative of the Japanese romanticists at that time.[24]

According to Yasuda, the Japanese romanticism originated from the counter movement against the Westernization of the society, and, above all, against the literature movement

---

22   Cf. Kierkegaard, Søren: Die Krankheit zum Tode, Jena: Eugen Diederichs, 1911, S. 67 f. (originally published in Kopenhagen in 1849).

23   Nietzsche, Friedrich: „Der Antichrist", in: Giorgio Colli und Mazzino Montinari (hrsg.): Friedrich Nietzsche: Sämtliche Werke, Kritische Studienausgabe in 15 Einzelbände, Bd. 6 (KSA 6), München: DTV de Gruyter, 1988, S. 179.

24   Cf. Okubo, Norio: Art. "YASUDA Yojuro", in: Dai hyakka jiten, vol. 14, Tokyo: Heibon sha, 1985, p. 1131; idem: Art. "Nihon roman ha", in: Dai hyakka jiten, vol. 11, Tokyo: Heibon sha, 1985, p. 482.

of naturalism.[25] As the political reform of Meiji Restoration started modernizing the Japanese society in the second half of the 19th century, the early stage of the Japanese modern literature took the form of naturalism under the influence of French literature at that time. The literary naturalism aimed at uncovering the dark side of the semi-feudal living, so as to reveal the tragic destiny of the ordinary people in it. This new trend of literature was integrated into the social-political movement of "Civilization and Enlightenment",[26] which tried to assimilate the Japanese society into the Western civilized one featured by pragmatism and utilitarianism.

Yasuda was deeply disappointed with these painful and vain efforts of the Japanese elites and intellectuals. He found out the hope, therefore, rather in the spiritual movement of romanticism, which arose in Japan in the last decade of the 19th century from the traditional conviction and world-view, indeed under the influence of the German nationalism, concervatism, reactionism, and romanticism, fighting against the modernization.[27] He modified the German version of the dichotomy between enlightenment and romanticism into his own formulation: current vice and fraud versus past glory; sound will and consciousness versus decay, prodigality, stray and confusion; scientific knowledge versus pain, sorrow, grief and anger; mount versus bottom; progress versus deadlock.[28]

What was the motive, then, for the Japanese romanticists to protest against the Western enlightenment? It was international circumstances that the Western Great Powers, first of all the United States, threatened and semi-colonized the Japanese society by means of the military power so as to force the Japanese government to sign the unequal treaties including extraterritoriality and deprivation of tariff autonomy. While the political and economical elites found it necessary to make the Japanese society modernize and strong enough to contest against the Western Powers, quite a few intellectuals, however, rejected the value and world-view of the Western because they found this as causing the unjust and unfair attitude of Westerners toward Japanese. From this anti-modern spirit arose the literature movement of Japanese romanticism. We could here find out a symbolic expression in Yasuda's words: "colonialist civilization and enlightenment",[29] with which he criticized that the Western Powers divided and colonized every region on the earth, appealing to

---

25  Cf. Yasuda, Yojuro: "Waga kuni ni okeru roman-shugi no gaikan", in: Kindai no syu-en, Tokyo: Shingaku-sya, 2002, p. 29 ff. ("Overview to the Japanese romanticism", in: The end of modern, first published in 1940; translation of the original Japanese text into English by H.K.)

26  Uete, Michiari: Art.: "Bunmei Kaika", Dai hyakka jiten, vol. 13, Tokyo: Heibon sha, 1985, p. 393 f.

27  Cf. Yasuda, Y., "Waga kuni ni okeru roman-shugi no gaikan", op. cit. FN 25, p. 32 f.

28  Cf. Yasuda, Yojuro: "Kon-nichi no roman-shugi", in: Eiyu to shijin, 4th printing, Kyoto: Shingaku-sya, 2001, p. 41 ff. ("Contemporary romanticism", in: Hero and poet, first published in 1935; translation of the original Japanese text into English by H.K.).

29  Yasuda, Yojuro: "Bunmei kaika no ronri no syu-en ni tsuite", in: Bungaku no tachiba, 2nd printing, Kyoto: Shingaku-sya, 2009, p. 17. ("To the end of the logic of civilization and enlightenment", in: Position of the literature, first published in 1939; translation of the original Japanese text into English by H.K.).

the humanity and the civilized order, though causing the inhumane poverty and misery in the underdeveloped nations which were deprived of autonomy.

In this way, the Japanese romanticism, parallel to the German one, appeared from the beginning as the counter movement against the modern civilization and rationalism.

## 3.2    Features of the Japanese Romanticism

Yasuda thought that the Japanese romanticism had developed from the social circumstances in first decades of the 20th century, where the ordinary people suffered from the widespread poverty, even though the government advertised Japan as having been one of the first-class powers since the victory of Russo-Japanese War in 1905.[30] While the possibility of success was open only for a limited number of political and economic elites who possessed the power and wealth enough to enjoy the modern culture, it was still so difficult for the majority of the people to make ends meet as in the semi-feudal era before modernization. In other words, the Japanese romanticists came from the premiss that the modernity and the Western civilization could not guarantee the prosperity of the people, but only bring about the poverty and misery, disparity and resentment among them. Yasuda, therefore, spoke of contemporary "despair", "suppression", and "eschatology",[31] from which those romanticist attitudes arose like as "enthusiasm for decay", combined with "quintessence of the national structure" and the "authentic ultra-nationalism".[32] Compared with the German nation as belated in terms of building its own nation state in the political aspect,[33] the Japanese nation was delayed in terms of building the civil society rather in the social-economic aspect.

Why were the Japanese romanticists, devoting to the literature, ultra-nationalists in their political position? It was surely because they found themselves possible only in their cultural tradition to develop their aesthetic creativity. They considered the national history to be ideal, through which the Emperor, "Ten-no", was the pure symbolic sovereign with no political power nor economic wealth, representing the purified beauty expressed in the literature form of the short poem with thirty-one syllables, "Tanka". [34] According to Yasuda, "the absolute pure art" could, certainly in this way, appear from "the sacred faithfulness" and "the aesthetic spirit of the old dynastic civilization".[35]

A further question would be why the "decadence" should be the standard for the romanticist aesthetic creativity? Although the word "decadence" literally means moral decay in pursuing pleasure and enjoyment, it came originally from the French "mouvement décadent"

---

30   Cf. Yasuda, Y., "Waga kuni ni okeru roman-shugi no gaikan", op. cit. FN 25, p. 34.

31   Yasuda, Y., "Waga kuni ni okeru roman-shugi no gaikan", op. cit. FN 25, p. 44.

32   Yasuda, Y., "Waga kuni ni okeru roman-shugi no gaikan", op. cit. FN 25, p. 43, 45.

33   See above 2-3.

34   Sasaki, Yukitsuna: Art.: "Tanka", Dai hyakka jiten, vol. 9, Tokyo: Heibon sha, 1985, p. 452 f.

35   Yasuda, Y., "Waga kuni ni okeru roman-shugi no gaikan", op. cit. FN 25, p. 39 f.

in the late 19th century, represented by P. Valéry and Ch.-P. Baudelaire, with the slogan "artiste ultra-raffiné (ultra-refined artist)".[36] Yasuda as a poet and critic took this French artistic movement seriously and tried to apply it to the Japanese context, indeed in the name of romanticism. He stood, therefore, for the aesthetic position of decadence, which should be the ethos of the intellectuals, in contrast to the ethos of political and economic elites oriented to the pragmatism and utilitarianism. He critically saw the bureaucrats and capitalists as having lost the traditional nobility, just as being an ugly upstart, snob and philistine.[37] From this criticism arose the "awareness of fiction",[38] in which Yasuda undertook his literary creation, instead of the awareness of reality, in that the political and economic elites were acting. While the reality would demand rationality and calculation as means to a pragmatic end, the fiction could contain contradictory emotions like as "brightness and vitality" in the future as well as "sorrow and anger", "grief and fear" in the past and present.[39]

Here could be summarized the features of the Japanese romanticism in three points. Firstly, as being artists, romanticists preferred being aesthetically excellent to being politically powerful or economically rich, oriented themselves rather to artistic creativity than to bureaucratic discipline or industrial productivity, so as to overcome the businesslike rationalism. Secondly, they identified their roots of the pure beauty in the traditional value and world-view, which the Emperor, Ten-no, represented, so as that they hated deeply the Western value and world-view as being ugly howsoever practical or pragmatic. Thirdly, they stood, in this way, for the ultra-nationalism combined with the contra-enlightenment in terms of their political position.

## 3.3    Romanticist Militarism?

The next question would be whether Yasuda supported, with no hesitation, the totalitarian militarism of the Japanese government in the first half of the 20th century, indeed in accordance with his ultra-nationalist position? In terms of this political question, Yasuda seemed to be complicated and somehow contradictory. While he considered, on the one hand, the Japanese hegemony in East Asia positively as liberating Asian nations from

---

36   Valde, Bernard: Art. „Décadence (idée de)", in: Encyclopaedia Universalis, corpus 5, Paris: Encyclopaedie Universalis France, 1984, p. 1019.

37   Cf. Yasuda, Yojuro: "Gendai nihon-bunka no hin-kon ni tsuite", in: Bungaku no tachiba, 2nd printing, Kyoto: Shingaku-sya, 2009, p. 233. ("To the poverty of the current Japanese culture", in: Position of the literature, first published in 1940; translation of the original Japanese text into English by H.K.) At this point, we can see the influence of Nietzsche to Yasuda; see also Nietzsche, Friedrich: „David Strauss der Bekenner und der Schriftsteller", in: Giorgio Colli und Mazzino Montinari (hrsg.): Friedrich Nietzsche: Sämtliche Werke, Kritische Studienausgabe in 15 Einzelbände, Bd. 1 (KSA 1), München: DTV, de Gruyter, 1988, S. 165.

38   Yasuda, Y., "Kon-nichi no roman-shugi", op. cit. FN 28, p. 36.

39   Yasuda, ibid.

Western colonization, he criticized, on the other hand, the totalitarian technocracy of the contemporary Japanese military and government for being driven by the Western mindset of pragmatism.

Related with the military aggression of Japan into the Northeastern China, Manchuria, in 1931 and the Second Sino-Japanese War in 1937, Yasuda expressed his support for this military deployment, speaking of the "reality of Empire",[40] which the Japanese government established in the mainland China through its "logic of the global concept" and "reform concept"[41] in accordance with "the idea and tradition of the national civilization"[42] and "the faith of the national civilization since the first day of the Japanese mythos".[43] He regarded the Manchurian Incident in 1931 as "the first step of dismantling the global ancient regime",[44] so as to insist that "the Japanese nationalism should never reverse the course of proceeding the Asian liberation".[45] Further in view of the outbreak of the World War II in Europe in 1939, he made a positive comment for the German aggression like this: "Germany declares the war not merely against the English nation, but it rather proclaims all the nations to be liberated from the super-national ruler who governs them, including the English".[46]

Though taking such an ultra-nationalist position, he, nevertheless, disagreed about the totalitarian policy of the Japanese government which mobilized art and literature for the sake of the military aggression. As the military government of Japan sent some writers to the front line in China as war correspondents, Yasuda criticized their reports for being "politicized literature" or "patronized literature",[47] as losing the artistic spirit. Further, as the Japanese government established the totalitarian scheme of the "Imperial Rule Assistance"[48] for its domestic politics in 1940, he saw his fellow writers falling into "the gloom of the current military literature as well as the depression of the assimilated literature".[49]

---

40  Yasuda, Y., "Bunmei kaika no ronri no syu-en ni tsuite", op. cit. FN. 29, p. 12.

41  Yasuda, ibid.

42  Yasuda, Yojuro: "Nihon no gendai-teki bun-mei no higeki", in: Bungaku no tachiba, 2nd printing, Kyoto: Shingaku-sya, 2009, p. 249 ("Tragedy of the Japanese contemporary civilization", in: Position of the literature, first published in 1940; translation of the original Japanese text into English by H.K.).

43  Yasuda, Y., "Nihon no gendai-teki bun-mei no higeki", op. cit. FN. 42, p. 250.

44  Yasuda, Yojuro: "Atarashii Rinri", in Kindai no syu-en, Tokyo: Shingaku-sya, 2002, p. 143 ("New Ethics", in: The end of modern, first published in 1941; translation of the original Japanese text into English by H.K.).

45  Yasuda, Y., "Atarashii Rinri", op. cit. FN 44, p. 147.

46  Yasuda, Yojuro: "Nihon no jo-tai ni tsuite", in: Bungaku no tachiba, 2nd printing, Kyoto: Shingaku-sya, 2009, p. 224 ("To the circumstances surrounding Japan", in: Position of the literature, first published in 1940; translation of the original Japanese text into English by H.K.).

47  Yasuda, Y., "Bunmei kaika no ronri no syu-en ni tsuite", op. cit. FN. 29, p. 16.

48  Kisaka, Jun-ichro: Art. "Yokusan taisei", Dai hyakka jiten, vol. 15, Tokyo: Heibon sha, 1985, p. 183.

49  Yasuda, Y., "Gendai nihon-bunka no hin-kon ni tsuite", op. cit. FN. 37, p. 235.

Yasuda was, thus, contradictory, once in standing for the nominal Asian liberation by means of aggression, whereas against the totalitarian mobilization of literature as being a servant of politics. At this point could be surely identified the political naivety of the Japanese romanticist who was not able to distinguish literature from politics, beauty from reality, as well as cultural glory from political extreme. Yasuda could not realize that the ultra-nationalist ideology, in which he had blind faith, was utilized to justify the military aggression and the mass killing on the sites of the war. He looked only at the bright side of the national tradition in terms of the aesthetic, and overlooked the decisive question whether his ultra-nationalist position might finally lead to terrorizing other nations. This horrible reality was regrettably the end result of the Japanese romanticist spirit, no matter how it came from the criticism of the Western civilization and enlightenment, liberty and humanity.

## 4      Comparison of German and Japanese Romanticism

It would now be meaningful again to take a look at the German romanticism in comparison with the Japanese one, though I must acknowledge that my consideration is not an exact one, because Plessner investigated the German romanticism rather objectively from his critical and philosophical point of view, whereas Yasuda was a romanticist himself who wrote poems and essays and therefore not critical and reflective. It would, nevertheless, be possible to some extent to clarify differences and similarities of romanticism between the both nations. In view of differences, I would point out that while the German romanticism directed criticism against those enlightened nations like as the United Kingdom, France, Netherland and the United States, which established the nation state and the humanist morality, the Japanese romanticism was, to the contrary, critical of the Western civilization as a whole including the German one, especially in terms of rationalism, pragmatism, and utilitarianism. Remarkable is also that the Japanese romanticism was not only influenced by the German one as seen in its naming, but also strongly by the French movement of decadence.

In spite of these differences, both the German and the Japanese romanticism had a lot of common characters. They were nationalist and reactionary, contra-enlightened and anti-humanist, so as to pave the way, at least on the mental level, for establishing the authoritarian up to the totalitarian regime, which deployed the political violence fully toward the World War II in which genocide and crimes against humanity were committed.

It has been suggested above, nonetheless, that Yasuda was not fully sympathetic toward the military dictatorship of the Japanese government at that time, which mobilized everything including culture and literature for the purpose of waging the aggressive war. This was the reason why he regarded the totalitarian machinery as being opposite to his ideal of the traditional aesthetic.

At this point, we could find out also some writers in Germany who were not liberal and democratic indeed, but took a critical attitude against the totalitarianism. An outstanding figure might be Ernst Jünger who was featured not as a romanticist indeed, but as an expressionist, at any rate cynical about the progress of the hypocritical Western civilization, strongly influenced by nihilism, value-relativism, and the death of the morality in Nietzsche's sense.[50] Nevertheless, he was also critical of Nazism so as to describe humans not being a human any more under a totalitarian regime.[51]

In this point of similarity between Yasuda and Jünger, we could find out that the romanticist attitude would not be necessarily connected to the political violence, even though it might often show a political naivety not to pay enough attention to egregious results of the totalitarian politics. This political naivety of romanticists is equivalent to what Carl Schmitt called "the occasionalist structure of the romanticism".[52] In this regard, though Carl Schmitt, as well as Martin Heidegger and many other intellectuals, participated in the NS regime also on the mental level of "decisionism",[53] they could not precisely be seen as approving the totalitarian violence, but rather just as finding themselves powerless in facing with the political reality.[54]

This remark would not mean that the romanticism-minded intellectuals at that time both in Germany and in Japan could escape their moral responsibility for the totalitarian violence, but rather should be responsible for what Karl Jaspers named the "moral... [and] metaphysical guilt".[55] I would interpret this Jaspers' concept as the moral and metaphysical responsibility of the intellectuals for paying attention to the gap between beauty and violence, their ideal in the national history and the reality they were facing with.[56] This

---

50  Cf. Jünger, Ernst: „Die totale Mobilmachung", in: Sämtliche Werke, Essays 1, Betrachtungen zur Zeit, Stuttgart: Klett-Cotta, 1980, S. 119 ff. (Erstdruck 1930).

51  Cf. Jünger, Ernst: „Auf den Marmorklippen", in: Auswahl aus dem Werk im fünf Bänden, 3. Bd., Stuttgart: Klett-Cotta, 1994, SS. 5-109 (first published in 1939).

52  Schmitt, Carl: Politische Romantik, 2. Aufl. München u. Leipzig: Duncker & Humblot, 1925, S. 115.

53  Krockow, Christian Graf von: Die Entscheidung. Eine Untersuchung über Ernst Jünger, Carl Schmitt, Martin Heidegger, Frankfurt am Main: Campus Verl., 1990, S. 44.

54  Cf. about Carl Schmitt, see above all Bendersky, Joseph: "Politische Romantik: Intellectual critique and enduring scholary influence", in: Quaritsch, Helmut (ed.): Complexio Oppositorum über Carl Schmitt, Berlin: Duncker & Humblot, 1988, pp. 465-490; about Martin Heidegger, see above all Safranski, Rüdiger: Ein Meister aus Deutschland: Heidegger und seine Zeit, Frankfurt am Main: Fischer, 1997, S. 258 ff.

55  Jaspers, Karl: Die Schuldfrage; Für Völkermord gibt es keine Verjährung, München: Pieper 1979, S. 21 (originally published in 1946; translation from German text into English by H.K.). See also May, Larry: "Metaphysical Guilt and Moral Taint", in: Larry May and Stacey Hoffman (eds.): Collective Responsibility, five decades of debate in theoreticaland applied ethics, Lanham: Rowman & Littlefield Publishers Inc. 1991, p. 239 ff.

56  The problem of the logical gap between ideal and reality, between normative and factual assertion, is known as Hume's law. See to this, Hume, David: A Treatise of Human Nature, reprint of the

would mean that, so far as a romanticist did not pay enough attention to this gap so as to stand for the totalitarian regime, then he should be criticized for being morally guilt; and that, even though some others did pay enough attention to it, they were still metaphysically responsible for being reflective and critical of the political reality that was once connected with their intellectual and political mindset.

## Conclusion

At the end of my report, I would try to draw lessons from the history of ideas of romanticism, in relation to our current global society consisting of the political and the economic elites, the intellectuals, and the people.[57]

We know that the intellectuals are, in general, critical of the political and economic mainstream. While political and economic elites often represent very character of the enlightenment and the civilization in facilitating the progress toward modernization and rationalization, some intellectuals, to the contrary, take a skeptical attitude toward freedom and fairness because of its hypocritical appearance in capitalism, by seeking for a counter ideal in their national history and/or in their religious belief. It would not be liberty, but authority, not humanity, but sacredness, which they might prefer. Supported by this cynical and nihilistic mindset prevailing among intellectuals up to usual people, new "reformative" agents, though substantially conservative and reactionary, could come to the political and economic stage, insisting on a breakthrough in the corrupt status quo and promising a new better world in accordance with their national and/or the religious ideal. This new kind of political and economic elites could abuse the critical thinking of intellectuals, in order to conceal the horrible reality resulting from their political violence. Here is the dividing point for the intellectuals, either to accept the facade of the new type of political elites by losing sight of the hidden back of their mask, or to keep critical eyes on what is happening in the political reality driven by elites.

I would personally share the moral attitude with the intellectuals in each nation and each civilization, who take pride in their own culture and respect their own tradition. I would, therefore, find it disastrous if all of the intellectuals in the world should adopt the moral values of the Western-Christian civilization, because our intellectual activities including literature and science would then lose the cultural diversity so as to become monotone to be dominated by those belonging to a certain civilization. I would, nonetheless, emphasize that the intellectuals should have faith in some common values in terms of humanity, which is the universal value of being human. This means that we should be

---

edition of 1888, Oxford: Clarendon Press, 1965, p. 469 f. (Book III, Part I, Section I; originally published in 1739.)

57   See above 1-2.

aware of the crucial point to divide intellectual criticism of the civilized society from the political aggression against humanity.

A historical lesson of the romanticism would say to us, intellectuals in philosophy of law, to be critical of society, and, at the same time, be sensible of political violence.

## The Author

**Hiroshi Kabashima**, Professor of Jurisprudence, Tohoku University, Sendai/ Japan; kabashima@law.tohoku.ac.jp

# A Penny for Your Thoughts
## The Conceptions of Justice in the Literature of Cora Coralina

Nuria López

### Abstract

This paper aims to demonstrate the different conceptions of Justice in the literature of Cora Coralina. The analysis comprehends each work of art as an expression of the thoughts of a specific artist in a specific moment of time. While it is impossible to collect thoughts, as research data for a deeper understanding the concept of Justice in our society by, we can definitely collect works of art as written evidence of these expressions. It provides an insight analysis, due to the fact that it considers the diversity of conceptions, making it possible to work with the great variations in the spectrum. The literature of Cora Coralina could be used as a sample of how uniquely one can perceive Justice in different contexts of life. Cora sang of the injustices and the justices of her life experiences – *my lost penny, my penny of happiness/ the bigger capacity of being myself, my constant affirmation*[1]. Our humanity is complex, and so are our thoughts. This paper gives a penny for Cora Coralina's thoughts of Justice as a sample of our complexity.

### Keywords

Justice; Literature; Cora Coralina

## Introduction

What is Justice? – This is a question to which the answer has been developed by philosophers from the ancient philosophy until modern days with the newest theories of Justice. Thus, there are several philosophical models that try to describe our relation with the idea of Justice.

---

1  All the translations are made by the author of this paper.

© Springer Fachmedien Wiesbaden GmbH, part of Springer Nature 2018
H. Kabashima et al. (Hrsg.), *The Idea of Justice in Literature*,
Wirtschaftsethik in der globalisierten Welt,
https://doi.org/10.1007/978-3-658-21996-3_11

It is important to highlight that all philosophical models are just abstract constructions, shining a light in order to assist us in the understanding of social relations. Therefore, instead of considering some models as right and some as wrong in describing a specific social circumstance, we should consider the description itself as the main observation point. A philosophical model should be able to channel our understanding of this social circumstance, being able to explain its complexities as precisely as possible.

However, to check the suitability of these abstract models in social relations it is not a trivial task. How can we determine if they are really suitable for the understanding of our societies?

Therefore, we should search for instruments that aid the observer to seek a correlation between those theoretical models and the social relations – and in the specific case of the idea of Justice, we should search for a correlation between the theoretical models of Justice and the conceptions of Justice the minds of actual people. It is possible, for example, to conduct an experiment, asking people about their feelings about Justice, which has been done by experimental philosophers. But there are plenty of others possibilities.

In this paper, we will propose an experiment by the analysis of works of literature, and actually present a proof with the literature of a Brazilian writer, Cora Coralina, that our idea of Justice could be much more complex.

## 1    New Approach in Law & Literature: Piece of Art, Piece of *Data*

Usually, literature works are used as allegorical pieces related to law and philosophy, universalizing the inferences that were drawn from the art. Contrary to that, the analysis in this paper comprehends each work of art as the expression of the thoughts of a specific artist in a specific moment of time. While it is impossible to collect thoughts as research data to know what is consider Justice in our society, *we can on the other hand definitely collect works of art as samples of the expressions of these thoughts.*

This provides researchers a wide variety of perspectives for their analysis, because it considers the diversity of conceptions, making it possible to work with the variations in the spectrum. So instead of building a universal concept of Justice to work within legal theory, we could build a more realistic cluster that is expected to shed light on the inherent irregularities of a complex society.

The idea of using a piece of art as a piece of data has an inspiration in the German philosopher Walter Benjamin, who explored the meaning of several pieces of art, constructing above them his philosophical models. Benjamin uses literature in a very interesting way – he digs for variables such as the past experiences of the author, the society he lives in, his influences, his economic situation, his social status and so on. All of these variables compose the subject (author) and the way he sees the world and expresses himself.

Furthermore, he points out, for example, the relation between the utility of a narrative, that could be a moral lesson, a practical suggestion, a proverb or a rule for living, and in each of this cases, the storyteller just *knows* to give advice. Benjamin says: *"Dieser Nutzen mag einmal in einer Moral bestehen, ein andermal in einer praktishen Anweisung, ein drittes in einem Sprichwort oder in einer Lebensregel – in jedem Falle ist der Erzähler ein Mann, der dem Hörer Rat weiß"* (1977, p. 442).

Benjamin creates the image of the storyteller going up and down a stairway from his own experience to reach the clouds of collective experience: *"Dabei ist allen großen Erzählern die Unbeschwertheit gemeint, mit der sie auf und ab bewegen. Eine Leiter, die bis ins Erdinnere reicht und sich in den Wolken verliert, ist das Bild einer Kollektiverfahrung, für die selbst der tiefste Chock jeder individuellen, der Tod, keinerlei Anstoß und Schranke darstellt"* (1977, p. 457). This way everything can be shared with others. The experiences are different, every individual has his own, but they are all communicable, able to influence others.

The storyteller, says Benjamin, takes advices, lessons, rules from his own experience and from the experience of others. And when he tells the story, those experiences make the way back to his listeners and become part of them: *"Der Erzähler nimmt, was er erzählt, aus der Erfahrung; aus der eigenen oder berichteten. Und er macht es wiederum zur Erfahrung derer, die seiner Geschichte zuhören"* (1977, p. 443).

The trajectory Benjamin describes for the narrative, or perhaps more precisely for the influence of the narrative is fundamental to help us observe how an individual is influenced by others and how he influences them back. It is a very important movement in Benjamin's work that makes clear how we grasp concepts from the world we are in contact with (immersed in ) with and also how we complete the world with our influence as well.

The literature of Cora Coralina is a unique kind of poetry, simple, *narrated* in the very meaning of *Erzählen*, generous, wise, full of experiences to share. If we have the benjaminian movement in mind, the experiences that compose her conceptions of Justice in each moment in her life will become clear – including the experiences of others, concepts that were shared with her and became part of her, of who she was.

## 2    What Could We Learn About Justice from Cora Coralina?

The literature of Cora Coralina could be used as a sample of how differently one can perceive Justice in different contexts in life. The reason for the choice of Cora Coralina is not only the great value of her poetry, which narrates her path of life, but also her profile, which is very distant from Academia.

Cora Coralina was born Ana Lins dos Guimarães Peixoto Brêtas (that is why in many of her poems she refers to herself "Aninha", short for "Ana") in the City of Goiás in the 20<sup>th</sup> of August 1889. At time her father was very ill and somehow her mother, as well as the people in the city, decide to point out she was the child of an old ill man, and how ungainly and ugly she was. Cora had a rugged childhood, filled with contempt. Even her sisters would not allow her to get closer.

While she grew up, in this "hard" environment, people pressured her into marriage, at the same time making her believe she was not beautiful enough to find a husband. When she was twenty years old, she met the man that would be her future husband. He was divorced and at that time, in Brazil, it was not possible to get a divorce and marry again (that law was approved just in 1977). Therefore, Cora ran away with him to the countryside of São Paulo, where they lived together for fourty-five years. During this period she lived a life of a housewife and they had together four children.

In her old age, after her husband's death and with an empty nest, she found herself alone and decided to move back to Goiás. In 1956 she moved back to the old house of her family and started a new activity: she baked candies for a living, a successful activity that she would pursue for more than twenty years. She decided also to try to publish her poetry. Her first book was published when she was seventy-six years old.

Her poetry, acclaimed in her last years of life, is a full narrative of the injustices she suffered and how she dealt with them. Nevertheless, it is worth noticing she did not define many of them as *injustices*. What the academic reader of this paper may find absurd, terrible social injustices, gender violence and so on, did not receive the adjective of *injustice/ unfairness* from Cora, for whom it was just the way things were. It will become clear in the analysis below, that she did not regard the fact that her only possible choice was being a housewife as an injustice; neither the fact that she was not beautiful enough to find a husband; she did not see as *injustice* the financial difficulties, the poverty, the hard work in the countryside. Her poetry shows she constantly compared her situation to that of others, showing gratefulness for having made the best of it.

For us, this provides a great insight in the life and believes of Cora and in how differently people can perceive Justice.

Philosophers are constantly researching the idea of Justice. Perhaps we should listen more carefully to what is being told outside the walls of our libraries. The idea of Justice is everywhere. Our academic work has to be able to explain or demonstrate social relations, illuminating why we perceive different attitudes and behaviours as *fair* and *unfair*.

If the concept of fairness is universal it should work for all – including people from different cultural backgrounds. Ergo, Cora Coralina is a perfect retest for theories of Justice.

Cora's poetry narrates her life experiences and the attitudes, situations, behaviours she finds *fair* or *unfair*. Digging into her literature we can find the variables that she gleans from the world around her and that expressly influenced her in her conceptions of Justice. Following Benjamin's approach, we can see in Cora's a central influence from her *situation* in time and place. Her expectations about her life guide her feelings about *fair* or *unfair* and are composed by what she can deduct from the society, family, her social and economic status and how she manages to construct her self-image. All of these variables build, stone by stone, her expectations and consequently her feelings about Justice.

## 3    Stone by Stone: The Construction of Ourselves, of *Others*, and of Our Expectations

When Cora Coralina looks back to the past to reconstruct her*self* and the world around her, she sees that "being more housewifely/ than intellectual/ I don't ever write/ conscious and reasoned, but/ driven for an uncontrollable impulse./ Being this way, I have the/ conscience of being authentic" [*Sendo eu mais doméstica do/ que intelectual,/ não escrevo jamais de forma/ consciente e raciocinada, e sim/ impelida por um impulso incontrolável./ Sendo assim, tenho a/ consciência de ser autêntica* (2013a, p.83)].

This is well-stablished in her poetry and opposes the theories of Justice, which usually share a philosophical background of *rationality* (in a strong sense of *Rationalismus*). Yet, Justice is a perception, a feeling, an u*ncontrollable impulse* people have when facing some specific situation. Modernity has been trying (and remains trying) to rationalize it, to find justifications for this or that idea of Justice, but they are commonly in conflict. How can such strong feelings break so easily in contact with the rule of modernity?

Our hypothesis in this paper is that perhaps we have been making the wrong quest. Perhaps our modern rules with which we have been measuring Justice are not applicable for this situation. The rules of modern reasoning and justification are too tight.

Justice could be seen as a much more dynamic idea, which each individual builds and re-builds in a non-ceasing way for itself. The movement described by Benjamin in *der Erzähler* of the impact a story has in each individual, a constant movement of back and forth between the storyteller and the listeners, so that what each one of them could extract from the story become part of them, that movement can guide us through the construction of the idea of Justice in each individual. That would explain why the strong idea of Justice, so chaotically constructed (and re-constructed), so fundamental for our societies, "breaks" so easily when confronted with the *ratio* of modernity. It is an ever-changing idea in every individual and between individuals in society.

The construction of this feeling sediments with what the individual apprehends from experience after experience. It is very clear the layers sediment in Cora's poetry especially about her childhood. She uses the metaphor of the penny for the misadventures of the past that she still carries on her heart and wishes never to forget it. She said: "(…) Today will be left for everybody a thousand *cruzeiros*[2]./ Always missing for me the penny from childhood. And for this/ I order to be made a brooch from a cooper penny/ and pin it in my dress besides my heart" [*"(…) Hoje sobrará para todos mil cruzeiros./ Me faltando sempre o vintém da infância. Bem por isso/ mandei fazer um broche de um vintém de cobre/ e preguei no meu vestido do lado do coração./"* (2013b, p. 35)]

The metaphor of the penny of copper describes her childhood and tells us much of her experiences as a child, growing up in a place she kept in her memory as sad, dark, hard, and very poor. She tells us about the old things she had, how everything was used, reused

---

2    Brazilian old currency.

as something else, carefully preserved. The scarce money was counted in pennies. This poetry *narrates* almost photographically the poverty that (still) exists among the enormous economic inequalities in Brazil.

She says: "Penny of copper.../ Old dark pennies/ (From black copper penny was named)./ Rusty oxidized./ I still see it,/ Still feel it,/ Still have it,/ in closed hand./ Sorrowful penny, dark, heavy,/ of my house,/ of my land,/ of my childhood,/ of the poor people, from that time./ Everything old, used, preserved,/ dusted, in the corners./ Taken to the deposit of the old house./ Blankets of faded uneven patchwork./ Corse grimy cloths, patched./ Pot and bowl, lipless plates,/ old shoes,/ flats, heelpiece/ were disputed,/ there was always someone who wanted them./ Pestle made with an ax,/ dig in stumps of aroeira./ Hands of pestle, crippled, rounded, fingerless./ Heavy hand of beat, sock; mill; break; pulverize./ Old hands, of a young lady, clawed, in rhythmic movements,/ alternate, continuous beats, compassed./ Domestic mill of pestle./, Forty pennies of réis[3] ...,/ Short money, scarce./ Sparing./ Of being saved./ Of an old time./ Of poor people./ Of my land./ Of my child-hood./ Penny of Cooper!.../ Economy. Savings./ The poor house./ Vest of old skirts/ of my great-grandmother./ Cut, sewn for me./ Helm of leftovers of baize./ Sedentary life. / Pride and greatness of the past./ In this period I raised myself./ Thence, this book – Penny of Copper, in a long gestation,/ unconscious or not,/ that comes from the remote childhood/ to the present old age." [*Vintém de Cobre... / Antigos vinténs escuros./ (De cobre preto foi batizado)./ Azinhavrados./ Ainda o vejo,/ Ainda o sinto,/ Ainda o tenho,/ na mão fechada./ Moeda triste, escura, pesada,/ da minha casa,/ da minha terra,/ da minha infância,/ da gente pobre, daquele tempo./ Tudo velho, gasto, conservado,/ empoeirado, pelos cantos./ Levados para o depósito do velho sobradão./ Colchas de retalhos desiguais e desbotados./ Panos gros-seiros encardidos, remendados./ Pote e gamela, pratos debeiçados,/ velhos sapatos,/ furados, acalcanhados/ eram disputados,/ tinha sempre alguém que os quisesse./ Pilões lavrados a machado,/ cavados em cepos de aroeira./ Mão de pilão, aleijada, redonda, sem dedos./ Mão pesada de bater, sociar, esmoer, quebrar, pulverizar./ Mãos antigas, de menina-moça, agarradas, em movimentos ritmados,/ alternados, batidas contínuas, compassadas./ En-genho doméstico de pilar./ "Quarenta vintém derréis..."/ Dinheiro curto, escasso./ Parco. Parcimonioso./ De se guardar./ De um tempo velho./ De gente pobre./ Da minha terra./ Da minha infância. / Vintém de Cobre!.../ Economia. Poupança./ A casa pobre./ Madrião de saias velhas/ da minha bisavó./ Recortadas, costuradas para mim./ Timão de restos de baeta./ Vida sedentária./ Orgulho e grandeza do passado./ Nesse tempo me criei./ Daí, este livro – Vintém de Cobre, numa longa gestação,/ inconsciente ou não,/ que vem da infância longínqua/ à ancianidade presente*] (2013b, p. 21-23).

And although she had experienced so deeply the economic inequality that still rules in Brazil, she did not look to the other face of this coin, this is, she narrates her poverty without voicing it as a complain. On the contrary, she sang of this time as a *"Pride and greatness of the past./ In this period I raised myself."*

---

3    Also a Brazilian old currency.

This does not mean that the economic status of Cora Coralina, the storyteller of our analysis, did not have an impact on her concept of Justice. Indeed, it does. Her economic status and all the situations described that were direct consequences of this status became part of her. The constant need for saving, the used things, the vest made from her great-grandmother's skirt, all of this became part of her, a part of composing her*self*. In this situation she *raised herself*. And that is the reason why such an unfair environment constitutes for her the *"pride and greatness of the past"*.

She did not mind her economic condition and even says the old vest made from a skirt of her great-grandmother made her happy. What she considered an injustice is the treatment she received from the grownups of her family and the city in general. Cora felt hurt and carried the scars of having been mistreated since a very young age. She tells us: "I used a child vest/ cut and sewn for me/ from an old skirt of my great-grandmother./ And how that vest/ made me happy!.../ I had a vest.../ I used an old vest/ cut and sewn for me/ from an old skirt/ of my great-grandmother./ I played, spanned, turned into wheel,/ and the old vest filled/ of balloon wind./ Aninha sang, *desentoada*[4], out of tune,/ silly I was./ My vest, balloon vest,/ spinning top, penny in hand./ The elderly exploited./ Ironic, sarcastic./ ,Play a conch, Aninha.'/ Aninha, the fool,/ roll on the floor,/ played a conch./ They laugh and say:/ ,she is really foolish'". [*"Eu vestia um mandrião*[5]*/ recortado e costurado para mim/ de uma saia velha da minha bisavó./ E como aquele mandrião/ me fazia feliz!.../ Eu tinha uma mandrião.../ Eu vestia uma antigo mandrião/ recortado e costurado para mim/ de uma saia velha/ da minha bisavó./ Eu brincava, rodava, virava roda,/ e o antigo mandrião se enchia/ de vento balão./ Aninha cantava, desentoada, desafinada,/ boba que era./ Meu mandrião, vento balão,/ roda pião, vintém na mão./ Os grandes exploravam./ Irônicos, sarcásticos./ "Faz caramujo, Aninha."/ Aninha, a boba,/ rolava no chão,/ fazia caramujão./ Riam e diziam:/ "é boba mesmo"* (2013b, p. 29-30)].

As she grew up, this violence just got worse, as she was considered ugly and goofy, and because of that was socially condemned not to marry. This psychologic violence contains so much prejudice it is hard to process. First of all, it shows how she lived in a society where marriage was the only possible choice for a woman. And so, taking this possibility from her was the same as condemning her to do nothing. They were clearly depriving her of an important social role – even before she had it. Secondly, the simple fact that marriage was the only social choice she was given is a violence against the construction of her*self* as a human being. Also, the reason why she was, in the opinion of *others*, condemned is because she was considered ugly – and this aesthetic social model was also a violence against Cora as still is for many woman all over the world.

Cora handled this social injustice this way: "Those elderly people exploited my silliness./ They used to say like this, turning face as if I were far away:/ ,Mrs. Jacinta has four *flowers*[6]

---

4   *Desentoada* is a neologism that could be closely translated as *"out of tune"*.

5   *Mandrião* in Brazilian portuguese is a child vest.

6   Cora uses the word *fulores* that is not really a word in Portuguese, but is phonetically similar to the word *flores*, that means *flowers*.

to say so./ Three find marriage soon, the other, I don't know, ugly lady don't marry easily.'/ I broke myself into tears. Gentle sob tears…/ ,This fool… Crybaby… No one even said that was her…'/ My great-grandmother scolded, consoled me with illusion words:/ Yes, I would marry. That was sure ugly girl, beautiful woman./ And gave me half of a cracker./ I consoled myself and hold to my great-grandmother./ I grew up with my fears and with tea from the root of *fedegoso*[7],/ prescribed by the knowledge of my great-grandmother./ Sure I lost the hideous appearance. I blushed/ found who wants me./ Yes, that he wasn't contaminated by the principles from Goiás,/ that a girl who read romances and declaimed Almeida Garret/ wouldn't be a good housewife." [*"Aquela gente antiga explorava a minha bobice./ Diziam assim, virando a cara como se eu estivesse distante:/ "Senhora Jacinta tem quarto fulores mal falando./ Três acham logo casamento, uma, não sei não, moça feia num casa fácil."/ Eu me abria em lágrimas. Choro manso e soluçado… / "Essa boba… Chorona… Ninguém nem falou o nome dela…"/ Minha bisavó ralhava, me consolava com palavras de ilusão:/ Sim, que eu casava. Que certo mesmo era menina feia, moça bonita./ E me dava a metade de uma bolacha./ Eu me consolava e me apegava à minha bisavó./ Cresci com os meus medos e com o chá de raiz de fedegoso,/ prescrito pelo saber de mina bisavó./ Certo que perdi a aparência bisonha. Fiquei corada/ e achei quem me quisesse./ Sim, que esse não estava contaminado pelos princípios goianos,/ de que moça que lia romance e declamava Almeida Garrett/ não dava boa dona de casa"* (2013b, p. 43-44)].

It is worth noticing that Cora did not confront those things that are for many of us terrible social violations. Those concepts also became part of her – *"I grew up with my fears"*. If the violence lives in a concept that is part of her, it should be hard to confront it. She deviate from the condemnation that was given to her, such as a course of a river when facing an obstacle – *"Sure I lost the hideous appearance"*. She then, believed she had reached her destiny, when she found a man that was not: *"contaminated by the principles from Goiás"*. If on the one hand she fought against the concepts she incorporated somehow, calling it *contaminated*; on the other hand, she chose to tell her story differently in the end of the poem, and suddenly she did not blamed the social standards of how a woman should look to be considered *beautiful*, but her love for literature - she said: *"that a girl who read romances and declaimed Almeida Garret/ wouldn't be a good housewife"*. The construction of the idea of Justice is a struggle of the concepts we can apprehend from the world. It is sometimes a hard struggle, which has also to do with the construction of the *self*.

Since Cora's companion was separated from his first wife and since Brazil's law at that time did not allow divorce, Cora had to run away in order to live with this man that was not *"contaminated by the principles of Goiás"*. So she left Goiás for a life that was not going to be easy.

They leave for the countryside of São Paulo, where she worked even harder. This period of fourty-five years is remembered by Cora for her identification with her social roles. She said: "My identification with the glebe and with its people./ Ranch woman am I. Workwoman,

---

7   A kind of herb known in Brazil for its healing properties.

baker, bee in her handicraft, good cooker, good washerwoman./ The glebe transfigures me, I am seed, I am stone./ Through my voice all the birds of the world sing./ I am a singer grasshopper of a long summer that is called Life./ I am an indefatigable ant, diligent, constructing my savings." [*Minha identificação com a gleba e com a sua gente./ Mulher da roça eu o sou. Mulher operária, doceira,/ abelha no seu artesanato, boa cozinheira, boa lavadeira./ A gleba me transfigura, sou semente, sou pedra./ Pela minha voz cantam todos os pássaros do mundo./ Sou a cigarra cantadeira de um longo estio que se chama Vida./ Sou a formiga incansável, diligente, compondo seus abastos*] (2013b, p. 110).

Of course it means she had a very simple life, for now a days standards a poor life, that demanded of her a massive workload, working with all her forces to help her family. This is clearly a portrait of the huge social and economic inequalities in Brazil. It is important to say that this kind of inequality has one great characteristic for researchers: it could be measured. Despite the objectivity of this injustice, it is interesting to notice that poverty may not be perceived as an injustice by some people. In other words, it is a huge social problem, it could be more objectively measured, but it may does not *feel* like an *injustice* to people in this situation.

It is a perplexing finding in one of Cora's poems: "Lord, make that I accept/ my poverty as it has always been./ That I don't feel what I don't have./ That I don't lament what I could have had/ and got lost for wrong paths/ and never came back./ Make, Lord, that my humbleness/ be as the desired rain/ falling,/ dark long night,/ in a thirsty land/ and in an old roof./ So that I can thank You,/ for my tight bed,/ my poor little things,/ my house of soil,/ stones and reassembled boards./ And that always is a bundle of wood/ under my stove of mud,/ and light, myself,/ the cheerful fire of my house/ in the morning of a brand new day that starts." [*Senhor, fazei com que eu aceite/ minha pobreza tal como sempre foi./ Que não sinta o que não tenho./ Não lamente o que podia ter/ e se perdeu por caminhos errados/ e nunca mais voltou./ Dai, Senhor, que minha humildade/ seja como a chuva desejada/ caindo mansa,/ longa noite escura,/ numa terra sedenta/ e num telhado velho./ Que eu possa agradecer a Vós,/ minha cama estreita,/ minhas coisinhas pobres,/ minha casa de chão,/ pedras e tábuas remontadas./ E ter sempre um feixe de lenha/ debaixo do meu fogão de taipa,/ e acender, eu mesma,/ o fogo alegre da minha casa/ na manhã de um novo dia que começa*] (2013a, p. 60).

Cora is very positive facing the obstacles of life. She uses the metaphor of the *stones* to talk about them. In one of her poems she says she collected the stones that came down on her and constructed a stair with them. It is clear that she embraces the difficulties of life as a part of the construction of her identity as a stronger person. In this poem it is also worth noticing that she says many things are made from *stone*, including her partner. There is an ambiguous meaning pointing to that man as insensitive and also as an obstacle. In her words: "*I collected all the stones/ that came down on me./ I raised a very high stair/ and up high I went./ I wove a flowered carpet/ and in the dream I lost myself./ A road,/ a bed,/ a house,/ a partner./ Everything was made from stone./ Between stones/ grew my poetry./ My life…/ Breaking stones/ and planting flowers./ Between stones that crushed me/ I raised the rough stone/ of my verses*". [*Ajuntei todas as pedras/ que vieram sobre mim./ Levantei uma escada muito alta/ e no alto subi./ Teci um tapete floreado/ e no sonho me perdi./ Uma estrada,/ um leito,/ uma casa,/ um companheiro./ Tudo de pedra./ Entre pedras/ cresceu minha poesia./ Minha vida…/ Quebrando pedras/ e plantando flores./ Entre pedras que me esmagavam/ levantei a pedra rude/ dos meus versos]* (2013a, p. 11).

This strength to overcome the difficulties of life comes also from her expectations and beliefs she apprehended and developed in the course of her life. One of these influences can be seen in a poem where Cora talks about her grandfather and his remarkable attitude facing difficult times. He had the belief that bad things "open the path" for good things. In other words, the bad things were a sign of good things to come. Also, he comes from bad things, while good things could bring confusion. The poem goes like this: "My grandfather used to say:/ When things get bad,/ it is a sign that the good is near./ The bad is always opening path/ for the good./ The wrong brings much experience/ and the good brings sometimes confusion: ‚Not always like this not never worst'./ My grandfather knew all the truths/ and spent the philosophy of whom lived a lot/ and learnt./ When the things were not very good,/ he said: tomorrow will be better./ And went down bended to his mountain mill." [*Dizia meu avô:/ Quando as coisas ficam ruins,/ é sinal de que o bom está perto./ O ruim está sempre abrindo passagem/ para o bom./ O errado traz muita experiência/ e o bom traz às vezes confusão:/ "Nem sempre assim nem nunca pior". / Meu avô conhecia todas as verdades/ e gastava a filosofia de quem muito viveu/ e aprendeu./ Quando as coisas não iam muito bem,/ ele dizia: amanhã estará melhor./ E descia curvado para o seu engenho de serra]* (2013b, p. 96).

Furthermore, she saw her four children as a motivation to overcome the difficulties of life. She wrote them a poem, which tells us since they were born; she took her strength and resistance from them. She said they were raised "in a school of struggle and work" and "then each one left for their best destiny". She felt the responsibility of being an example of work and courage.

After they left "for their best destiny", Cora, who was a widow, found herself alone and decided to go back to her hometown – her last example of work and courage: restarting her life, at an old age, alone, in the city that treated her so badly in her youth. Her poem says: "A day, has been./ I was young, full of dreams./ Rich of an immense poverty/ that limited me/ between eight women that ruled me./ And I left in the search of my destiny./Nobody offered me a hand./ Nobody helped me and everybody threw stones at me./ Stripped. Stoned./ Alone and lost on the uncertain paths of life./ And I was walking, walking…/ And children were born./ And they were fragile and tiny,/ needing care,/ growing up slowly./ And they were the stone where I stood,/ shield against the storm that came over me./ They were, in their infant fragility,/ post and foundation, walls and roof,/ security of a home/ that the wind of insanity/ threatened to collapse./ Children, tiny and fragile…/ did I carry them, did I feed them?/ No. They were the one who carried me,/ who fed me./ They were chains, moorings, emplacements./ They were so strong./ The built my resistance./ Children, you were bread and water in my desert./ Shadow in my loneliness./ Refuge of my nothing./ I removed stones, broke the edges of life and planted rose trees./ You were, for me, seed and fruit./ In your childish unconsciousness./ You were unity and aggregation./

You grew up in a school of struggle and work,/ then,/ each one left for their best destiny,/ And the old mother alone/ should still give one example/ of work and courage./ My last debt of gratefulness/ to my children./ I did the walk back to the ancestral roots./ Went back to the origins of my life./ I wrote the ,Chant of the Return'./ It was meant to be./ I made a beautiful name as a confectioner, greater glory./ And in the rough stones of my cradle, i engraved poems." [*Um dia, houve./ Eu era jovem, cheia de sonhos./ Rica de imensa pobreza/ que me limitava/ entre oito mulheres que me governavam./ E eu parti em busca do meu destino./ Ninguém me estendeu a mão./ Ninguém me ajudou e todos me jogaram pedras./ Despojada. Apedrejada./ Sozinha e perdida nos caminhos incertos da vida./ E fui caminhando, caminhando.../ E me nasceram filhos./ E foram eles frágeis e pequeninos,/ carecendo de cuidados,/ crescendo devagarinho./ E foram eles a rocha onde me amparei,/ anteparo à tormenta que viera sobre mim./ Foram eles, na sua fragilidade infante,/ poste e alicerce, paredes e cobertura,/ segurança de um lar/ que o vento da insânia/ ameaçava desabar./ Filhos, pequeninos e frágeis.../ eu os carregava, eu os alimentava?/ Não. Foram eles que me carregaram,/ que me alimentaram./ Foram correntes, amarras, ambasamentos./ Foram fortes demais./ Construíram a minha resistência./ Filhos, fostes pão e água no meu deserto./ Sombra na minha solidão./ Refúgio do meu nada./ Removi pedras, quebrei as arestas da vida e plantei roseiras./ Fostes, para mim, semente e fruto./ Na vossa inconsciência infantil./ Fostes unidade e agregação./ Crescestes numa escola de luta e trabalho,/ depois, cada qual se foi ao seu melhor destino,/ E a velha mãe sozinha/ devia ainda um exemplo/ de trabalho e de coragem./ Minha última dívida de gratidão/ aos filhos./ Fiz a caminhada de retorno às raízes ancestrais./ Voltei às origens da minha vida,/ escrevi o "Cântico da Volta"./ Assim devia ser./ Fiz um nome bonito de doceira, glória maior./ E nas pedras rudes do meu berço/ gravei poemas*] (2013b, p. 76-77).

Yet, the way back to Goiás was not easy. It seemed to be a dark road for her. A road "in the night of her life" she walked with an unlit candle. So, why return to a city that mistreated her in the past? Why return to a city of a sad childhood? The answer may be in the verses below. She went to her "lost penny, her penny of happiness, the bigger capacity of being herself, her constant affirmation". The poverty of her childhood, the humiliation, and the misadventures of the past *are* her affirmation as a person. She apprehends these painful experiences and they become one.

Cora went back to Goiás to find herself: "What are you looking for, Aninha?/ What strength made you waste chains of affections/ and brought you back to the lapidary stones of the past?/ Alone, without fear, twenty-seven years have been passed.../ My lost penny, my penny of happiness./ Bigger capacity of being myself, my constant affirmation./ Walker, always walking./ On my little foots,/ my flat flip flops./ So dark the night of my life.../ Indifferent or watchful./ So much balk./ Ahead, marking the way the candle unlit." [*Que procura você, Aninha?/ Que força a fez despedaçar correntes de afetos/ e trazê-la de volta às pedras lapidares do passado?/ Sozinha, sem medo, vinte e sete anos já passados.../ Meu vintém perdido, meu vintém de felicidade./ Capacidade maior de ser eu mesma, minha afirmação constante./ Caminheira, caminhando sempre./ Nos meus pés pequenos,/ meus chinelinhos furados./ Tão escura a noite da minha vida.../ Indiferentes ou vigilantes./ Tanto tropeço./ Na frente, marcando o caminho a candeia apagada./ (...)]* (2013b, p.51).

In Goiás, she returned to the house she grew up in, and had to work baking confectionery to survive. Even with a hard life, she felt blessed and said she was receiving the pennies she planted in the past. Cora described herself as a singing grasshopper and diligent ant, stock between writing poems and baking confectionary, blessed by angels that help her to work: "What have I been if not singing grasshopper and diligent ant/ of this long summer that is called Life.../ My candies, my pans of copper.../ My guarding angels, valorous and assured./ Little Radar... My familiar ghosts, my fictionalized/ permeated the candies' sells./ Before, far away, in the past, giving birth to children and raising children/ and planting rose bushes, lilies, and palms, avencas and palm trees,/ in Jaboticabal, land of my learn of living,/ land of my children./ My people from Jaboticabal. My Guardian Angel, little Radar,/ watchful to the pan, herding the bees in my candies,/ warning me at the right time. Sometimes, putting out the fire,/ a way of helping that only little Radar knew. In other times, way before,/ I already planted a penny of copper that I watered with love/ with the hope of it multiplying. Pieces of pennies/ running to Aninha." [*Que tenho sido, senão cigarra cantadeira e formiga diligente/ desse longo estio que se chama Vida.../ Meus doces, meus tachos de cobre.../ Meus anjos da guarda, valedores e certos./ Radarzinho... Meus fantasmas familiares, meus romanceados/ de permeio à venda dos doces./ Antes, lá longe, no passado, parindo filhos e criando filhos/ e plantando roseiras, lírios e palmas, avencas e palmeiras,/ em Jaboticabal, terra de meu aprendizado de viver,/ terra de meus filhos./ Minha gente de Jaboticabal. Meu Anjo da Guarda, Radarzinho,/ atento ao tacho, tangendo as abelhas que se danavam nos meus doces,/ dando aviso certo na hora certa. De outras me apagando o fogo,/ um modo de ajudar que só Radarzinho sabia. Em outros tempos, muito antes/ tinha já plantado um vintém de cobre que regava com amor/ na esperança de haver crias. Porção de vinténs/ correndo para Aninha*] (2013b, p. 47-48).

She would still be a confectioner until her last days. This activity is discussed in many of her poems. During this period in Goiás, at the age of seventy-six she would succeed in publishing her first book. This book caught the attention of the most famous poetry writers of Brazil, Carlos Drummond de Andrade, who wrote her an open letter in an important newspaper. From this moment on she became more and more famous as a writer. Yet, she still had to work as a confectioner, while receiving people for all over the country interested in her poetry. What we may think of as an exhausting routine was described by this indefatigable woman this way: "I made candies for fourteen years in a row./ I earned the needed money./ I had commitments and hadn't resources./ I made a beautiful name as a confectioner, my greater glory./ I made friends and customers. I wrote books and told stories./ Truths and lies. It was the best time of my life./ It was so full and so fertile that made me forget the word/ ,I am tired'./ Tired maybe the washerwoman of the Red River of my town./ Maybe the woman of the ranch of São Paulo, not even her./ I've never heard from the washerwoman the expression ,I am tired'./ Yes, her fear: do not have a costumer and a bundle of clothes to wash and iron./ Your constants, when in a time off: ,Thanks God!'/ Your day started with the dawn and continued with the night./ I had workers and ranches. I planted and reaped through their warm hands./ I have never heard of anyone: ‚I am tired'." [*Fiz doces durante quatorze anos seguidos./ Ganhei o dinheiro necessário./ Tinha compromissos e não tinha recursos./ Fiz um nome bonito de doceira, minha glória maior./ Fiz amigos e fregueses. Escrevi livros e contei estórias./ Verdades e mentiras. Foi o melhor tempo da minha vida/ Foi tão cheio e tão fértil que me fez esquecer a palavra/ "estou cansada"./ Cansada talvez a lavadeira do rio Vermelho da minha cidade./ Talvez a mulher da roça de São Paulo, nem mesmo ela./ Nunca ouvi da lavadeira a expressão "estou cansada"./ Sim, seu medo: faltar a freguesa e trouxa de roupa para lavar e passar./ Suas constantes, quando na folga: "Graças a Deus!"/ Seu dia começava com a aurora e continuava com a noite./ Tive trabalhadores e roçados. Plantei e colhido por suas mãos calosas./ Jamais ouvi de algum: "Estou cansado"*] (2013b, p. 49).

If we look carefully to this poem, we will be able to see to whole benjaminian movement. First, she says how much she worked to honor her, and that time was so full and fertile that it made her to forget the words "I am tired". It is the first movement, from the experience that is being told by the storyteller to the reader. Then, she is influenced by the experience of others. She compares herself with the washerwoman of her city that never complains about being tired. And for comparison, it almost as if Cora did not *deserve* to feel tired, since a harder worker is not.

This game of back and forth we do all the time, comparing ourselves to others, and our concepts to the concepts of others, is of fundamental importance because it describes the dynamic of the construction of ourselves, of others and of our expectations about *life* and what is *fair or unfair* in it.

She would bake and write until the end of her life. The years took much of her vision and made it hard to recognize the ones she loved and to read her beloved books. Still, she left as beautifully as she lived: "Everything in me is fading./ My strength of a woman of fighting gives up by saying:/ I am tired./ The clarity turns into mist and haze./ The beloved book: the black of the letters blur,/ the parallel lines warp./ The words dance,/ the distance is made lampshade./ I don't recognize friendly faces, family./ A thin veil is incorporating the retinal field./ Slowly as calm sheep pass the known figures/ that I don't know anymore./ It's the cataract turning into pall the vision that is made shadow./ I feel thy courage of a woman of fight giving in,/ and I confess myself:/ I am tired." [*Tudo em mim vai se apagando./ Cede minha força de mulher de luta em dizer:/ estou cansada./ A claridade se faze m névoa e bruma./ O livro amado: o negro das letras se embaralham,/ entortam as linhas paralelas./ Dançam as palavras,/ a distância se faze m quebra-luz./ Deixo de reconhecer rostos amigos, familiares./ Um véu tênue vai se incorporando no campo da retina./ Passam lentamente como ovelhas mansas os vultos conhecidos/ que já não conheço./ É a catarata amortalhando a visão que se faz sombra./ Sinto que cede meu valor de mulher de luta,/ e eu me confesso:/ estou cansada.*] (2013b, p. 235).

## 4    Conclusions

There are many philosophical models about our conceptions of Justice, but it is hard to demonstrate which ones are more or less helpful to make us understand *Justice*. How can we *test* our ideas of Justice? This paper presents a new approach in this matter by presenting pieces of art as an expression of the thoughts of that artist in that specific moment of time. Therefore, it uses a piece of art as a piece of data.

Here, we worked with the literature of the Brazilian writer Cora Coralina. She was a strong woman, a housewife, and a hard worker until her last days, leading a life far away from the walls of Academia. In her poetry, she narrates her life stories and shows much of her ideas about Justice. For that, her profile and distinguished poetry, she is an optimal choice to confront our philosophical models of Justice. Are our abstract models enough to handle the ideas of a simple woman of the countryside of Brazil?

In this analysis, we took the time to learn with the complexity of our storyteller. Facing what are, in a macro perspective, huge injustices, such as poverty, gender violence and social exclusion, it is interesting to notice she did not perceive those things as *unfair* in each singular situation.

Also, we use a movement that Walter Benjamin describes in his *Erzähler* – where the storyteller takes his lessons of life from his experiences and from the experiences of others, in a way that those experiences become a part of him, and when he tells the story, his listeners apprehend the lessons being told, so that they become part of them.

We reproduced this movement in the analysis of Cora's poetry, in order to understand the life experiences that become part of her and compose her ideas of Justice.

Cora's conceptions of Justice do not fit in ours philosophical models of Justice, which are not even close to the complexity of our life experiences. It shows that each subject, notmatter where she lives or who she is, is a complex subject that apprehends from experiences and learns from them. *It shows our philosophical models should work with a much wider spectrum of concepts of Justice, if they want to handle the complexity and the diversity of the subjects. Our academic work has to be able to help us to a better understanding of our social relations.*

Cora Coralina's poetry is an elegant demonstration of how different people can be and how rich can be the spectrum of conceptions of Justice. We gave a penny for her thoughts about Justice and it was worth it.

### Acknowledgments

This work is financially supported by the National Counsel of Technological and Scientific Development (Conselho Nacional de Desenvolvimento Científico e Tecnológico- CNPq) grant nº 142138/2014-2.

## References

BENJAMIN, Walter. Der Erzähler. *In* Gesammelte Schriften II, 2, Frankfurt am Main: Suhrkamp, 1977.
CORALINA, Cora. Meu livro de cordel. 18th edition, São Paulo: Global, 2013a.
CORALINA, Cora. Vintém de cobre: meias confissões de Aninha. 10th edition, São Paulo: Global, 2013b.
CORALINA, Cora. Villa Boa de Goyaz. 2nd edition, São Paulo: Global, 2003.

## The Author

**Nuria López**, PhD Candidate. Master in Philosophy of Law at Pontifical Catholic University of São Paulo – PUC/SP (Brazil). Email: nuria.lcs@gmail.com

# Justice without Formulas
## Interpretations of Polish Nobel Prize Winners in the 20th Century

Tomasz Stawecki

## Abstract

The author suggests that lawyers' perceptions of justice differ from those which we very often find in the literature. It is particularly true in case of the literature of nations which arises under the rule of foreign rulers, and they do not have their own deeply legitimized legal orders. Writing about the idea of justice novelists and poets of such nations or communities are keen to seek fairness or basically intuitive acts of "giving others their dues", rather than justice as acting in accordance with more detailed rules, formulas, or simply the binding law.

In seeking that special concept of justice, the reference is made to the Polish literature of the 20th century with the focus on four artists, who as literary representatives of Poles have been granted Nobel Prize in literature: H. Sienkiewicz (1905), W. Reymont (1924), C. Miłosz (1980) and W. Szymborska (1996).

May be, an analogy might be noticed with contemporary immigrants to Europe or various "excluded groups".

## Keywords

Justice, formulas of justice, righteousness, fairness, phronesis, compassion, forgiveness, Polish Nobel Prizewinners, novelists, poets

## 1    Known and Forgotten Ways of Understanding Justice

When we reflect on justice in the descriptive approach, namely, when we ask what people commonly call justice, the first thought and response is the opinion that justice is defined very differently and understood in various ways. The acceptance of this position without any reservations (radical version) leads to the conclusion that the idea of justice is a matter of extremely subjective interpretations. In such a case, we usually claim that everyone as-

© Springer Fachmedien Wiesbaden GmbH, part of Springer Nature 2018
H. Kabashima et al. (Hrsg.), *The Idea of Justice in Literature*,
Wirtschaftsethik in der globalisierten Welt,
https://doi.org/10.1007/978-3-658-21996-3_12

signs their own meaning to the idea of justice, most frequently, one that is consistent with their own interests, expectations or accepted vision of the social world.

The second, moderate view of the multitude of ways of understanding justice suggests that, despite there being many individual concepts, a common denominator or common place (*topos*) can be found in disputes about justice. Particular points of view are most frequently reconciled in the conviction that the idea of justice can be reduced to a *general rule or formula*, which is acceptable to many. Examples of such a conciliatory approach are the classical definitions of justice, formulated by Ulpian, a Roman jurist (170–223 AD), who claimed that justice is "rendering to everyone his due" (*iustitia [est] suum cuique tribuere*) or "the constant and perpetual will to render to every man his due" (*iustitia est constans et perpetua voluntas ius suum cuique tribuere*).[1] This principle has been developed through the ages. Today, we find a similar solution, *inter alia*, in a well-known essay by Chaïm Perelman "*Concerning Justice*", in which he reconstructs six current conceptions of justice: (i) to each the same thing; (ii) to each according to his merits; (iii) to each according to his work; (iv) to each according to his needs; (v) to each according to his rank; and (vi) to each according to his legal entitlement.[2]

Many more, similar examples of the treatment of justice as activities which are consistent with the established rule can obviously be found, especially in the works of the legal philosophers. This general rule or formula is often equated with the law as a set of legal norms (rules). In such a case, it is just to act strictly in compliance with the applicable law. After all, lawyers have a tendency of emphasizing connections between the idea of justice and positive law and for highlighting two key functions of the idea of justice. Justice then becomes a prospective model for positive law, as well as a criterion for its *a posteriori* evaluation. If the law proves to be inconsistent with the accepted understanding of justice, we remember the principle of St. Augustine and St. Thomas Aquinas, according to which an unjust law is not a law (*lex iniusta non est lex*) or Gustav Radbruch's rationalistic reinterpretation from the middle of the 20th century: "a grossly unfair law is not a law" (*lex iniustissima non est lex*). Chaïm Perelman, as mentioned above, also emphasizes the double-sidedness of this relationship: "[justice] is invoked to protect the established order as well as to justify its overthrow. And so, justice is a universal value."[3] This juxtaposition of the idea of justice, sometimes called the natural law or the divine law, on one side and human law (positive law) on the other side, is a well-known literary concept dating back to at least the times of

---

1   See, for example: Vlastos, Gregory, The Theory of Social Justice in the Polis in Plato's Republic; [in] North H. F. (ed.), Interpretations of Plato. A Swarthmore Symposium (Leiden: E.J. Brill, 1977), 5.

2   Perelman, Chaïm, Concerning Justice, [in:] The Idea of Justice and the Problem of Argument (New York: The Humanities Press, 1963, originally published as: De La Justice, 1945), 6.

3   Perelman, Chaïm, Justice (New York: Random House, 1967), 3. Perelman also adds: "justice is [however] far from being an exclusively revolutionary value. The courts of justice are shields that protect the established order; its guardians are the judges, whose role is to apply the law and to punish those who violate it." (p. 4)

Antigone from the tragedy by Sophocles. In addition, the belief in justice as following an agreed principle or formula with respect to the law or against the law is so strong that the lawyer and philosopher, Perelman proposes that the principle of the Rule of Justice should be adopted and applied alongside the principle of the Rule of Law.[4]

The belief about the universality of justice as an action that is *consistent with a specific rule* reinforces the expectation of the authors of individual theories or concepts of justice that they will be considered the "one right answer" to questions on this. Philosophers have repeatedly emphasized that this conviction could have been an illusion. If parties enter into peace or surrender to the settlement of a court in the case of a conflict or dispute, in the name of justice, this does not mean that they see and evaluate the events binding them and the judicial sentences in the same way. "The opposing camps simply do not have t h e s a m e conception of justice. Having noted that justice is a universal value—that is to say, one that is universally acknowledged—we must (…) add that the notion is also *confused*."[5]

However, the desire to arrive at an understanding as to what justice is was and still is strong. We encounter this way of thinking not only in the area of philosophy and legal philosophy, but also in the opinions of greater populations. Modern scholars of European culture emphasize, for instance, that "in Western iconography, Justice is blindfolded and holds aloft a balance scale. The blindfold represents impartiality—because Justice cannot see the people before her, her decisions will not be prejudiced by their appearance. The scale represents the use of publicly accepted principles—all can see as Justice weighs the punishment to the crime."[6] We should add from ourselves that the vast majority of images or statues of Themis, the goddess of justice, are portrayed with an additional attribute—a sword, which symbolizes power and the ability to punish those who breached the divine and human laws. Therefore, the figure of Themis has the objective of symbolizing the commonality of convictions and ways of thinking about justice.

The uniformity of the ways of presenting the idea of justice seems to have not only ancient roots, but also support in modern philosophy. Many authors, both in Germany during the 19th century and today—especially because of the Kantian influences in John Rawls' "A Theory of Justice"—believed that the universality of the idea of justice is reflected in the universality of Immanuel Kant's categorical imperative. This view is popular to

---

4     Perelman, Justice, 35-45. Perelman's interests in issues of justice were not incidental. He was born in Warsaw (in 1912) to a Jewish family, whereas he lived through the Second World War in Belgium. Commentators emphasize that his legal philosophy was a reaction to the horrors of the Nazi and Stalin wartime crimes. This comment is also a further illustration of one of the arguments of this article that philosophical, moral and legal positions are embroiled in historic events and the experiences of the individual authors-philosophers.

5     Perelman, Justice, 4.

6     Leung, Kwok, and Morris, Michael W., Justice Through the Lens of Culture and Ethnicity, [in:] Handbook of Justice Research in Law, edited by Joseph Sanders and V. Lee Hamilton, Plenum Publishers, New York 2000, p. 343.

this day, even if, according to experts, it is based on an erroneous interpretation by the philosopher from Königsberg.[7]

However, it appears that, despite all the advantages of reducing justice to acting in compliance with a specified rule, formula or principle, this idea has a more extensive meaning. It is worth noting that, as early as in Greek mythology, the domain of justice was placed in the hands of the two goddesses. The first was Themis, the Titan goddess, personification of the order of things established by law, order and equity, she was also described as prophetic divinity.[8] She was the divine voice (*themistes*), who first instructed mankind on the primal laws of justice and morality, such as the precepts of piety, the rules of hospitality, good governance, conduct of assembly and pious offerings to the gods. Before Roman times, Themis was often represented as seated beside Zeus' throne, advising him on the precepts of divine law and the rules of fate. The second goddess, responsible for introducing justice among mankind was Dike (or Dicé), the daughter of Themis and Zeus. In the tragedians Dike appears as a divinity who severely punishes all wrong, watches over the maintenance of justice, and pierces the hearts of the unjust with tie sword made for her by AEsa. In this capacity she is closely connected with the Erinnyes, though her business is not only to punish injustice, but also to reward virtue.[9] She was recognized as the goddess of justice, fair judgements and the rights established by custom and law; in other words: personification of Natural Law, or Justice, and Shame. Dike was also identified with Dikaiosyne (Righteousness)[10] and was seen as being in opposition to Adikia (Injustice).

Therefore, in the earliest period of our reflection, the idea of justice had at least two faces. Even in the case of Aristotle, we encounter the suggestion that justice can mean either acting according to the binding laws or acting fairly, treating other people equally.[11] In the former

---

7    O. Höffe, Kant's Principle of Justice as Categorical Imperative of Law, [in:] Kant's Practical Philosophy Reconsidered, International Archives of the History of Ideas / Archives Internationales d'Histoire des Idées, 2010, Volume 128 of the series, 149-167.

8    Smith, William (ed.), Anthon, Charles (revisions, corrections, additions) Dictionary of Greek and Roman Biography and Mythology, (New York: Harpers & Brothers, Publ., 1884), 870, at: http://www.columbia.edu/cu/lweb/digital/collections/cul/texts/ldpd_10482899_000/ ldpd_10482899_000.pdf. In Greek, the word themis referred to divine law, the rules of conduct long established by custom. Unlike the word nomos, the term was not usually used to describe laws of human decree.

9    Dictionary of Greek …, 255. See also: Graves, Robert, The Greek Myths, Vol. 1 (London: Penguin Classics, 2012), 104.

10   In ancient Greek the equivalents of the contemporary notion of justice were dike or diaiosunê. See: Miller, F. D., Aristotle's Philosophy of Law, [in:] A History of the Philosophy of Law from the Ancient Greeks to the Scholastics, F.D. Miller, Jr., and C.-A. Biondi (eds.), A Treatise of Legal Philosophy and General Jurisprudence, Volume 6, Editor-in-Chief: E. Pattaro, Dordrecht: Springer, 2007), 103-104.

11   Looking from a different angle: "the term 'unjust' is held to apply both to the man who breaks the law and the man who takes more than his due, the unfair man. Hence it is clear that the law-abiding man and the fair man will both be just. 'The just' therefore means that which is lawful, and that which is equal and fair, and 'the unjust' means that which is illegal and that

case, justice requires reference to a specific measure or standards, but in the latter, it rather refers to a standard which is not specified in detail: to an intuitive sense of fairness.[12] It is something more than a distinction of distributive and retributive or restorative justice.

Roman and Medieval philosophers, including Thomas Aquinas, are responsible for many philosophers and lawyers referring to Aristotle's philosophy of justice in later centuries. However, it is notable that they concentrated on the first aspect of his concept of justice—the search for a formula or measure—and not on the second. The idea of "acting in a fair way" was clearly neglected, probably as being excessively imprecise for the needs of the changing world. Perhaps the English concept of equity, as opposed to justice administered by the courts adjudicating on the basis of the common law, was the differentiating exception.

However, it is not the objective of this article to search for answers to the question of why the idea of "acting in accordance with the binding laws" has dominated our thinking about justice. Meanwhile, the *initial hypothesis* which I raise in this article is the assertion that lawyers' perceptions of justice differ from those which philosophers normally accept, as well as that we very often find an illustration of the idea of justice in the literature which is different from the visions of lawyers and legal philosophers. In this sense, the lawyers/ practitioners and lawyers/legal philosophers can find a special way of thinking about justice in literary texts, which has remained clearly forgotten, especially in continental Europe.

## 2      Justice and Literature

The search for forgotten notions of justice can be an important task of the "Law and Literature" stream. After all, this is not an easy task for lawyers. The famous American judge, Benjamin N. Cardozo, author of the essay from which this stream of research about the law took its name,[13] indicated that the literature [fiction] can be useful to judges because it helps improve the form of the judicial opinion and only indirectly, the content of the judgement. The legal reasoning, the judgement and then the opinion issued by the judge must be precise and convincing. "The opinion will need persuasive force, or the impressive virtue of sincerity and fire…" It is not in the literature that a judge should look for models of justice, but in previous court judgements, although the boundary between the content

---

which is unequal or unfair." Aristotle, The Nicomachean Ethics, transl. R. Rackham, (Cambridge, Mass.: Harvard Univ. Press, 1926, reprint 1994), Book V, i.8., p. 257. It is worth noting that it was only J. Rawls in his famous "A Theory of Justice" clearly combines both aspects into a single concept: "justice as fairness" (Oxford-London: Oxford University Press, 1972), § 3, 11 ff.

12   Some commentators suggest that Aristotle often used terms "fairness" and "equality" (ἴσος, ἀγίσος, ἰσότης) as synonyms (e. g. Gromska, Daniela (translation and comments to: Etyka Nikomachejska [The Nicomachean Ethics, Polish ed.], Warsaw: PWN. 1996), 168.

13   Cardozo, Benjamin N., Law and literature and other essays and addresses (New York: Harcourt, Brace and Co., 1931), 3-40, in particular 9.

and the form of the text is not sharp at all. Work on the form will primarily enable the judge to improve his assertions and his arguments, not just the essence of the judgement. However, today, eighty years after the publication of B. N. Cardozo's essay, we are convinced that we can and should go much further.

However, an important assumption is made in this article that the study of justice in the literature requires the rejection of the concept of autonomy of the text. It is true that frequently, "the text speaks for itself" and it is unnecessary to study the historic and social circumstances of the emergence of such a text, the author's experience, events and social objectives. I believe that this does not apply to a reflection about justice in the majority of cases. They are usually a reaction to various forms of actual injustice, and often also an expression of dreams, demands or programs formulated by the author because of his experiences of injustice. Literary texts, in which reference is made to justice, are therefore entangled in the historical and social contexts, as well as the personal experiences of the authors. It is only by taking these contexts into account that they can be fully understood.[14]

The analysis of Polish literature will elaborate on and illustrate this assumption. Regardless of whether or not the novels, short stories or poems were written in Poland or abroad, they express the experiences of the Polish nation since the 19th century. To explain most briefly the historical context of such an understanding of justice, we have to remember that Poland had been under the authority of invaders, foreign rulers and governments imposed from outside for the last two hundred years. Poland had been divided among three authoritarian regimes: Russia, Prussia (later Germany) and Austria, from 1795, through the whole of the 19th century, until 1918. After 1939, Poland fell under the totalitarian regime of Nazi Germany (until 1945), after which it was under the power of the Soviet Union (in the latter case, until the fall of the communist system in 1989). Political authorities, public institutions and, in particular, positive law were all regarded as coming from outside and imposed on Poles [the Polish nation].[15] Such laws and institutions could not be deemed as just, unless we view justice very narrowly with pure legalism.

The objective of the analysis of the idea of justice in Polish literature which arose over two centuries in conditions of a lack of independence, the inability to build its own, fully free state and the lack of democratically or even ideologically legitimized law is not to remember the historical wrongs. It is also not an attempt to build a further "theory of tran-

---

14   Czesław Miłosz, a contemporary Polish poet, mentioned later in the article, claimed: "Every poet depends upon generations who wrote in his native tongue; he inherits styles and forms elaborated by those who lived before him. At the same time, though, he feels that those old means of expression are not adequate to his own experience" (Miłosz, Czesław, Nobel Lecture, (New York, Farrar Straus Giroux, 1981), 5. In fact, the "poet's experience" may refer not only to an influence on the form of the poetry, but also to its content.

15   The few exceptions, such as, for example, French family law, which were introduced in the central part of Poland by Napoleon in 1809 and tolerated by the Russian tsars or Prussian (German) GAMS, do not change the picture for the better.

sitional justice,[16] a sociologically-oriented theory which looks to the future, even though it has the experience of wounds from the past. This article only looks at the past. It is an attempt to show that an understanding of the idea of justice in the literature can differ, if countries are examined in which the principle of the rule of law has not been practiced for many years, while the law imposed on the public was not legitimized. I believe it is worth distinguishing the mainstream theories of justice from the different concept of justice in the literature: one that is worshipped by people living in territories under foreign domination, most frequently the control of another state and other ruler. It may also be the case of people who live in their national system, but are excluded from society, because of their race, skin color, cultural or political identity, religion or economic poverty. Living in such reality, writers and poets are usually ready to reject the legal order of the enemy or of the despot and would rather emphasize the crime, tortures and evil perpetrated on the nation or group conquered or subjected by the invader or ruler(s) instead of developing a virtue of loyalty to a ruler.

A feeling of injustice, particularly gross injustice, does not necessarily need to arise from direct coercive actions. The literature of the Holocaust would serve as an example. It was not until Hannah Arendt, who showed in a philosophical study, the book reporting the Eichmann trial, that even an unimaginable evil can take the form of a common clerk's acts.[17]

Anticipating further detailed considerations, the hypothesis may be stated that, in the literature of nations which arises under the rule of other rulers, which do not have their own, legitimized laws, the idea of justice, which rather seeks fairness or completely intuitive acts of "giving others their dues", gains acknowledgement, rather than justice as acting in accordance with more detailed rules, formulas, or simply the binding law. I understand that the borderline between these two interpretations of justice is not sharp, however I believe it is worth to see the difference. This is the key hypothesis of this article.

In seeking that special concept of justice, let's make reference to the Polish literature from the end of the 19th century and the whole of the 20th century. It would be a good idea to quote two authors and two poets, as literary representatives of Poles, all being Nobel Prizewinners in literature: Henryk Sienkiewicz (Nobel Prize in 1905), Władysław Reymont (Nobel Prize in 1924), Czesław Miłosz (Nobel Prize in 1980) and Wisława Szymborska

---

16    ">Transitional justice< is an expression … coined in 1991 at the time of the Soviet collapse and on the heels of the late 1980s Latin American transitions to democracy. In proposing this terminology, [the] aim was to account for the self-conscious construction of a distinctive conception of justice associated with periods of radical political change following past oppressive rule." See: Teitel, Ruti G., Transitional Justice Globalized, The International Journal of Transitional Justice, 2008, Vol. 1-4, available at: http://papers.ssrn.com/sol3/papers.cfm?abstract_id=2143194, as well. See also Czarnota, Adam, On the beauty of confusions, or transitional justice and the rule of law, [in:] Wielowymiarowość prawa [Multidimensionality of the law], J. Czapska, M. Dudek, M. Stępień (eds.), (Toruń: Adam Marszałek Edition, 2014), 137-144.

17    Arendt believes, however, that doing justice requires clear and general rules to be applied. Arendt, Hannah, Eichmann in Jerusalem. A report on the banality of evil, New York: The Viking Press, 1963), 7-8.

(Nobel Prize in 1996). The fact that these authors were awarded by the Swedish Academy of Sciences shows that their writing or poetry proved to be understandable to readers from other countries, readers who developed in other cultures and with different historical, political and legal experiences. All these prizewinners in the area of literature lived and wrote at different historical times, opposing different enemies, but each made reference to the idea of justice in their works of art.

There is no suggestion in this article that these four authors consistently wrote about justice as the most important issue and, all the more so, that they represented as a uniform theory of justice. Reflections on the works of the four Polish Nobel Prizewinners should also not be understood as a deep analysis of a very rich literary output of each one of these authors. It is a rather modest search for traces of the idea of justice. All four presentations below constitute purely illustrations of specific perceptions of justice in great literary works.

In this article, all disputes and discussions on the artistic value of works of the Nobel Prizewinners in literature are—in principle—left aside. Almost all of the 111 winners (since 1901) were highly criticized, while some were praised for the timeless value of their writings. The aim of this article is only to have a look for the idea of justice in the writings of Polish novelists and poets who did not enjoy a sovereign state practicing the rule of law principle.

## 3      Values of the Christian Civilization Before the Idea of Justice

The first concept of justice, which we find in the works of the Polish Nobel Prizewinners in literature, was presented by Henryk Sienkiewicz (1846-1916). He is mostly known in Poland as the author of historical novels glorifying the virtues of Polish knights fighting German, Cossack, Swedish, Turkish and Tatar invaders in the 15th century (novel "*The Teutonic Knights*", sometimes translated as "*The Knights of the Cross*") and in the 17th century (the trilogy: "*With Fire and Sword*", "*The Deluge*", "*Sir Michael*"). These novels led to the creation of various myths intended to keep up the Polish national spirit at times when Poland was not an independent state. Sienkiewicz's glorification of national heroes was not one-sided; a commentator of his novels wrote: "[a] distinctive trait is Sienkiewicz's habit of never shutting his eyes to the faults of his compatriots; rather, he exposes them mercilessly, while he renders justice to the abilities and courage of the enemies of Poland. Like the old prophets of Israel he often tells his people strong truths."[18]

However, the work of art that was awarded the Nobel Prize by the Swedish Academy was the novel entitled "*Quo vadis?*" (1896). It was a novel about the persecution of Christians

18   af Wirsén, C.D., Presentation, [in:] Frenz Horst, (ed.), Literature 1901-1967. Nobel Lectures including presentation speeches and biographies of the prizewinners (Amsterdam—London—New York: Elsevier Publ. Co., 1969), 37. This opinion was at least partly supported by the idea of Poland being "the bulwark of Christendom" against the Turks and the Tartars, as well as any possible threat to Europe coming from the East.

in Rome in the 1st century AD, in Emperor Nero's times. The novel was highly popular. The official announcement was made, however, that Sienkiewicz had been awarded the Nobel Prize "because of his outstanding merits as an epic writer."[19] The members of the Swedish Academy were not guided by the compassion for Poles deprived of sovereignty and basic liberties and freedoms, but they took into account the universal artistic values of Sienkiewicz's novel. C.D. af Wirsén, the Permanent Secretary of the Academy, in his "Presentation" [of the Nobel Prize], declared that "in every nation there are some rare geniuses who concentrate in themselves the spirit of the nation; they represent the national character to the world. Although they cherish the memories of the past of that people, they do so only to strengthen its hope for the future."[20]

The City of Rome described in the novel "*Quo vadis?*" was populated by various characters: educated and sophisticated pagans, including philosophers (Epicureans and Stoics), poets and Nero portrayed as a dilettante crown with all his vanity, false exaltation and capricious cruelty, as well as by Christians drawing strength from their faith. However, the novel was received as a zealous defense of the Catholic faith at the end of the 19th century. These were the times of the comeback to the philosophy of Thomas Aquinas, as well as of the pontificate of Pope Leo XIII. The Pope was the author of the encyclical "*Rerum Novarum*" (1891), in which he presented the stance of the Catholic Church regarding the workers and the economic system of the time.

However, Sienkiewicz did not take part in the discussion about the possibility of introducing and elaborating on the concept of distributive justice in the new areas of social life. Different ideas expressed in "*Quo vadis?*" had significant relevance. The most appealing was the *concept of forgiveness* of even the greatest sins and the idea of resignation from revenge as a reaction to earlier injustice, which were present in "*Quo vadis?*" as well as in other books.[21] There are numerous examples in the prize-winning novel. Glaukos, ex-slave, good Christian and finally martyr, twice forgives all harms done by the traitor Chilon Chilonides.[22] Similarly, the Roman aristocrat, Vinicius, discovers a principle not previously known to him and which he did not understand: "The Lord forgives you and I forgive you." It was an amazing idea in the world of Greek and Roman civilization: not the strength of the sword and the fist that should rule the world, but the morality of Christians, believers in Jesus, the poor carpenter from Palestine. In *Quo vadis?* Peter the Apostle summarizes these ideas: "*The Lord has punished Babylon with fire, but His mercy will be on*

---

19  Frenz (ed.), Literature 1901-1967, 34.

20  af Wirsén, Presentation, 36.

21  See: Zacharska, Jadwiga, Sztuka przebaczania według Sienkiewicza, [The art of forgiveness according to Sienkiewicz], [in:] Stępnik, Krzysztof, Bujnicki, Tadeusz, Henryk Sienkiewicz w kulturze polskiej [Henryk Sienkiewicz in Polish culture], (Lublin: Maria Curie-Skłodowska University Publ., 2007), 43 ff.

22  Similarly, in the novel "The Teutonic Knights" ("Krzyżacy") a Polish knight named Jurand, blinded and mutilated by a high-ranking Teutonic monk, Sigfrid, does not repay him by taking his life or by mutilation, but cuts the bonds and sets him free.

*those whom baptism has purified and whose sins are redeemed by the blood of the Lamb.*"[23] Justice is then, even in the most difficult times, not the key idea. Therefore it is not *iustitia commutativa* that should guide people when a drastic evil happens. Instead of the pair: crime and punishment, Sienkiewicz recommends the relationship of cruelty and mercy.[24]

The commentators of Sienkiewicz's novels emphasize that the Christian stance of love to one's neighbors, which leads to the ability to forgive those who are the source of great harm, constituted for Sienkiewicz not only an alternative to the ancient pagan tradition but also to the modern utilitarian concept of happiness, harm and justice, as well as the capitalist economy, according to which all actions should be evaluated from the point of view of their social consequences and the rule of law which is applicable in the given state. The philosophy of Christian mercy was also intended to serve as a barrier to the spread of socialist ideas and the principle of justice related to needs, work and merits for the entire community. Facing contemporary problems Sienkiewicz looks for inspiration in the rising Christian ideas, rather than in studies of the official laws of countries of his time or the promotion of ideological illusions.

## 4      Life in Poverty and Precarious Justice of the Community

Another interpretation of the idea of justice may be found in the novels of the second Polish Nobel Prizewinner in literature: Władysław Reymont (1867-1925). He received the prize in 1924 "for his great national epic, *The Peasants.*" Reymont started writing it in

---

23   Sienkiewicz, Henryk, Quo Vadis: A narrative of the time of Nero, [Volume II], transl. Curtin, Jeremiah, (EasyRead Large edition, 2006, available at Google.books), 188.

24   In the novel Quo Vadis? an echo can be heard of the criticism by St. Paul the Apostle of the inhabitants of the Greek Corinth. In his first epistle to the community of Christians living in that city, Paul points out not only their sins of excessive permissiveness ("For me there are no forbidden things…"), especially in the sexual sphere, but also "the recourse to [seeking justice at] the pagan courts." The Apostle tries to embarrass his brothers in faith that they are fighting for their earthly interests before the city courts according to human law instead of surrendering to the judgement of the most staunch members of the Christian community:

"Is one of you with a complaint against another so brazen as to seek judgement from sinners and not from God's holy people? / Do you not realize that the holy people of God are to be the judges of the world? / And if the world is to be judged by you, are you not competent for petty cases? / Do you not realize that we shall be the judges of angels? /—then quite certainly over matters of this life. / But when you have matters of this life to be judged, you bring them before those who are of no account in the Church! (…) / it is a fault in you, by itself, that one of you should go to law against another at all, / why do you not prefer to suffer injustice, why not prefer to be defrauded?"
(The First Epistle of St. Paul the Apostle to the Corinthians, Chapter 6 [http://www.catholic. org/bible/book.php?id=53&bible_chapter=6]; the epistle of St. Paul is cited in the translation accepted in the Catholic Church, because this is almost certainly what Sienkiewicz used).

1897 (according to some commentators in 1901), but, for personal reasons, completed the four parts between 1902 and 1909. The plot of the book takes place at the end of the 19th century, at a time of Poland's partition. The novel shows a rich and simultaneously very realistic image of the life and culture of Polish peasants from the end of the 19th century. The extremely poor conditions of the lives of the villagers depicted in "*The Peasants*" lead readers, particularly critically-oriented readers, to find a rough psychological outline of the main characters of the novel. As Per Hallström wrote, most of them "have extremely little of what ordinarily is called character. Among the men, only few have even the raw material of character in mental energy and firmness; and their working up of this material inspires but little respect. The manliness which consists in self-discipline, a sense of responsibility, and a *personal grasp of the idea of right*, has barely attained any development beyond collective and vague mass feeling" (emphasis added).[25] This is a central case of the analysis of "*The Peasants*" if the idea of justice is to be discovered and reconstructed.

The commentators emphasize that, in his novel, Reymont tries to avoid simple moral assessments of his characters and he is far from formulating strong examples of good and just behavior. Likewise, Reymont does not restrict himself to the matter-of-fact realism.[26] Therefore, the novel "*The Peasants*" does not present a simple teaching of basic moral ideas, including justice. In the story of love and passion, violence and reconciliation, hatred, cowardice and forgiveness, the reader has to draw his own conclusions.

A better-defined stance in this respect was presented by Reymont in his earlier and less known book entitled "*Sprawiedliwie*" ("*Justly*", "*Righteously*"), published in 1899 and considered to be the prologue to "*The Peasants*". The plot of this novel focuses on a story of a young man, Jasiek Winciorek ("Johnny"), living in a poor village somewhere in the peripheries of the Russian Empire. His story is full of dramatic experience. Jasiek beat up the village clerk in defense of his fiancée's honor and, as a result of false accusations, he is sentenced to three years behind bars.[27] He escapes from prison after a year, goes into hiding and falls ill. In order to avoid prison again, he intends to emigrate illegally to America. However, other villagers provoked by the village administrator and encouraged by the promise of a reward for catching Jasiek, get in the way of Jasiek, his mother and his fiancée in his

---

25  Hallström, Per, [in:] Frenz Horst, (ed.), Literature 1901-1967 …, 215.

26  The Peasants are interpreted as the end of Reymont's Realism (Naturalism), which is comparable with the works of Flaubert in France, Turgenev and Tolstoy in Russia, Henry James in America and the beginning of a new philosophy of literature. See: Krzyzanowski, Jerzy R., Wladyslaw Stanislaw Reymont (New York: Twayne Publishers, Inc., 1972), 16-17, 73, 77, 85, 90. Per Hallström, the Chairman of the Nobel Committee of the Swedish Academy, in his "Critical Essay" prepared in lieu of a presentation speech (no official ceremony took place) stated that "The Peasants" "rather than turning out to be a naturalistic novel, has taken on epic proportions—certainly naturalistic in method, but epic in scope." P. Hallström, Ibidem, 214.

27  From Jasiek's and his neighbors' point of view, prison was not a symbol of materialized justice, but rather as a form of pure violence introduced and practiced by the occupiers and their collaborators.

attempt to escape to America. They catch him and hand him over to the Russian soldiers.[28] The main character did not want to give up easily and, as a form of revenge, he set fire to the houses in his home village. His act led to a cruel reaction of the villagers who threw him on the roof of his own burning house. They were guided by the elementary principle of justice: harm for harm, "an eye for an eye"; even the villagers seemed to be empowered by the feeling of revenge. Nevertheless, even the mother watching the death of her beloved son in despair whispered: *"Righteously!, Righteously!"*[29] She agreed to the argument of the village community which administered a punishment illegally, but in accordance with a general conviction of justice.[30] A crime against one's own community is inexcusable.

Similar stories of punishment through banishment or even death of a community member for a deviation from accepted village customs, pitiless settlement of harms inflicted and suspected, as well as fire, which has absolute "cleaning" power, can all be found in the prize-winning novel *"The Peasants"*. Therefore, Reymont presents a different idea of justice to Sienkiewicz: there is no place for mercy in small communities. Instead, there is absolute subordination to the will of the majority of the community. The rights of the community member are neither protected by positive law nor by the clerks of the Russian Tsar. The latter are obviously only guided by the instructions and injunctions of the higher authorities or by the complete discretion of uncontrolled powers.[31] The grounds for justice, in which common people believe, are therefore very weak: the unforeseeable *will of the majority* led by interest-guided and ruthless leaders.

The novel *"The Peasants"* has equally a realistic, as well as a symbolic, allegoric dimension. In an interesting interpretation of 1926, Polish critic Jan N. Miller, found the novel to be a modern version of universal myths and archetypes, associating Antek [Anthony]

---

28  In 19th century Russia, certain functions of the state police outside larger cities were performed by military units. There was no rule of law in the Russia of the Tsars.

29  Some commentators interpret its tragedy as a classical motive: "A rustic Niobe." Krzyzanowski, 72.

30  Perelman comments on the relationship between cruelty and justice: "Aristotle's main purpose, however, is to examine justice not as virtue in general, but as a specific virtue distinct from all others. As such, this virtue encompasses a sense of equality. It embodies a striving for rationality in action. If the notion of justice is interpreted in its *wider sense*, one might say it is just to be charitable and *unjust to be cruel*; but if the notion is taken in its *narrow sense*, it becomes conceivable for *justice to coincide with cruelty* and charity with injustice, since the just action is one that provides equal treatment for all those who are equals, and the unjust action one that favors or disfavors some people over others." (Perelman, Justice, 7; emphasis added).

31  Readers may wonder whether Reymont's distance to the Russian authorities, referred to by the novelist as "the watchmen", was a result of political tension and Reymont's attempt to avoid intervention from the occupier's censorship. See: Krzyzanowski, 60. It was not an abstract threat. In his biography, Reymont mentioned "I was socialist and the punishment was inevitable. The Russian authorities expelled me from Warsaw after suspecting me of having taken part in the strike…" (Reymont, Władysław, Autobiography, [in:] Frenz, Horst (ed.), Literature 1901-1967, 215).

with Hercules and Jagna [≈Jane] with Aphrodite, and so on.[32] However, none of them has direct contact with Themis and Dike.

In all this, Reymont does not pretend to be an ideologist. He does not preach noble ideals, does not call for perfecting virtues. He comes closer to Hobbes and the image of the state of nature in which "Man is a wolf to man." The conclusion is therefore pessimistic: if there is no legitimized law which would set clear rules of conduct, then justice is reduced to power and the unpredictable will of the majority. This does not mean that the sense of justice disappears completely, but its criteria are, at most, intuitive and its content is reduced to purely a negative order to repay.

## 5      Value of Justice and a Threat to Tyrants

A person living in today's America or Europe, even if they follow contemporary literature, is most likely not to come across names like Sienkiewicz or Reymont. There is a greater chance that he has heard about Czesław Miłosz (1911-2004), a Polish poet who was awarded the Nobel Prize in literature in 1980. The better knowledge of Miłosz may be a result of the greater time proximity: many of us still remember the beginning of the 1980s, while the possibility of remembering the dawn of the 20th century is very slight for obvious reasons.

Miłosz can also be more easily recognizable because he lectured on literature in the USA for over 25 years (including at Berkeley). Above all, the year 1980 in Poland was marked by the birth of the independent "Solidarity" trade union and a major rebellion of the shipyard workers in Gdańsk, as well as in hundreds of other factories and institutions, against the communist regime which, after a decade, led to the fall of the communist system in Europe.

Miłosz was acknowledged as a national bard. Miłosz was said to have actually worked for the People's Republic of Poland as a cultural attaché in America in the immediate post-War years, but, by 1951, he had broken with the regime, gone into exile in Paris and his writings had been banned in Poland. However, his work was widely circulated in samizdat editions and he went on to become an almost mythical figure among the dissident community. His 1953 study of totalitarian ideology, *"The Captive Mind"*, had dared to face up to both its subtle attractions, as well as its mechanisms of enslavement. In his poetry, particularly his autobiographical works, his depictions of an idealized and peaceful homeland provided solace to a nation living in an uncertain world under foreign domination.[33]

Miłosz had already come to be known as a poet before 1939. He spent the War years and the Nazi occupation in Warsaw, taking part, among others, in the Warsaw Uprising, through which the Polish Home Army [*Armia Krajowa*] tried to liberate the city in 1944. Warsaw's tragedy lasted two months and ended in disaster: more than 200,000 inhabitants

---

32   Krzyzanowski, Ibidem, 83.

33   Wroe, N., A century's witness, Guardian (10 November 2001), available at: http://www.guardian.com/books/2001/nov/10/poetry.artsandhumanities

were killed while the city was devastated. However, the poet does not fall into despair, but tries to reconcile his own vision of poetry and the tasks of the poet with the tragic experiences of the Polish People. In the poem "In Warsaw" (1945),[34] he writes:

*What are you doing here, poet, on the ruins*
*Of St. John's Cathedral this sunny*
*Day in spring? (...)*
*You swore never to be*
*A ritual mourner.*
*You swore never to touch*
*The deep wounds of your nation (...)*
*But the lament of Antigone*
*Searching for her brother*
*Is indeed beyond the power*
*Of endurance. (...)*
*Leave*
*To poets a moment of happiness,*
*Otherwise your world will perish.*
*It's madness to live without joy*
*And to repeat to the dead*
*Whose part was to be gladness*
*Of action in thought and in the flesh, singing, feasts,*
*Only the two salvaged words:*
*Truth and justice.*

However, despite the terrible experience of the whole nation, Miłosz looks for fundamental social governance and refers to timeless and universal values: to *truth and justice*. Neither of the values—it can be said—are understood as a direct subject of practical knowledge (*techne*); they have to constitute the foundation of social existence and be recognized by moral knowledge (*phronesis*).[35] Perhaps, when referring to ancient inspirations, this is why Miłosz does not refer to Aristotle, but to Antigone, the heroine of Sophocles' tragedy who, in the name of divine order, defied King Creon's order.[36] Her attitude in defense of

---

34   Miłosz, Czesław, Wiersze [Poems], vol. 1, (Kraków, Wydawnictwo ZNAK, 2001), 229.

35   For the difference in the Greek tradition between theoretical knowledge (episteme), practical knowledge (techne) and moral knowledge (phronesis) see: Gadamer, Hans-Georg, Truth and Method, Second, Revised Ed., transl. revised by J. Weinsheimer and D. G. Marshall, (London—New York: Continuum, 2004), 312-315.

36   In the translations of Sophocles' tragedy into modern languages, "divine order" is most commonly referred to as being derived from the gods (in general), or from Zeus and the goddess of Justice seated next to him. Antigone, by defying Creon's order, challenges his legitimacy: "Yea, for these laws were not ordained of Zeus, / And she who sits enthroned with gods below, / Justice, enacted not these human laws." (Sophocles' Antigone, transl. by F. Storr, BA, (Cambridge, MA: Harvard

the hallowed principles of order among people (the obligation to bury her brother who was killed in battle), is a symbol of faithfulness to such order, precisely fairness, and equal treatment for everyone, even traitors.

Miłosz also returns to these two fundamental values, truth and justice, in later poems. He also emphasizes that they do not come from religious thinking, so, in this sense, they are not competing, for example, with divine mercy, or love of one's neighbor, as suggested by Henryk Sienkiewicz. They are also not, as in the case of Reymont, a justification for defending the existing order, even one which is full of cruelty, violence and disregard for the weak. Truth and justice constitute the ethos of society, a community of rational entities with elementary ethical sensitivity. The role of the poet is to reach out for the truth, to call an evil an evil, but also to refer to justice so that we notice the harm caused to others. Miłosz writes, *inter alia*:

> *Human reason is beautiful and invincible.*
> *No bars, no barbed wire, no pulping of books,*
> *No sentence of banishment can prevail against it.*
> *It establishes the universal ideas in language,*
> *And guides our hand so we write Truth and Justice*
> *With capital letters, He and oppression with small. (…)*
> *Beautiful and very young are Philo-Sophia*
> *And poetry, her ally in the service of the good. (…)[37].*

However, Miłosz does not limit himself to the indication of the core values that they are the subject of human longings or intellectual utopia. Justice may also constitute grounds for criticizing the government, stigmatizing the evil which they commit. The belief in such a role of the idea has been included, albeit without directly naming these values, in his most well-known poem entitled "You who wronged" (1950).[38] The poet appeals in it to a dictator, a tyrant:

> *You who wronged a simple man*
> *Bursting into laughter at the crime,*
> *And kept a pack of fools around you*
> *To mix good and evil, to blur the line,*

---

University Press, 1912.) Similarly, other classic editions. There are translations, however, which, instead of Justice as a source of rights, directly specify goddess Dike. See: Sofokles, Antygona, transl. Morawski, Kazimierz, 12th ed., Wrocław-Warszawa-Kraków: Ossolineum, 24.

37  Miłosz, Czesław, Incantation, [Zaklęcie], transl. Miłosz, Cz., Pinsky R., [in:] Czesław Miłosz, Poezje wybrane. Selected poems, transl. D. Brooks [and others] (Kraków: Wydawnictwo Literackie, 1996), 195. This poem was written in 1968 in Berkeley, California, where Miłosz lectured on Slavic literature.

38  Milosz, Czesław, You Who Wronged, [in:] The Collected Poems: 1931-1987, transl. R. Lourie, (New York, The Ecco Press, 1988).

*Though everyone bowed down before you,*
*Saying virtue and wisdom lit your way,*
*Striking gold medals in your honour,*
*Glad to have survived another day,*
*Do not feel safe. The poet remembers.*
*You can kill one, but another is born.*
*The words are written down, the deed, the date.*
*And you'd have done better with a winter dawn,*
*A rope, and a branch bowed beneath your weight.*

Miłosz writes to the ruler: if you caused harm or evil to another person, even the smallest, your fault will not be forgotten ("the poet will remember")! You, tyrant, will be punished for your sins, even if you intended to cover your first wrongdoing with another crime. And you will not find help among the flatterers, servants and the court surrounding you. There is a certain *type of justice*, which, as in the stories about the mythical Oedipus or the biblical Job, will reach out to everyone who has harmed another person.

Someone may argue that this kind of justice is metaphysical, though the poet does not proclaim that it will be brought by God. Justice materializes out of the state, even against it. This justice is independent of laws, notwithstanding the manner of their creation. And it will not be the state's courts which will bring such justice. It is not derived from any particular ideology or religion.[39] It is not based on detailed rules which are subject to interpretation and official methods of application. Its dimensions extend current time and territorial borders of individual countries.

## 6      Justice as Passion and the Excellent Distance

Miłosz wrote the majority of his novels and poems since 1950 abroad, far from his homeland and far from the nation whose member he was until the last days of his life. Therefore, it was probably easier to believe in the idea of justice while living in Paris or Berkeley, California. The fourth Polish Nobel Prizewinner (1996) was Wisława Szymborska (1923-2012), a poetess spending most of her time in Kraków in communist Poland.[40] It could be said that she does not fit into this presentation: the People's Republic of Poland was formally a sovereign state, internationally recognized and using national symbols: a red

---

39   However, in his famous book entitled "The Captive Mind" (1953) Miłosz explains "the vulnerability of the 20th century mind to seduction by socio-political doctrines and its readiness to accept totalitarian terror for the sake of a hypothetical future" (Wroe, A century's witness, 3).

40   For several years, communism in Poland was not an imposed order and a symbol of evil for Szymborska. She was a member of the Communist Party until 1966 and it can be assumed that she had no reason to emigrate.

and white flag, as well as a white eagle (in the republican version: without a golden crown on the eagle's head). For most Poles, however, the second half of the 20th century (until 1989) was a time of political dependence. Poland was a part of the Soviet system: in the political, economic and military sense. What might a poet say under such circumstances? Szymborska's response had numerous components, very often paradoxically combined: hope, love, skepticism, distance, simplicity and multidimensionality of human life. The Swedish Academy did not hesitate and granted the Nobel Prize in literature "for poetry that with ironic precision allows the historical and biological contexts to come to light in fragments of human reality."

Szymborska did not converse with the rulers. She rather preferred to concentrate on humankind and, at her later stage of writing—on the individual. Szymborska fulfilled herself and made it clear to us that "what attracts people to poetry today is not its potential for making statements but rather its art of asking questions."[41] Therefore, we hardly find political manifestos in her books, as in case of Miłosz, but instead read her "questions put to myself."

However, this does not mean that Szymborska did not raise serious or even painful issues. She notices, for example, that the contemporary world still tolerates and uses tortures as a form of coercion:

> [...] Nothing has changed.
> The body still trembles as it trembled
> before Rome was founded and after.
> in the twentieth century before and after Christ.
> Tortures are just what they were, only the earth has shrunk
> and whatever goes on sounds as if it's just a room away.[...][42]

So nothing has changed. Despite talks on human rights, international commissions and public protests, justice systems are powerless and useless. The victims of tortures do not know the word "justice" and evil is so banal, as Hannah Arendt noticed. And the perpetrators of tortures, diligent officials have probably never read Miłosz's poem "You who wronged [a simple man]."

Szymborska seemed to ask why was there no emotion at all, when we were watching TV reports presenting victims of tortures. There was no warning, no horror and no serious reflection while we were watching Adolf Hitler's first photography:

---

41    Barańczak, Stanisław, Afterword, [in:] Szymborska, Wisława, Nic dwa razy. Wybór wierszy [Nothing Twice. Selected poems], selected and translated by S. Barańczak and C. Cavanagh (Kraków: Wydawnictwo Literackie, 1997), 389.

42    Szymborska, Wisława, Tortures, [in:] The People on the Bridge [1986], reprinted in: Szymborska, Nothing, 281.

*And who's this little fellow in his itty-bitty robe?*
*That's tiny baby Adolf, the Hitlers' little boy!*
*Will he grow up to be an L.L.D.?*
*Or a tenor in Vienna's Opera House? [...]*[43]

Is justice an example of utopia, a dream which will never come true? We believe in it; furthermore, we are sure it is there and it is very important... but we still do not take it seriously:

*Island where all becomes clear.*
*Solid ground beneath your feet.*
*The only roads are those that offer access.*
*Bushes bend beneath the weight of proofs. [...]*
*For all its charms, the island in uninhabited [...]* [44]

Szymborska asked questions about our indifference, why we do not react to the evil we face or the evil we have already experienced. They were questions asked of herself, but of course we can repeat them to ourselves. It is a matter of interpretation; why did she decide not to give answers to these questions? Because she was a poetess, living a little above the everyday life, or because her country was a part of the totalitarian system and she was afraid of being directly involved in politics? Szymborska suggested her own answer: poets are not religious or political leaders. "Poets, if they're genuine, must also keep repeating *"I don't know."* (emphasis added)[45] One of the commentators added: "Never associating herself with any poetical school, she [Szymborska] created her own craft of writing and her own language that keeps a distance from great historical events, the biological conditioning of human existence, the social role of the poet, and also from philosophical systems, ideologies, truths taken on faith, habits, stereotypes and inhibitions. It is also a language of compassion for those who have been wronged, of delight at the beauty of human life with its keen beauty, illogicality and tragedy. It is a language of well-considered judgements and muffled emotions ..."[46] Someone, and particularly a poetess, who excelled in keeping the necessary distance from social life issues, is not the best candidate for writing treatises of justice, its rules, core principles and necessary procedures.

---

43  Szymborska, Wisława, Hitler's first photography [1986], reprinted in: W. Szymborska, Nothing, 269.

44  Szymborska, Wisława, Utopia, [in:] A Large Number [1976], reprinted in: W. Szymborska, Nothing, 226.

45  Szymborska, Wisława, Nobel Lecture: The Poet and the World, Stockholm, December 7, 1996 (available at: http://www.nobelprize.org/nobel_prizes/literature/laureates/1996/szymborska-lecture.html).

46  Dąbrowska, Krystyna, Wisława Szymborska—The Poetry of Existence, (text of 2007, published again after the death of the poetess; available at: http://culture.pl/en/article/wislawa-szymborska-the-poetry-of-existence).

But maybe the answer is different, less sophisticated. Perhaps Szymborska did not appeal to us, did not sound the trumpets, because, until 1989, she had not experienced her life in a democratically ruled society, under the principle of the rule of law and with deep respect of justice in the public sphere. In such countries people tend to stay asleep in a way and to look at a photograph of one-year-old Adolf Hitler to see only a tiny baby.

# 7      Fairness and Equality as Forms of Justice and Intuitive Law

We find four ways of looking at justice in the novels and poems of the four Polish Nobel Prizewinners in literature: as a value that is subordinate to Christian mercy, as an argument for the merciless enforcement order within the community, as grounds for the existence of a community that is known because of the *phronesis* and as utopian and simultaneously necessary human passion. None of these concepts is as accurate or specific as the theories developed by legal philosophers. However, they are not ideas-ephemeris, literary wordplay or elusive emotions. The conviction that we cannot stop in our efforts in searching for it and that the way to discovering it is our ethical intuitions is probably common to them all.

The common genesis of these concepts of justice is also consistent and not incidental: they were formulated by creators, who wandered around the world without their own free state, or could not even count on a legal order which would provide legitimized principles and rules for organizing a community and settling conflicts.

Can such an understanding of justice can gain the acknowledgement of lawyers? It seems that it can, because similar ideas appeared, even in this environment. They were proposed, among others by Rudolf Stammler, but primarily the Polish legal theorist from the turn of the 19th and 20th centuries—Leon Petrażycki. He is only remembered today as the author of the psychological theory of the law, which, because of the methodology accepted over a hundred years ago, seem anachronistic. However, it is precisely Petrażycki who pointed out that most people do not have direct sources of knowledge about the law, but merely imagine an external authority ordering specific conduct. Petrażycki calls such emotions positive law. At the same time, Petrażycki indicates we equally frequently follow emotions justified by our autonomous conviction that "this is what should be done." This is precisely intuitive law, which, for centuries, has borne the name of none other than justice.[47] Petrażycki noted that *intuitive law* (which he directly recognized as the emotion

---

47    See, among others: Motyka, Krzysztof, Leon Petrażycki Challenge to Legal Orthodoxy. Volume presented at the 23rd World Congress of Philosophy of Law and Social Philosophy in Kraków, Poland (August 1–6, 2007), (Lublin, Towarzystwo Naukowe Katolickiego Uniwersytetu Lubelskiego Jana Pawła II [Editor: Academic Association of the John Paul II Catholic University of Lublin], 2007), especially 37-39. See also Northrop, F. S. C., Petrazycki's Psychological Jurisprudence: Its Originality and Importance, original: 104 University of Pennsylvania Law Review, 1956, 651 ff; also available as: Yale Law School. Faculty Scholarship Series. Paper 4372 (http://digitalcommons.law.yale.edu/fss_papers/4372).

of justice) can undermine positive law laid down by governments and parliaments. The inconsistency of the two legal orders can even lead to revolution. Intuitive law can also contribute to the development of positive law, as it inspires change and sets its directions. For these reasons, not only philosophers, but also lawyers should not disregard intuitive law or the idea of justice understood as *fairness and equality*, even when they do not give us clear rules and formulas for awarding everyone that which is rightfully due to him. Writers and poets suggest ways of understanding such justice.

## The Author

**Tomasz Stawecki**, professor of legal theory at the Faculty of Law and Administration, University of Warsaw, Poland; e-mail: t.stawecki@wpia.uw.edu.pl. The first version of this paper was presented at the XXVII World Congress of Philosophy of Law and Social Philosophy: "Law, Reason and Emotion", Washington, D.C., United States, July 27 – August 1, 2015, during the Special Workshop: The Idea of Justice in Literature / Die Idee der Gerechtigkeit in der Literatur.

# VI
# The Idea of Justice in Graphic Novels

# Rule of Law and State of Exception in Arts
## A Study of *V for Vendetta*

Marcelo Maciel Ramos and Bernardo Supranzetti de Moraes

**Abstract**

This study takes the graphic novel V for Vendetta as a reference for the debate on the relationship between citizens and a Government based on authoritarian laws, in which we can identify a "Rule of Law" not at all democratic. Moreover, it proposes a discussion over the strategies that in the plot are used to overcome the state of exception, in a dialogue with the political theories of Walter Benjamin, Carl Schmitt e Giorgio Agamben. Published in the 80s in England, V for Vendetta was written as a critical instrument against the government of Margaret Thatcher, marked by authoritarian and conservative elements. In the graphic novel, revolution and anarchy seemed to be the only way to promote a real change in the authoritarian government (in the state of exception) of the story. It is an interesting illustration that provokes the reader to the polarization of two ideas: on the one hand, the call for a strong and centralized power able to promote order and to fight war and instability; on the other, the apology of anarchy as a resource to fight the subjection of citizens and despotism. In order to discuss those ideas we resort to authors such as Hardt and Negri that claim that we can live in a world dominated by the masses. V for Vendetta is an up-to-date story that can be useful for the discussions on State of Exception and Rule of Law. One can easily find some of its elements in today's society, such as the constant struggle of certain groups against the illegitimate control of the State. Besides, it provide us with a striking example of a literary work that exceeds its own pages and have become a symbolic living part of our time, as the mask of the protagonist has been used for many protesters around the globe.

**Keywords**

Rule of Law; State of Exception; Authoritarian Regime; Anarchism; V for Vendetta

## Introduction

This paper takes the graphic novel *V for Vendetta*—a very renowned work made by Alan Moore and David Lloyd—as a reference for the debate on the relationship between citizens and a Government based on authoritarian laws, in which we can identify a "Rule of Law" not at all democratic. Moreover, we propose a discussion over the strategies that in the plot are used to overcome the state of exception, in a dialogue with the political theories of Giorgio Agamben, Michal Hardt and Antonio Negri.

Published in the 80s in England, *V for Vendetta* was written as a critical instrument to describe the period lived by the country when Margaret Thatcher was in power. A time haunted by the fear of a possible nuclear war and with little hope for the future. Thatcher's government was marked by authoritarian and conservative elements, such as the limitation of political and social rights.

Revolution and anarchy seemed to be the only way to promote a real change in the authoritarian government (in the state of exception) of the story. It is an interesting illustration that provokes the reader to the polarization of the ideas of order to fight war and instability, and anarchy as a resource to fight subjection and despotism. In order to discuss those ideas we resort to authors such as Hardt and Negri that claim that we can live in a world dominated by the masses.

*V for Vendetta* is an up-to-date story that can be useful for the discussions on state of exception and Rule of Law. One can easily find some of its elements in today's society, such as the constant struggle of certain groups against the illegitimate control of the State. Besides, it provides us with a striking example of a literary work that exceeds its own pages and has become a symbolic living part of our time, as the protagonist's mask has been used in many political demonstrations around the globe.

## 1    The Graphic Novel *V for Vendetta*

The graphic novel *V for Vendetta* is a powerful and terrifying story about the loss of freedom and democracy in an imaginary totalitarian world that uses elements of our own reality.

*V for Vendetta* was created by Alan Moore and David Lloyd, being published originally in ten editions, from September 1988 to May 1989. Its publication took place in the government of Prime Minister Margaret Thatcher, known for her authoritarian and conservative policies. It was a time when the State itself disseminated through the media the fear of nuclear war, helping establish a scenario of uncertainty about the future[1].

---

1    EVANGELISTA, Michele Aparecida; ARAUJO, Patrícia Vargas Lopes. A máscara que virou um símbolo. Revista História Viva, n. 52, 2014, p. 76

Subjects such as homosexuality, the rise of minorities, police power and many others delicate issues of that time were presented in *V for Vendetta*, in a direct defiance to the government.

According to one of the authors:

> Since Dave and I both wanted to do something that would be uniquely British rather than emulate the vast amount of American material on the market, the setting was obviously going to be England. Furthermore, since both Dave and I share a similar brand of political pessimism, the future would be pretty grim, bleak and totalitarian, thus giving us a convenient antagonist to play our hero off against[2].

The story is set in a future England, in the decade of 90's, after a third world war, ravaged by chaos. Through political and ideological manipulation of a fascist party, an authoritarian government emerges to establish order, hunting civil rights and enforcing a strong censorship on the media, violently repressing their opponents.

As in George Orwell book *1984*[3], *V for Vendetta* portrays a world where the State oversees and persecutes its citizens. The instruments of exception are numerous: curfews, forbidden news, generalized censorship, and State agents working as "eyes", "ears", "noses" and "fingers" of a fascist and controlling government.[4] The official propaganda, stamped by the walls of London, is "Strength through purity, purity through faith". The State's strength works for only one truth, the government's truth. Every divergence is submitted to a violent process of purification. Those who opposed the government were sent to rehabilitation camps, where they were interrogated, tortured and served as test subjects for experiments and the construction of biological weapons.

The main character of the story is V, a figure that always presents itself wearing a mask, without reveling his/her real name, gender or any physical characteristics.[5] V fights against

---

2    MOORE, A. Behind the painted smile. In: MOORE, Alan; LLOYD, David. V for Vendetta. New York: DC Comics, 1990 [Text originally published in October 1983 in the magazine Warrior #17], p. 269-270

3    "V for Vendetta" has many clear references of "1984". Alan Moore repeatedly mentions the book by George Orwell as a source of inspiration. One of the similar characteristics between the two works is that both stories take place in a dystopian future, where an authoritarian government constantly oversees their citizens and even more. In the graphic novel we are able to observe the cameras overseeing people, as described in the Orwell's book.

4    GRANUZZIO, Patricia Magria; CERIBELLI, Renata de Fátima. V de Vingança – uma vendeta contra a homofobia e o fascismo. Revista do curso de Letras da Uniabeu. Rio de Janeiro, v. 1, n. 2, 2010, p. 120

5    The fact that we are working with a graphic novel allows for the fact that we never get to know that information about "V," since we are dealing with a form in which the characters communicate through speech balloons, and we do not know if V has a voice of male or female. As the character throughout the entire story is costumed, we have no gender information about him/her. This element is very important for the plot breakthrough, since V is made to be not just one person, but an idea. In the movie based on the graphic novel, this element is not preserved

the permanent state of exception established by the authoritarian regime of the dictator Adam Susan.

The graphic novel *V for Vendetta* is permeated by symbolic elements and circumstances that provide excellent material for reflection about political and legal fundamental concepts: on one side, one can find the composition of a state of exception in the form of an authoritarian and dictatorial government, and, on the other hand, one can identify the struggle for freedom fought by an anti-hero who sees no other way than terrorism and anarchy.

From Agamben's reflections about the state of exception and Hardt and Negri reflections about multitude, we aim to discuss in this paper the authoritarian and anarchic elements undertaken on the story of *V for Vendetta*.

## 2      *V for Vendetta* and the State of Exception

By using the argument of an urgent need to maintain peace after a critical political moment, the government in the graphic novel *V for Vendetta* suppresses any kind of popular participation or control by the Parliament in the political decisions of the State. The dictator, "the Head", has in his hands the absolute control of the government. So, the question is: can we identify this government as a state of exception? In order to answer that, it is necessary to make some preliminary clarifications.

The state of exception can be understood in two ways: in a narrower sense, as a planned and controlled mechanism of power concentration in the case of emergencies, and in a broader sense, as a concrete movement of usurpation or illegitimate suspension or unregulated normal exercise of power.

The state of exception is not a new fact in History. According to Jorge Gouveia, although we do not know all exception mechanisms in ancient Greek's political organizations, it arises in the *praxis* of political power, in an attempt to strengthen it in the face of danger to the community[6]. Among the ancient Athenians, we find the example of *aesymnète* who was an "elected tyrant", a temporary monarch to whom were transferred the control and defense of the city, being given numerous exceptional prerogatives. The *aesymnète* was limited timewise, because it was only indented to face a critical political moment. Besides that, he was forbidden to change the existing laws. The state of emergency in theory could not suppress rights.

This state of exception, a type of elective tyranny, exceptional and limited by their own political rules, should not be confused with the tyrannical regimes in which there is a

---

because of the film form. In the movie, V is impersonated by Hugo Weaving, portraying the character with male voice and masculine features.

6     GOUVEIA, Jorge Bacelar. O Estado de Excepção no Direito Constitucional: entre a eficiência e a normatividade das estruturas de defesa extraordinária da Constituição. Coimbra: Almedina, 1998, p. 110.

permanent absence of control on the exercise of power. Aristotle called attention to this difference in his work *Politics* by claiming that *aesymnète* was "an elective tyranny, unlike the existing monarchy among the barbarians"[7]. While among those last ones, what you see is a hereditary tyranny that does not submit itself to the laws, the *aesymnète,* despite his autocratic powers, was freely chosen and exercised his powers under the law[8].

Among the ancient Romans, we can find several regulated mechanisms of exception. In the first era of Rome, citizens could constitute a commission of ten men, the *decenviri,* that received from the city exceptional and unlimited power to establish a new law[9]. Later, the Senate assumes the prerogative to declare the *iustititum*, which meant literally a "standstill or suspension of the law"[10], through the attribution of *imperium* powers to a dictator who would concentrate military and civil powers for a period of six months, in order to deal with an external or internal threat.

Even today there are countless exception mechanisms provided by States. The declaration of an "Emergency State" exists in several Laws throughout the globe. In Brazilian Law, Articles 136 to 139 of the Federal Constitution establish those mechanisms. Article 136 and 137 list specific situations by which the President may declare a "state of defense" or a "state of siege", which restrict rights of citizens in the event of "serious and imminent institutional instability", "major natural calamities" or war[11].

---

7 ARISTÓTELES. Política. Trad. Mario da Gama Kury. Brasilia: Editora UNB, 1985. 1285b.

8 "(...) there are certain differences between these forms of tyranny, though they are of the same nature of the monarchy exercised within the law and their holders to exercise monarchical power with the consent of the subjects, while being identical to the tyranny for rule despotic and arbitrarily" ARISTÓTELES. Política. Trad. Mario da Gama Kury. Brasilia: Editora UNB, 1985, 1295a.

9 "The decenviri legibus scribundis (decêmviros) had unlimited power to implement a new constitution, with the remaining authorities suspension, and defined themselves, especially by their number ten, wielding extraordinary power for a day in succession." GOUVEIA, Jorge Bacelar. O Estado de Excepção no Direito Constitucional: entre a eficiência e a normatividade das estruturas de defesa extraordinária da Constituição. 1ª Edição. Coimbra: Almedina, 1998, p. 119

10 AGAMBEN, Giorgio. State of Exception. Translated by Kevin Attell. Chicago: The Universty of Chicago Press, 2005, p. 41

11 Constitution of the Federative Republic of Brazil: "Article 136.  The President of the Republic may, after hearing the Council of the Republic and the National Defense Council, decree a state of defense to preserve or to promptly re-establish, in specific and restricted locations, the public order or the social peace threatened by serious and imminent institutional instability or affected by major natural calamities. Paragraph 1. The decree instituting the state of defense shall determine the period of its duration, shall specify the areas to be encompassed and shall indicate, within the terms and limitations of the law, the coercive measures to be in force from among the following: I - restrictions to the rights of: a) assembly, even if held within associations; b) secrecy of correspondence; c) secrecy of telegraph and telephone communication; [...]. Article 137. The President of the Republic may, after hearing the Council of the Republic and the National Defense Council, request authorization from the National Congress to decree the state of siege in the event of: I - serious disturbance with nationwide effects or occurrence of facts

Another example is the "USA PATRIOT Act" signed in October 2001 by George W. Bush, President of the United States of America at the time. This act was created as a response to the September 11 attacks, legalizing authoritarian measures that could be used by security agencies and by the American intelligence. Without any need for a judicial authorization, the US government can intercept phone calls, e-mails and other types of communication of suspected individuals supposedly involved with terrorism, regardless of his/hers nationality. The USA PATRIOT Act covers other situations, such as the circumstances of arrested foreigners in the country. Without any need for proof or evidence, the "*Attorney general*" can keep arrested suspects on the grounds of threatening national security. We emphasize that it is not necessary for the act of terrorism or the real threat itself to take place in order to place the suspect in captivity.

These exception mechanisms served or serve to suppress or suspend the laws or institutional powers in case of emergency and disturbance of peace. In general, situations in which such mechanisms may be used are restricted: invasion, war, internal instability, etc. However, the regular suspension of political normality, that is, the state of exception in a restricted or legal sense, is often converted into an illegitimate state of exception, in a normalization of the political anomaly, in a permanent authoritarian regime.

That's exactly what happens in *V for Vendetta*. After a nuclear war, Adam Susan emerges as the hope for restoring the "normality". However, from the moment that the sovereign power is in the hands of the dictator, he reveals his conservative and authoritarian nature, normalizing the exception in the form of a totalitarian and exclusionary State.

This is the danger to which authors like Giorgio Agamben and Slavoj Zizek alert us. From the moment that some basic rights are suspended for the guarantee of the system itself, the opportunity for authoritarian figure's to rise is created and the state of exception tend to become permanent and violence the general rule.

The story *V for Vendetta* begins with V saving Evey Hammond, a young 17 year old who was being chased by the "fingermen", government men allowed to kill in the name of social peace. On that scene, Evey was about to be raped and killed when V appears and rescues the young woman from the agents of the State.

---

that evidence the ineffectiveness of a measure taken during the state of defense; II – declaration of state of war or response to foreign armed aggression. Sole paragraph. The President of the Republic shall, on requesting authorization to decree the state of siege or to extend it, submit the reasons that determine such request, and the National Congress shall decide by absolute majority. [...] Article 139. During the period in which the state of siege decreed under article 137, I, is in force, only the following measures may be taken against persons: I – obligation to remain at a specific place; II – detention in a building not intended for persons accused of or convicted for common crimes; III – restrictions regarding the inviolability of correspondence, the secrecy of communications, the rendering of information and the freedom of press, radio broadcasting and television, as established by law; IV – suspension of freedom of assembly; V – home search and seizure; VI – intervention in public utility companies; VII – requisitioning of property". In:<http://www.stf.jus.br/repositorio/cms/portalStfInternacional/portalStfSobreCorte_en_us/anexo/constituicao_ingles_3ed2010.pdf> last access in June 2015

**Image 1**   V saves Evey from the "Fingerman"
Source: MOORE, GIBBONS, 1990, p. 11-12[12]

12   MOORE, Alan; LLOYD, David. V for Vendetta. New York: DC Comics, 1990, p. 11-12

In the graphic novel, the dictator Adam Susan has control of the State's intelligence, the police apparatus and the "fingermen". The violence perpetrated by the State is said to be at people's service and it is justified by the need to maintain order and to promote progress. Before attacking Evey, the "fingermen" justify their action by calling upon the law. They make it clear that the defense of the interests of the State, according to is legal dispositions, is their prerogative.

In addition to repression and terror, the dictator Adam Susan manages to captivate people with fiery speeches about progress. His motto "England prevails!" is repeated to exhaustion. The fifth chapter of the first part of the graphic novel[13] is narrated by the dictator himself, where it becomes clear the mindset of the character and the criticism made by the authors to the English government. In order to justify the government's propaganda—"strength through purity, purity through faith" –, Adam Susan declares: "I believe in strength. I believe in unity. And if that strength, that unity of purpose, demands a uniformity of thought, word and deed then so be it."[14]

The extremism of the dictator, Adam Susan, is exposed in the following scene:

> *"I lead the country that I love out of the wilderness of the twentieth century. I believe in survival, in the destiny of the Nordic race. I believe in fascism. Oh yes, I am a fascist, what of it? Fascism. A word whose meaning has been lost in the beatings of the weak and the treacherous. (...) I will not hear talk of freedom. I will not hear talk of individual liberty. They are luxuries. I do not believe in luxuries. The war plait paid to luxury. The war plait paid to freedom. The only freedom left to my people is the freedom to starve. The freedom to die, the freedom to live in a world of chaos. Should I allow them that freedom? I think not.*[15]

In this passage, we can identify that war is the justification for the state of exception and to the suspension of rights and freedom. In the dictator's mind, everything makes sense. The concentration of power in his hands is the logical thing to do, so England can thrive once again.

Illegitimate and extreme violence is the regular instrument of a state of exception. In *V for Vendetta,* the most shocking violence is the one perpetuated in concentration camps.[16] They operate as real laboratories. In the rehabilitation camps, as they are called in the plot, experiments are performed in those who are not part of the "Nordic race". People who are against the government are interrogated, tortured and killed.

---

13  Division made by "Editora Panini" in hardcover translated version of the series. This variant was the one that we use as the basis of this work.

14  MOORE, Alan; LLOYD, David. V for Vendetta. New York: DC Comics, 1990, p. 37

15  MOORE, Alan; LLOYD, David. V for Vendetta. New York: DC Comics, 1990, p. 37-38

16  Alan Moore and David Lloyd make it clear in the graphic novel that this is an allusion to the Nazi concentration camps, which is one of the greatest examples of state of exception in History. Often mentioned in the works of Agamben and Zizek.

**Image 2**   Dictator Adam Susan and an obvious allusion to Nazism
Source: MOORE, GIBBONS, 1990, p. 37[17]

In this environment of extreme exclusion and political exception, V rises as a savior, who has gotten his/her freedom after blowing up the wing where he/she was imprisoned by the State.

## 3      Against the Violence of the Exception: Anarchism and Multitude

V uses different tactics to confront the government. The first one that is shown in the graphic novel is a "terrorist attack". At the very beginning, just after saving Evey from the fingermen, V explodes the Parliament and, then, the "Old Bailey", the English criminal court. Another method used is the invasion of the State's institutional communication channels, such as television and radio.

---

17    MOORE, Alan; LLOYD, David. V for Vendetta. New York: DC Comics, 1990, p. 37

**Image 3**   V explodes the Parliament
Source: MOORE, GIBBONS, 1990, p. 14[18]

At first, those strategies seem not to work. The dictator Adam Susan uses all his power to prevent V from attacking again, so that the people doesn't start to question and think about her/his actions.

Besides, V sees the demobilized population as a big obstacle to his/her plans to overthrow the tiranic government:

> *But the people are so cowed and disorganized, a few might take the opportunity to protest, but it'll just be a voice crying in the wilderness. Noise is relative to the silence preceding it. The more absolute the hush, the more shocking the thunderclap. Our masters have not heard the people's voice for generations, Evey, and it is much, much louder than they care to remember.[19]*

About the apathetic population, to whom V calls for manifest, Andityas Matos offers us an argument that fits perfectly to the analysis of the work *V for Vendetta*:

> "Obviously, the comprehensive category called 'people' is not more than the other face of a bloody sovereign, serving as mostly of the times, as magical expression that uncritically legitimate the established authority"[20].

It is noteworthy how an abstract and evasive concept of people serves to justify a state of exception. Moreover, such a concept serves to vacate the real political meaning of the real

---

18   MOORE, Alan; LLOYD, David. V for Vendetta. New York: DC Comics, 1990, p. 14

19   MOORE, Alan; LLOYD, David. V for Vendetta. New York: DC Comics, 1990, p. 194

20   MATOS, Andityas Soares de Moura Costa. A multidão contra o Estado. Revista Brasileira de Estudos Políticos, Belo Horizonte, v. 108, jan./jun. 2014, p. 152.

people. On his first invasion of the TV station, V complains about the lack of resistance against the government by the people, saying that passivity legitimizes the authoritarian rules of Adam Susan. In order to inflame the masses, the masked hero claims, ironically, that the people should be fired, since it is not bringing any results for the "company". For him, inert people is as bad as dictators, once its lack of action supports the unjust acts of the government. After all, without opposition, why would the political order change?

At the end of the plot, V gives an ultimatum to the people, challenging it to act or live the same life. Then, the population finally rebels and starts to attack the police.

**Image 4**   Sequel of the people striking the police
Source: MOORE, GIBBONS, 1990, p. 258-259[21]

Due to its symbolic content, this scene is a milestone. V longed for this moment throughout the whole story. He knew that if the population did not change its attitude, he alone
could not promote a real change. That is the moment when people take action, when they
become real citizens again.

The importance of *V for Vendetta* is that it has become a symbol of the struggle against
an oppressive system. Given the political background of Alan Moore, the character V is
an anarchist and tries to show that anarchy is the solution against a state of exception.

Nevertheless, we must ask ourselves: could anarchy be a solution for real life politics?

---

21   MOORE, Alan; LLOYD, David. V for Vendetta. New York: DC Comics, 1990, p. 258-259

**Image 5** V talks to the people about the Anarchy
Source: MOORE, GIBBONS, 1990, p. 258[22]

Anarchy cannot be understood only by the lack of government, but by the lack of rules. Matos explains that anarchy isn't just absence of dominion as in the Greek etymology of *an-archia*. It is "also an *a-nomia*, which means, a lack of government that leads to a lack of law regulating the sharing of commonwealth"[23].

The aspiration of V was a government truly of the people, a country without oppressive laws, a society ruled by the masses. However, once the masses were actually in power, one might wonder if they can still be identified by the evasive and abstract concept of people. For Matos, in that case, the masses cease to be the people and become the "multitude".

> The multitude corresponds to a new form of social intelligence that, for those who are outside, seems chaotic, irrational and anarchic. However, for those who participate in it, the multitude identifies with a social structure that tends to preserve the greatest degree of individuality, the democratic self-management and the spontaneity, opposing all hierarchical and centralized types of usufruct of social power[24].

Seemingly chaotic, the multitude is a new concept that authors such as Antonio Negri and Michael Hardt have been developing to explain some new forms of political expression. For

---

22   MOORE, Alan; LLOYD, David. V for Vendetta. New York: DC Comics, 1990, p. 258

23   MATOS, Andityas Soares de Moura Costa. A multidão contra o Estado. Revista Brasileira de Estudos Políticos, Belo Horizonte, v. 108, jan./jun. 2014, p. 154.

24   MATOS, Andityas Soares de Moura Costa. A multidão contra o Estado. Revista Brasileira de Estudos Políticos, Belo Horizonte, v. 108, jan/jun 2014, p. 152.

them, "in a more general sense, the multitude defies any kind of representation because it is an incommensurable multiplicity"[25]. It is opposite to the concept of people, which is precisely what we see in the plot prior to the moment that V provokes a revolution among the population. It is exactly the false and abstract unity of the people that are present in the major speeches of England's authoritarian government of the graphic novel.

The multitude, explains Hardt and Negri, is genuinely a "social active actor"[26]. However, it is not a mass without focus. "The multitude needs a political project to bring into existence. Once we have examined the conditions that make the multitude possible, then, we have to investigate what kind of political project can bring the multitude into being."[27]

The motivations of the multitude in *V for Vendetta* are very similar to the motivations that Hardt and Negri present in the three books of the "Empire"[28] series: to denounce the maintenance of exclusion and false democracy that capital imposes on the globalization era, ceasing the autonomy of the State. For that reason, the multitude is a possibility, a potentiality, and it is not yet a reality, like in the graphic novel:

> Like the flesh, the multitude is then pure potentiality, unformed life force and an element of being. Like the flesh, the multitude is oriented towards the fullness of life. The revolutionary monster that is named multitude and appears at the end of modernity continuously wants to transform our flesh into new forms of life[29].

It may not be exactly what Moore and Lloyd had in mind at the plot when the people finally released themselves from an authoritarian government. However, it was no longer a mass that was conducted by a ruler who decreed the state of exception. It was a population, which, according to the authors of *V for Vendetta*, was anarchic, that no longer needed a government ruled by a "visionary man with fire in his belly". When Evey becomes V, she makes a speech that explains what anarchy is for the people: "In anarchy, there is another way. With anarchy, from rubble comes new life, hope reinstated. They say anarchy's dead, but see... Reports of my death were.. Exaggerated"[30].

---

25  NEGRI, Antonio. Para uma definição ontológica da Multidão. Revista Lugar Comum, Rio de Janeiro, n. 19-20, jan/jun 2004, p. 17

26  NEGRI, Antonio. Para uma definição ontológica da Multidão. Revista Lugar Comum, Rio de Janeiro, n. 19-20, jan/jun 2004, p. 18

27  HARDT, Michal; NEGRI, Antonio. Multitude: War and democracy in the age of empire. Nova York: The Penguin Press, 2004, p. 212

28  Such authors wrote three books about the "Empire", which is the capitalist culture that the Western world, a globalization that excludes and that takes the autonomy of the States. The first book is "Empire," published in 2000. The second is "Multitude", published in 2004. The last book is "Commonwealth" published in 2009.

29  NEGRI, Antonio. Para uma definição ontológica da Multidão. Revista Lugar Comum, Rio de Janeiro, n. 19-20, jan/jun 2004, p. 19

30  MOORE, Alan; LLOYD, David. V for Vendetta. New York: DC Comics, 1990, p. 258

**Image 6**   V as Evey seen the last terrorist attack against the State
Source: MOORE, GIBBONS, 1990, p. 262

The chaos and anarchy insufflated by V took place when the dictator's died. People rose up to face the police forces of the State. Realizing they were the true owners of sovereignty, they were willing to rule.

> Such a configuration is conceivable, step by step, by an *an*-árquico man. More than a product of a meticulous social reconstruction project as planned by Marxism, the *an*-árquico man consists in the unexpected result of a tragedy. Our time is especially propitious to radical transformations arising from tragedies, which should not be confused with cosmetic revolutions that change things so that everything remains as it is[31].

---

31   MATOS, Andityas Soares de Moura Costa. A multidão contra o Estado. Revista Brasileira de Estudos Políticos, Belo Horizonte, v. 108, jan/jun 2014, p. 158.

*V for Vendetta* is not just a story about the fight against an oppressive State. It is a provocation that makes us wonder about our reality. It presents a future that could actually happen. Not surprisingly, it has become a landmark for Western culture, providing symbols that have been used in various movements against governments. One of this symbols was the Guy Fawkes' mask wore by V.

On November 5, 1605, Guy Fawkes was caught in the basement of the English Parliament with a large amount of explosives. In collusion with other unhappy Catholics, he intended to blow up the Parliament and kill King James I. But, denounced by an anonymous letter, the terrorists saw their plan foiled. Fawkes was tortured and executed before the Parliament on 31 January 1606. Such personality inspired David Lloyd to create the famous V mask, which is never taken off by the protagonist of the plot.

For the authors, the choice of Guy Fawkes as the alter ego of V was perfect:

> We knew that V was going to be an escapee from a concentration camp where he had been subjected to medical experiments but then I had the idea that in his craziness he would decide to adopt the persona and mission of Guy Fawkes—our great historical revolutionary.[32]

After the adaptation of the graphic novel to movie screens, the masks began to be seen in various demonstrations around the world, even becoming the symbol of the group *Anonymous*[33]. A famous quote of the movie[34] deeply represents the idea behind the secret group: "People should not be afraid of their governments. Governments should be afraid of their people".

The masks have been also used in the *Occupy* movement in locations across the globe: New York, Chicago, Madrid and others cities. It made the author himself, Alan Moore, to write an article for BBC about the fact that one of the many symbols of his work could be find in many popular protests:

> It also seems that our character's charismatic grin has provided a ready-made identity for these highly motivated protesters, one embodying resonances of anarchy, romance, and theatre that are clearly well-suited to contemporary activism, from Madrid's Indignations to the Occupy Wall Street movement[35].

---

32  Interview given by David Lloyd for BBC, access on < http://www.bbc.com/news/magazine-15359735> Last access on 12/17/2016

33  International group of hackers (people who invade other computers via the World Wide Web) which held several protests online, invading government websites and creating other types of movements in the network. The group struggle for freedom of expression, not only in the virtual world, and for an Internet freedom.

34  The movie V for Vendetta was released in 2005, directed by James McTeigue and Hugo Weaving portrays the main character V.

35  MOORE, Alan. Viewpoint: V for Vendetta and the rise of Anonymous. BBC, published on <www.bbc.com/news/technology-16968689.png> in 10/02/2012. Last access in July 2014.

The illustrator—and creator of the V mask—David Lloyd, once said that the mask has become an icon as it was Che Guevara in a more recent past:

> The Guy Fawkes mask has now become a common brand and a convenient placard to use in protest against tyranny—and I'm happy with people using it, it seems quite unique, an icon of popular culture being used this way. [...]Che was as imperfect as V as a revolutionary and as a human being, but he was as dedicated to his ambitions as V. V is too sophisticated a creation to be a copy of Che, but he doesn't suffer in a comparison with him. Though he does, of course, as created character and not a real one![36]

**Image 7**   V talks to the people through the Television. The *Anonymous* group announces they threats in videos very similar way

Source: MOORE, GIBBONS, 1990, p. 113[37]

Such repercussions demonstrates the impact, range and different uses of the symbolic and discursive elements mobilized in the movie and in the graphic novel *V for Vendetta*, especially of V's image in contemporary society. It reinforces the perception of cinema and

---

36   This citation is formed by two interviews given by David Lloyd in 2011. Both can be accessed complete in the following links: <http://www.bbc.com/news/magazine-15359735> Last access on 12/17/2016. And < http://comicsalliance.com/v-for-vendetta-anonymous-david-lloyd/> http://comicsalliance.com/v-for-vendetta-anonymous-david-lloyd/

37   MOORE, Alan; LLOYD, David. V for Vendetta. New York: DC Comics, 1990, p. 113

graphic novels as transmitters of ideas and worldviews, constituting symbolic objects for theoretical reflections[38].

> Symbols direct our thoughts and deeds; rouse buried shapes beneath our waking minds. All magic is symbolic, from Corn Doll to the Vau-Dau rite. Why, consciousness itself is naught but symbols; metaphors which build upon themselves and thus extend their metaphysical domain.[39]

The symbolic meaning of the Guy Fawkes mask had a repercussion that has surpassed the historical fact itself. Nevertheless, one can quickly identify the mask as a reference to an act of rebellion against the government. Besides, "because there are innumerable things beyond the range of human understanding, we constantly use symbolic terms to represent concepts that we cannot define or fully comprehend".[40]

Many often refer to the political significance of the mask without knowing its origins. However, this is not really important. Some symbols such as V's mask embodies ideas that go beyond their context of creation. That is the case of *V for Vendetta*. As our hero states in the graphic novel, he could not be killed, because he was just an idea, and ideas are bulletproof.

**Image 8**   "Ideas are bulletproof"
Source: MOORE, GIBBONS, 1990, p. 236[41]

---

38   EVANGELISTA, Michele Aparecida; ARAUJO, Patrícia Vargas Lopes de. A máscara que virou um símbolo. Revista História Viva, nº 52, 2014, p. 81

39   MOORE, Alan; CAMPBELL, Eddie. From Hell. Paddington: Eddie Campbell Comics, 2000, p. 108

40   JUNG, Carl G. Man and his Symbols. New York: Anchor Press, 1988, p. 21

41   MOORE, Alan; LLOYD, David. V for Vendetta. New York: DC Comics, 1990, p. 236

## Conclusion

*V for Vendetta* is the evidence that Comics can deal with complex political issues in a way that can be easily understood. It has a clear pedagogic potential that could be use as resource for political and legal education. More than that, it provokes the reader to think about all the matters it addresses and to rethink his own reality.

Topics such as *state of exception* and *anarchy* are not always approachable for most, as these concepts are often studied as abstract categories by those that have a privileged access to a higher education level.

As Comics popularizes the debate on political and legal issues, they fulfill an educational and social purpose. By addressing those topics in an understandable way, graphic novels such as *V for Vendetta* become an essential tool to promote critical questioning of governments structures and policies. The fact that V's mask has become a constant symbol in several political demonstrations around the world proves our point.

Comics can not only make legal and political debates more understandable and democratic, but they can also be a useful educational resource in an era where graphic and dynamic Medias tend to attract students in a way that text books alone cannot do.

## References

AGAMBEN, Giorgio. State of exception. Translated by Kevin Attell. Chicago: The Universty of Chicago Press, 2005

ARISTÓTELES. Política. Trad. Mario da Gama Kury. Brasilia: Editora UNB, 1985.

BENJAMIN, Walter. "Crítica da Violência. Crítica do Poder", trad. de Willi Bolle, in: W. Benjamin, *Documentos de Cultura, Documentos de Barbárie*, org. W. Bolle, São Paulo: Cultrix/EDUSP, 1986

EVANGELISTA, Michele Aparecida; ARAUJO, Patrícia Vargas Lopes de. A máscara que virou um símbolo. *Revista História Viva*, n° 52, 2014

GOUVEIA, Jorge Bacelar. O Estado de Excepção no Direito Constitucional: entre a eficiência e a normatividade das estruturas de defesa extraordinária da Constituição. Coimbra: Almedina, 1998

GRANUZZIO, Patricia Magria; CERIBELLI, Renata de Fátima. V de Vingança – uma vendeta contra a homofobia e o fascismo. *Revista do curso de Letras da Uniabeu*. Rio de Janeiro, v. 1, n. 2, 2010.

HARDT, Michal; NEGRI, Antonio. Multitude: War and democracy in the age of empire. Nova York: The Penguin Press, 2004

JUNG, Carl G. Man and his Symbols. New York: Anchor Press, 1988

MATOS, Andityas Soares de Moura Costa. A multidão contra o Estado. *Revista Brasileira de Estudos Políticos*, Belo Horizonte, v. 108, jan./jun. 2014

MOORE, Alan; CAMPBELL, Eddie. From Hell. Paddington: Eddie Campbell Comics, 2000

MOORE, Alan; LLOYD, David. V for Vendetta. New York: DC Comics, 1990

MOORE, Alan. Viewpoint: V for Vendetta and the rise of Anonymous. BBC, published on <www.bbc.com/news/technology-16968689.png> in 10/02/2012. Last access in July 2014

NEGRI, Antonio. Para uma definição ontológica da Multidão. *Revista Lugar Comum*, Rio de Janeiro, n. 19-20, jan./jun. 2004

ZIZEK, Slavoj. Welcome to the desert of the real! Five essays on September 11 and related dates. London: Verso Books, 2002

## The Authors

**Marcelo Maciel Ramos**, Professor at the Faculty of Law of *Universidade Federal de Minas Gerais* (UFMG) in Belo Horizonte, Brazil. Ph.D. in Law and LL.M. at UFMG. Visiting researcher at the *Institut de la Pensée Contemporaine* of *Université Paris-Diderot* (France), and at *University of Kent* (England).

**Bernardo Supranzetti de Moraes**, LL.M. student at the Faculty of Law of *Universidade Federal de Minas Gerais* (UFMG). Bachelor's degree in Sciences of the State at UFMG.

# The Idea of Justice in Legal Philosophy

# Der Sinn des Rechtsgedankens
## (Gerhard Sprengers Radbruchsche Formel[*])

Marijan Pavčnik[*]

### Abstract

Dominik Smole's (1929–1992) Antigone „seeks the inmost meaning of some thought." She is "a gentle flower that opens just to shed its petals." (Ismene) The symbolic power of Antigone's deed tells us that the range of legal argumentation ends where the *sense of law* ends. It is in the character of law and its nature not only that so-called law is not law any more if it is humanly intolerable. These are extreme cases that are typical of authoritarian political systems. In political systems that accept the rule of law and are based on it, it is the opposite direction that is natural. Its basic characteristic is that it seeks to find the right measure, which is humane and takes into account that law is about mutual and interdependent relations that are tolerable to both sides.

### Keywords

the argument of non-law, the symbolic meaning of Radbruch's formula, legal sense, sense of justice, mutuality, coexistence.

## 1     Sprengers Ansicht

Der berühmte Artikel von Radbruch *Gesetzliches Unrecht und übergesetzliches Recht* (1946) gehört zu den am meisten zitierten im europäischen Kontinentalraum.[1] Unter den Sekundärquellen genießt auch Sprengers Abhandlung *50 Jahre Radbruchsche Formel oder: Von der Sprachnot der Juristen* keineswegs geringe Aufmerksamkeit. Bereits die Worte,

---

[*]     Der Aufsatz basiert auf drei Kapiteln des Referats, das der Verfasser auf dem Kolloquium zum Gedanken an Gerhard Sprenger (1933–2012) anlässlich der 80. Wiederkehr seines Geburtstages am Zentrum für Interdisziplinäre Forschung (Bielefeld) gehalten hat.

[1]     Darüber siehe auch Paulson, 2006: 17 ff.

© Springer Fachmedien Wiesbaden GmbH, part of Springer Nature 2018
H. Kabashima et al. (Hrsg.), *The Idea of Justice in Literature*,
Wirtschaftsethik in der globalisierten Welt,
https://doi.org/10.1007/978-3-658-21996-3_14

dass es sich um die *Sprachnot der Juristen* handelt, lassen aufhorchen. Sprenger spricht über eine ziemliche begriffliche Ungenauigkeit, die sich vor allem darauf bezieht, wie man den Maßstab, der die Formel inhaltlich auffüllt, erfassen und verschärfen kann. Ist das „Natur-/Vernunftrecht" (R. Alexy), geht es um „naturrechtliche Grundsätze" (H. Rittstieg), befindet man sich bei „vorpositiven Menschenrechten" (J. Hruschka) oder gar bei „Moral" (gegenüber dem „Recht" – J. Limbach, H. Lecheler) usw. (Sprenger, 1997: 3)? Vielsagend ist auch die Definition des Bundesgerichtshofs über die „allen Völkern gemeinsamen, auf Wert und Würde des Menschen bezogenen Rechtsüberzeugungen" (BGHSt 40, 241 ff.; Sprenger, 1997: 3).

Sprenger stimmt mit Kaufmann überein, der auf *horror iuris naturalis* aufmerksam macht. Der Jurist „ist im Grunde seines Herzens froh", so Kaufmann, „wenn er die ihm gestellten Aufgaben ohne Zuhilfenahme naturrechtlicher Erwägungen lösen kann" (Kaufmann, 1984: 1). Sprengers und Kaufmanns Kritik haben vor sich einen schwachen (gefügigen) Juristen, der keine Verantwortung für (konkrete) Rechtsentscheidungen übernehmen will. Ein solcher Jurist fühlt sich am sichersten, wenn er sich hinter dem Gesetz und dem konkreten Fall verstecken kann, die so eindeutig sein sollen, dass eine mechanische Rechtsentscheidung möglich ist.

Das zentrale Problem ist es, dass das Recht als normatives System keinen (unverfügbaren) inhaltlichen Ausgangspunkt hat, den man objektiv unanfechtbar feststellen und anschließend auch konkretisieren könnte. Das Berufen auf Naturrecht, objektive Wertordnung oder Menschenwürde als den Ausgangsrechtswert braucht eine entsprechende inhaltliche Ergänzung. In allen drei Fällen gibt es auch Leergut, dass alles Andere als argumentativ unantastbar ist. Im Gegenteil: in diesen und anderen Fällen handelt es sich um „Behältnisse", deren Inhalt nicht unfehlbar vorgegeben ist.

*Mutatis mutandis* kann man das auch für die Radbruchsche Formel sagen, bei der sich die Frage stellt, wie man die Maßstäbe „Erträglichkeit" und „Unerträglichkeit" definieren sollte. Eine charakterische Stelle bei Sprenger ist etwa die folgende:

> „‚Erträglich kommt von ‚tragen' – *Radbruch* ging, um es bildlich zu wenden, von einer gewissen ‚Tragfähigkeit' aus, und zwar nicht der Tragfähigkeit eines Gegenstandes, etwa einer Brücke, die man berechnen kann, sondern von der ‚unberechenbaren' Tragfähigkeit des Menschen. Unberechenbar ist jetzt nicht im Sinne von schwankend und unvorhersehbar, sondern im Sinne von ‚in wissenschaftlich-rechnerischer Größe' nicht meßbar zu verstehen. Es geht hier nicht um logische, eher anthropologische, weniger um rationale, denn irrationale Faktoren. *Erträglich ist auf den Menschen zugeschnitten* und meint hier *für ihn tragfähig*, und das heißt soviel wie: *zumutbar*. Wir haben es offenbar mit einem ‚menschlichen' Maß zu tun" (Sprenger, 1997: 5).

Der Punkt, bei dem man sich befindet, muss uns sagen, dass der Gegensatz zwischen dem positiven Gesetz und der Gerechtigkeit (als übergesetzlichem Recht) „ein so unerträgliches Maß erreicht, daß das Gesetz als ‚unrichtiges Gesetz' der Gerechtigkeit zu weichen hat." (Radbruch, 1946: 216) Der Maßstab der Unerträglichkeit ist menschlich und man kann ihn nicht mathematisch genau ausmessen und bestimmen. Wie man es auch drehen mag, befindet man sich (auch) im Bereich des Subjektiven. Sprenger spricht nicht aus metaphysischen Höhen, obwohl er weit davon entfernt ist, dass ihm die *positiv*rechtliche Sicht des Rechts genügte. Sprengers Gedanke ist in einer Realität, die auch eine Wertrealität ist, verwurzelt, und in dieser Realität ist der Mensch, der unablässig die letzten Gründe sucht, „am Ende auf sich selbst verwiesen." (Sprenger, 1997: 5)

Sprenger ist unerbittlich und setzt fort:

> „In seinem Streben nach ‚objektiver' Wahrheit erlebt er (der Mensch – zugefügt von M. P.), sobald er erkennt, dass er diese Wahrheit nicht erreicht, den Rückwurf auf seine Subjektivität, die sich um sich selbst kümmern muß. Der Mensch muß lernen, sich als jemand zu begreifen, der an der Begründung dieser ‚Wahrheit' selbst beteiligt ist: er ist es, der jenes Übergreifende inszeniert, dem er sich dann wiederum unterwirft" (Sprenger, 1997: 5).

Und was sollte hier bedeuten, dass der Mensch das Übergreifende inszeniert, „dem er sich dann wiederum unterwirft"? Das Niveau, das der Mensch braucht, ist ein einigermaßen fester inhaltlicher Ausgangspunkt, der in einer bestimmten Zeit und in einem bestimmten Raum allgemein als legitim akzeptiert wird. Das Suchen nach dem Ausgangspunkt sollte nicht „in verlassene ethische Hochebenen" führen, sondern „in die farbige lebensdichte Menschenwelt des Alltags" gerichtet sein (Sprenger, 1997: 6). Der Alltag

> „enthält einen reichhaltigen und vielfältigen Bestand an religiöser, ethischer, allgemein kultureller und sozialer Orientierung, in der sich der Mensch immer schon vorfindet und der ergänzt wird durch mannigfache eigene Erfahrung im Umgang mit der Welt und den Mitmenschen – ein Bestand, der sich in bereitliegenden Verhaltensmustern, in Brauch und Gewohnheit bekundet, deren Funktionieren im wesentlichen auf Gegenseitigkeit gestellt ist und deren Erfüllung ein sinnvolles Dasein verspricht. Diese sittlichen Grundsätze verkörpern die Summe einer unendlichen Vielzahl von Vorentscheidungen mit den Gehalten sozialethischer Erfahrung, tradiert aus den Normerlebnissen vieler Generationen. In ihnen gehorcht das Individuum zugleich der Gesellschaft, die in ihm ist und ihm in seinem alltäglichen Umgang mit der Welt zugleich immer mitbegegnet." (Sprenger, 1997: 6)

Für Sprenger ist es typisch, dass er *Gegenseitigkeit* als ein wesentliches Element des Rechts besonders hervorhebt. Leben kann man nur *miteinander*. Lebensfälle, vor die wir gestellt sind und auf die wir rechtlich reagieren, sind oft miteinander vergleichbar und in diesem Sinne auch identisch. Dabei kommen immer wieder neue Fälle auf, die neue und geänderte Entscheidungen fordern. Die Werttradition, auf die man sich stützt, muss man im Hinblick auf das Zeit- und Raumgeschehen und auf die Verantwortung gegenüber der künftigen Generation ergänzen und ausbauen. Eine zusätzliche Schwierigkeit besteht darin, dass sich auch Wertansichten mit der Zeit ändern (vgl. Pavčnik, 2011: 74-75).

Das unablässige Suchen nach „richtigem Recht" und nach „richtigen Antworten" wird oft von Wagnis und Zweifeln begleitet. Das Suchen ist nicht nur eine Reproduktion des bereits gültigen Rechts, das Suchen ist immer auch die Produktion von neuen Entscheidungen. Es liegt in der Natur der Sache, dass man richtiges Recht *„nur im persönlichen*

*Einsatz und mit dem Risiko des Scheiterns* [erreichen kann. ...] *Bekenntnis tritt an die Stelle von Erkenntnis.*"[2]

In dieser Situation befindet man sich gleich in einem ungeschützten Raum, wo jeder die Verantwortung für seine Entscheidungen übernehmen muss. Und gerade darin liegt der Sinn der „Inszenierung des Übergreifenden". Es wird gerade deshalb inszeniert , dass man einen einigermaßen festen Boden erhält, auf dem man stehen und Rechtsentscheidungen treffen kann. Sprenger hat sehr wohl recht, dass dieser Boden auch subjektiv ist. In diesem Kontext erhalten auch abstrakte Formulierungen wie „Freiheit", „Gleichheit" und „Solidarität" eine neue ethisch-sittliche Dimension. Freiheit ist „verantwortete Freiheit", Gleichheit ist „adäquate Gleichheit" und Solidarität ist „zumutbare Solidarität" (Sprenger, 1997: 6).

## 2      Einige offene Fragen

Das Argument des gesetzlichen Unrechts weist mehrere Gesichter auf, bei denen es sich zu verweilen lohnt. Das Argument ist eine scharfe Kritik des apologetischen Rechtspositivismus und teilweise auch des wissenschaftlichen Rechtspositivismus, der den tatsächlichen Inhalt des Rechts nicht wahrhaben will. Dem wissenschaftlichen Rechtspositivismus kann man nicht vorwerfen, dass er wegen seiner positivistischen Haltung für die Gräueltaten und Missbräuche, die im Namen des „Rechts" geschehen, verantwortlich wäre. Verantwortlich sind jene, die Entscheidungen treffen und sie auch ausführen.[3] Was bei wissenschaftlichem Positivismus störend sein kann, ist, dass er nicht ausdrücklich seine Reichweite bestimmt. Wenn er das tut – so handeln Hart und auch Kelsen auf seine Weise – liegt der Schwerpunkt des Problems bei der Frage, ob der positivistische Ansatz selbst von guter Qualität ist.

Das Unrechtsargument – ich spreche darüber im Sinne der Radbruchschen Unerträglichkeitsformel – ist eine Kritik des selbstgenügsamen Gesetzespositivismus. Der Inhalt des Arguments beruht nicht auf einem ewigen und unveränderlichen Naturrecht, mit dem positives Recht in Einklang sein muss, sondern auf Grund- bzw. Menschenrechten, wie sie in einzelnen Geschichtsperioden gelten. In Radbruchs Fall geht es um Grund- bzw.

---

2    An dieser Stelle ist Fn. 48: „G. Radbruch, in: Rechtsphilosophie, aaO (Fn. 4), S. 100."

3    Siehe Philipps, 2007: 195-196: „Der Ausdruck ‚Stoppbedingung', den man anstelle von ‚Grundbedingung' verwenden kann, erinnert mich an etwas, das fast ein halbes Jahrhundert her ist. Ein Freund von mir und ich – wir waren Assistenten von Werner Maihofer – sind damals von Saarbrücken nach Mainz gefahren, um einen Vortrag von Hans Kelsen zu hören. An die Einzelheiten des Vortrags erinnere ich mich nicht mehr, wohl aber an eine Szene, die sich daran anschloss. Ein Student fragte Kelsen in deutlich kritischer Weise, ob der von ihm vetretene Positivismus nicht wieder zu einer Diktatur wie der vergangenen führen könne. Kelsen antwortet: ‚Ob eine solche Diktatur wieder eintritt, das hängt von keiner Rechtstheorie ab, sei sie nun positivistisch oder nicht. Das hängt nur davon ab, ob Menschen, jetzt die Menschen Ihrer Generation, rechtzeitig ‚Halt!' sagen.'"

Menschenrechte, die zusammen mit dem modernen Staat entstanden. Diese Rechte sind „in den sogenannten Erklärungen der Menschen- und Bürgerrechte" zusammengefasst und so stark verankert, dass „in Hinsicht auf manche von ihnen nur noch gewollte Skepsis den Zweifel aufrechterhalten kann." (Radbruch, 1945: 210)[4]

Die Radbruchsche Unerträglichkeitsformel ist in erster Linie ein Falsifizieren des gesetzlichen Rechts, von dem behauptet wird, dass es Recht ist. In diese Richtung ging auch das slowenische Verfassungsgericht, das in einigen Fällen entschied, dass bestimmte „Rechts"akte kein Recht sind, weil sie im Gegensatz zu allgemeinen, von zivilisierten Völkern anerkannten Rechtsprinzipien sind (Pavčnik, 2015: 51-52). Das Unrechtsargument behauptet also nicht, dass etwas Recht ist, sondern dass etwas *kein* Recht ist. Kaufmann stellt wohlbegründet fest: „Jedenfalls ist unsere Erkenntnis beim Falsifizieren sehr viel sicherer als beim Verifizieren." (Kaufmann, 1995: 83) Doch auch beim Falsifizieren muss man vorsichtig sein. Die Rechtssicherheit erfordert, dass man nur das falsifiziert, was direkt in die Augen springt – das ist nur das, was „unerträglich" ist (Radbruch), was eine „grobe Störung" ist, weil es sich um „eine auffallende, offenkundige, schwere Unmenschlichkeit" (Pitamic) handelt, oder gar ein „extremes Unrecht" (Alexy[5]) darstellt.

Es wäre naiv zu denken, dass die Falsifizierung auf keinem Maßstab beruht, den man verifizieren muss. Wir haben gerade darüber gesprochen und gesehen, dass die Grundlagen der Falsifizierung die Grund- bzw. Menschenrechte und die allgemein gültigen Grundsätze des Völkerrechts sind. In beiden Fällen geht es um Rechte und Grundsätze, die positiv und somit rechtlich stärker sind als das Gesetz, das in Gegensatz zu ihnen steht. Die Tatsache, dass sie rechtlich stärker sind, gibt ihnen die Natur eines *übergesetzlichen Rechts*, mit dem Gesetze und andere Vorschriften in Einklang stehen müssen.[6]

Die allgemein gültigen Grundsätze des Völkerrechts sind ins slowenische Recht inkorporiert und ein Bestandteil davon.[7] Von ihnen muss man „die von den Kulturvölkern anerkannten allgemeinen Rechtsgrundsätze" (allgemeine Rechtsgrundsätze) unterscheiden. Über diese Grundsätze spricht Art. 38 des Statuts des Internationalen Gerichtshofs.[8] Diese Grundsätze sind die Grundlage für das Funktionieren des Rechts schlechthin, während die allgemein gültigen Grundsätze des Völkerrechts „in der internationalen Praxis ent-

---

4    Siehe auch Radbruch, 1948: 147: Die völlige Leugnung der Menschenrechte entweder vom überindividualistischen Standpunkt (‚Du bist nichts, Dein Volk ist alles') oder vom transpersonalen Standpunkt (‚Eine Statue des Phidias wiegt alles Elend der Millionen antiker Sklaven auf') aber ist absolut unrichtiges Recht."

5    Alexy, 2009: 159: „Extremes Unrecht ist kein Recht."

6    Über allgemein gültige Grundsätze des Völkerrechts siehe Degan, 2000: 70-76, Škrk, 2007: 281-289, und Türk, 2007: 59.

7    Siehe Art. 8 und 153/2 der Verfassung der Republik Slowenien.

8    Für diese Grundsätze hat sich der Ausdruck allgemeine Rechtsgrundsätze eingebürgert, weil die Aufteilung auf zivilisierte und unzivilisierte Völker veraltet ist und nicht mehr gebraucht wird (Türk, 2007: 59, Anm. 44). Siehe auch Degan, der über allgemeine Grundsätze des Rechts spricht (Degan, 2000: 70).

standen" sind und sich „als allgemein gültige Verpflichtungen der Staaten durchgesetzt" haben (Türk, 2007: 76).

Eine Frucht der Falsifizierung ist es, dass man gesetzlichem Unrecht die Rechtsgültigkeit aberkennt. Wenn man anstatt eines „Rechts", das als Unrecht qualifiziert wird, ein neues Recht aufstellt, handelt es sich um einen Akt der Verifizierung des Rechts. Der Akt der Verifizierung ist wesentlich schwieriger als der Akt der Falsifizierung und die Verifizierung „zeitigt durchweg weniger genaue Ergebnisse" (Kaufmann, 1995: 85). Man steht also vor einer schwierigen Frage, die uns ermahnt, dass man möglichst umsichtig handeln sollte und dass man im Namen der Beseitigung von Ungerechtigkeiten keine neuen schaffen darf. Es gibt keine vollkommene Rechtssicherheit. Wenn man Rechtssicherheit nicht opfern will, kann man sich dem edlen Ziel der Gerechtigkeit nur nähern, ohne es gänzlich erreichen zu können. Dazu fordert auch Radbruch auf:

> „Die Annahme gesetzlichen Unrechts und die Anerkennung übergesetzlichen Rechts müssen auf die äußersten Fälle jener Art beschränkt bleiben, wie sie den Anlaß zu ihnen gegeben haben: auf Fälle eines flagranten, für niemand ernstlich bestreitbaren, schlechthin verbrecherischen Mißbrauchs in Gesetzesform." (Radbruch, 1949: 33)

Das Unrechtsargument wird in der Regel in einem Rechtsstaat angewendet, der auf Unrecht aus vergangenen Zeitabschnitten reagiert, die wenigstens in einem bestimmten Umfang unrechtlich waren. In derartigen Fällen sind die Akte der Falsifizierung in der Zuständigkeit des Gesetzgebers, der das früher geltende Recht durch ein neues ersetzt. Eine bedeutende Rolle kommt auch den Gerichten zu, insbesondere dem Verfassungsgericht, das die strittigen Gesetze (und andere allgemeine Rechtsakte) aufhebt oder sie für Unrecht erklärt. Die Gesetze, die Unrecht sind, können keine weiteren Rechtsfolgen haben, deshalb muss man individuelle Rechtsakte, die darauf beruhen, für ungültig erklären oder wenigstens aufheben.

Das Unrechtsargument ist immer empfindlich und man muss es wohlabgewogen und sehr zurückhaltend anwenden. Im Verwaltungsrecht muss man etwa einen nicht rechtlichen Akt (z. B. ein Nationalisierungsgesetz) aufheben und anschließend ein neues Gesetz über Denationalisierung erlassen, das das Verfahren und die Art und Weise der Wiedergutmachung bestimmt.

Im Strafrecht sind Rechtsfragen auf eine bestimmte Weise menschlich noch verschärft. Die Radbruchsche Formel bietet eine Grundlage, um gesetzliches Unrecht zu falsifizieren, sie kann jedoch nicht sagen, wie man anstatt des Unrechts neues gesetzliches Recht verifizieren kann. Das ist die Aufgabe des Gesetzgebers, welcher *Lex certa*, das Schuldprinzip, das Rückwirkungsverbot, die Verjährung, die Verhältnismäßigkeit und noch einige andere Grundsätze berücksichtigen muss. Diese Fragen, obwohl sie von großer Bedeutung sind, kann man hier nicht erörtern. Streng genommen geht es auch um Fragen, die die Radbruchsche Formel selbst unmittelbar nicht löst, sie gibt jedoch eine feste Anweisung dafür. Die Anweisung sagt, dass man von *positiv* akzeptierten und geltenden Maßstäben ausgehen soll, die *bereits zu der Zeit, auf die wir reagieren, gültig waren*. Es wäre nicht rechtlich, wenn man heute geltende Maßstäbe *ex post facto* in die Zeit und Verhältnisse einbrachte, in denen es diese Maßstäbe noch nicht gab.

Das Unrechtsargument ist ein juristisches und/oder ein moralisches Argument. Es ist ein moralisches Argument für alle, die scharf zwischen Recht und Moral unterscheiden; für sie ist moralische Ungerechtigkeit ein Argument, das sie legitimiert, das unmoralische positive Recht auf eine legale Weise zu ändern. Die typischsten Befürworter sind edle Rechtspositivisten. Deren Begründung ist es, dass sie als Wissenschaftler am Inhalt des Rechts nicht interessiert sind. So sagt Kelsen, dass er nicht weiß, was Gerechtigkeit ist, doch setzt er gleich hinzu, hinter dem Maßstab der rechtlichen Gerechtigkeit stehe „die Gerechtigkeit der Freiheit, die Gerechtigkeit des Friedens, die Gerechtigkeit der Demokratie, die Gerechtigkeit der Toleranz." (Kelsen, 2000: 52)

Wenn das Unrechtsargument auch ein juristisches Argument ist, steht man auf dem Standpunkt, dass „Unrecht" keine Rechtsfolgen haben soll. Diese These ist mit jenen Rechtswissenschaftlern vereinbar, die das Recht auch inhaltlich behandeln und zugleich Rechtsteilnehmer (z. B. Richter) sind, die in konkreten Fällen rechtlich entscheiden, zu verstehen versuchen. *Mutatis mutandis* muss man das auch für Rechtsteilnehmer sagen, insbesondere für alle jene, die machtbezogene Rechtsentscheidungen treffen.

Typische Rechtsteilnehmer, die machtbezogen entscheiden, sind Richter. In einem Rechtsstaat, wo die Gerichte die Verfassungsmäßigkeit und Gesetzlichkeit der Rechtsakte sichern, gewinnt ihre Rolle an Gewicht. Wenn ich mich nur auf Staaten mit einem Verfassungsgericht (konkret auf den Staat Slowenien) beschränke, muss man sagen, dass in den Staaten dieser Art ein Mechanismus errichtet ist, mit dem man sehr gut auf ein mögliches gesetzliches Unrecht reagieren kann. Ein Richter, der glaubt, dass das Gesetz, das er anwenden soll, Unrecht (also gesetzliches Unrecht) ist, wird das Verfahren unterbrechen und sich mit einem entsprechenden Antrag an das Verfassungsgericht wenden.[9]

In einem modernen Staat ist der Katalog der Grund- bzw. Menschenrechte so umfangreich, dass er eine genügend breite Grundlage für das Beseitigen von rechtlichen Unregelmäßigkeiten (einschließlich des gesetzlichen Unrechts) bietet. Der Verfassungskatalog der Grund- bzw. Menschenrechte positiviert die Errungenschaften des rationalistischen Naturrechts und öffnet somit die Tür dafür, dass auch die Radbruchsche Formel zu einem Bestandteil des gültigen Rechts wird. Es ist keine Übertreibung, wenn man sagt, dass dadurch Naturrecht in Verfassungsrecht eingetreten ist, wie der Titel von Hassemers Abhandlung (Hassemer, 2002: 135-150) lautet. Naturrecht, das in Verfassungsrecht eintritt, ist kein überpositives Recht, sondern ein integraler Teil des positiven (Verfassungs)rechts.

Die Radbruchsche Formel hat somit noch eine weitere Dimension, wodurch sie sich heute ganz besonders auszeichnet. Die Formel macht uns feinfühlig darauf aufmerksam, dass jedes Recht inhaltlich fraglich sein kann:

---

9    Siehe Gesetz über Verfassungsgericht (der Republik Slowenien), Art. 23.

„Ein guter Jurist würde aufhören, ein guter Jurist zu sein, wenn ihm in jedem Augenblick
seines Berufslebens zugleich mit der Notwendigkeit nicht auch die tiefe Fragwürdigkeit seines
Berufes voll bewußt wäre." (Radbruch, 1999: 105)
„Uns Juristen aber ist das Schwierigste auferlegt: an unseren Lebensberuf zu glauben und doch
zugleich in irgendeiner tiefsten Schicht unseres Wesens immer wieder an ihm zu zweifeln."
(Radbruch, 1999: 105)

In dieser Bedeutung hat die Radbruchsche Formel einen symbolischen Wert: ihr Wert
*übersteigt* die Bedingungen, in denen sie entstand und auf die sie reagierte. Sie ist nicht nur
für den Gesetzgeber und andere Rechtsgeber bestimmt, sie gilt auch dem Verstehen des
Gesetzes und dessen Verwirklichung. Ein Gesetz, auch ein Strafgesetz, ist nur selten (wenn
überhaupt) so eindeutig, dass sein Verstehen eine reine Rekonstruktion „des Gedankens"
(d. h. der Norm), den es mitteilt, ist.[10] Es liegt in der Natur der Gesetzesauslegung, dass
sie – mal mehr und mal weniger – auch das „Zuendedenken eines Gedachten" ist (Radbruch, 1999: 108). Rechtsnormen sind nicht automatisch gegeben, Rechtsnormen sind erst
die Bedeutung des Gesetzestextes. Smoles Antigone würde, wie der Page berichtet,[11] das
literarisch so beschreiben, dass man den Sinn des (geschriebenen) Gedankens finden soll.


## 3    Symbolische Bedeutung der Radbruchschen Formel

Smoles Antigone (1929–1992), die gerade erwähnt wurde, ist eine der ausgezeichneten
Reinterpretierungen von Sophokles' Antigone.[12] Das zentrale Merkmal von Smoles Antigone
(aus dem Jahr 1959) ist es, dass Antigone nicht auf der Szene erscheint. Bei der physischen
Abwesenheit von *Antigone* ist der Protagonist des Dramas *Kreon*, der im Vergleich zu
*Sophokles'* Helden wesentlich weniger geradlinig und prinzipiell und darum umso prag-
matischer ist („und – überhaupt," sagt er, „tut innerhalb der vorgeschriebenen Grenzen/
was euch beliebt …"[13]), auch ein philosophisch und menschlich Zweifelnder („Und nicht
zuletzt: auch der König, der trotz allem auch ein Mensch ist,/ schläft besser, wenn er zuerst
Mensch und zuletzt König ist./ Jetzt aber genug des Geschwätzes. Geschäfte warten auf

---

10   Siehe von Savigny, 1840: 214. Die Auslegung ist für ihn eine „Reconstruction des dem Gesetze
     inwohnenden Gedankens."

11   Smole, 2009: 14, Vers 118: „beharrlich sucht sie den Sinn eines Gedankens."

12   Steiner, 2003: 170: „As I noted above, the Sophoclean chorus tends to fall away from spoken
     ‚Antigones' after the sixteenth century and such scholary treatments as Garnier's. There are
     exceptions. Among the most intriguing is Domik Smole's Slovene Antigone, first staged in
     1960. Here, the heroine never appears. It is via the chorus and several secondary personae that
     we experience the terror and moral-political meaning of her fate."

13   Smole, 2009: Verse 142-143.

uns"[14]), doch trotz der Zweifel schließlich unerbittlich, wenn es um die Grundlagen der Macht geht:

> „Alles, was dieser sanfte Rebell erreichen kann, ist, meinen Kopf abschlagen/ – falls ich es ihm gestatte – um danach selbst König zu werden./ Der König also bleibt erhalten, auch unsre Ordnung und unsre Gesetze bleiben,/ die Welt bleibt auch, zwar etwas verändert, nicht aber eine völlig andere./ Wer jedoch die Welt von Grund auf ändert, ohne diese Ordnung, ohne/ diese Gesetze und ohne jeglichen König,/ wer sich dünkelhaft neue Pläne, die er vom Himmel heruntergeholt, ausdenkt,/ und nicht nach meinem Kopfe strebt, nach diesem Kopf hier,/ sondern überhaupt die Notwendigkeit des Königs bezweifelt,/ der ist ein Feind. Der König muß mit ihm hart umgehen,/ weil Friede und Wohlstand nicht, wie lauer Sommerregen,/ von Himmel fallen: eine vernünftige Macht schafft sie hier auf Erden."[15] Und auch: „Keine Maße habe ich, denn ich bin der König." – „Ich bin also der König."[16]

Über Antigone berichten andere, die zu ihr gehen und mit ihr sprechen. Von tragender Bedeutung ist der bereits erwähnte Bericht des Pagen, dass Antigone beharrlich sucht, weil sie hinter den Sinn des Gedankens kommen will, mit dem sie sich Kreons Befehl, dass Polyneikes kein Grab haben darf, widersetzt. Antigone findet schließlich Polyneikes und bestattet ihn auch. Sie ist, wie Ismene sagt, „eine zärtliche Blume, die sich öffnet und gleich wieder verblüht."[17]

Dieses etwas längere Zitat aus der, wenn ich sie so nennen darf, slowenischen Antigone führe ich einerseits deshalb an, weil wir über Antigone auch mit Professor Sprenger gesprochen haben, und andererseits auch deswegen, weil das Verhältnis von Recht und Literatur ein Thema war, das dem Professor am Herzen lag. In seinem Buch *Literarische Wege zum Recht* (2012) liest man, dass literarische Beschäftigung mit einem Einzelfall „unendlich ‚sensibler‘, ist als ein Rechtsschema, das Lebensfälle typisiert (Sprenger, 2012: 130). Die Frage der Lebenserträglichkeit oder -unerträglichkeit von Recht ist sicher eine von den sensiblen Fragen, bei denen Literatur helfen kann.

Sprenger hatte immer viel Gefühl für Rechtssensibilität. In zwei Abhandlungen über das Rechtsgefühl – eine ist rechtstheoretisch (Sprenger 2003), die andere gehört zu den literarischen Zugängen zum Recht (Sprenger 1998) – beleuchtete er auf seine Weise den Hintergrund der Radbruchschen Formel und deutete somit klar an, wie man sich mit dem Maß der Rechtlichkeit auseinandersetzen kann.

Sprengers Suche nach dem Sinn des Gedankens „Recht" schlägt den Weg ins Feld der vor-rechtlichen Ordnung ein, d. h. auf das Gebiet von „recht", worauf auch Recht beruht. Im Feld der vor-rechtlichen Ordnung kommt eine bedeutende Rolle dem Rechtsgefühl zu, das immer auch emotional und intuitiv ist. Sprenger stellt sich die Frage, was Rechtsgefühl

---

14 Smole, 2009: Verse 947-950.

15 Smole, 2009: Verse 639-650.

16 Smole, 2009: Verse 2087 und 2270.

17 Smole, 2009: Vers 2259.

ohne Recht ist und wie es aussehen könnte. Das Erkennen des Rechtsgefühls und seiner Elemente ist von wesentlicher Bedeutung für das Begreifen von Recht.

Sprengers Intellekt befindet sich innerhalb des In-der-Welt-seins und ist sich bewusst, dass „Gefühle und Stimmungen" existieren und dass es deshalb sinnlos wäre, sie im Namen von reiner Rationalität – insoweit diese überhaupt möglich ist – abzulehnen. Im Leben und im Recht ist auch die „Logik" des Herzens von Bedeutung.[18] „Die Stimmung (das Gefühl) begreift nicht und versteht nichts", betont er (indem er sich auf Max Müller beruft),

> „aber sie ermöglicht Begreifen und Verstehen; sie ist ein Vorgang, der, wenn er geschieht, nicht durch mich und in mir bzw. meinem Bewußtsein geschieht und abläuft, sondern ein Vorgang, der mit mir und auf mich zu geschieht, *der Vorgang des Seins, durch den Begreifen, Verstehen und Bewußtsein erst grundgelegt werden.*"[19] (Sprenger, 2012: 97)

In der vor-rechtlichen Ordnung kann das Leben normal ablaufen, wenn „recht" tief empfunden und natürlich ist. Die Grundelemente, die von der Ordnung gewährleistet werden müssen, sind Gleichheit und Gegenseitigkeit.

Gleichheit und Ungleichheit entstehen im menschlichen Miteinander, d. h. im Verhältnis, in dem der Mensch die Gesellschaft formt und die noch origineller ihn formt (Sprenger, 2003: 229-330). Für das Ineinandergreifen ist es charakteristisch, dass der Mensch im Anderen „den Anderen *als sich selbst*" erfasst (Sprenger, 2003: 330).[20] Der Maßstab der Gleichheit ist Gerechtigkeit, die seit Aristoteles als distributive (austeilende) und kommutative (ausgleichende) Gerechtigkeit bekannt ist. Den Inhalt der Gleichheit (Gerechtigkeit) kann man „*ohne Rücksicht auf die Person und ihre Situation im Leben*" (Sprenger, 2003: 329) weder bestimmen noch verwirklichen. Erst der konkrete Fall ist es, der Gleichheit als Gerechtigkeit eingehender determiniert und sie dynamisiert. Die inhaltliche Aktualisierung der Gleichheit „vollzieht sich als *Gegenseitigkeit*" (Sprenger, 2003: 331).

Sprenger denkt existenzialistisch und gräbt wie ein Maulwurf in der Wirklichkeit und im Menschen, der hier und jetzt lebt. Der Kern des Rechts ist in einem gegenseitigen und mehrseitigen Verhältnis, in dem man *gegenseitig* ist. Rechtsverhältnisse sind Verhältnisse der Koexistenz. Die Gegenseitigkeit ist somit „*der allgemeine Bestimmungsgrund des Verhaltens zum Mitmenschen*" (Sprenger, 2012: 100). In dieser Qualität definiert er sie auch „als *kategoriale Voraussetzung für die Begegnung mit Anderen*" (Sprenger, 2003: 333). Die Gegenseitigkeit beruht auf Verlässlichkeit und Vertrauen, die die Bedingung für ein entsprechendes Mit-einandersein sind. Sobald das Beisammenleben auch auf Zwang beruht, weist die Gegenseitigkeit ein Defizit auf (Sprenger, 2003: 332). Wenn es überhaupt keine

---

18  Vgl. Pascal, Pensée 277/1: „Le cœur a ses raisons que la raison ne connaît point."

19  An dieser Stelle ist Fn. 49: „Müller (1964), S. 110 (Hervorhebungen G. S.)." Sprenger beruft sich auf die Arbeit von Max Müller: Existenzphilosophie im geistigen Leben der Gegenwart, 3. Aufl., 1964.

20  Siehe auch die ausgezeichnete Abhandlung Des Menschen Maß: der Andere. – Gedanken zu Humanität und Recht (Sprenger, 1997a: 25 ff.).

Gegenseitigkeit gibt, weil das „Ich" den „Anderen" mit den Füßen tritt, ist man schon in den Bereich von Unrecht abgeglitten.[21]

Die Gegenseitigkeit braucht Normen, die sagen, wie verschiedene Verhaltensweisen miteinander in Einklang sein sollen. Wenn es keine Normen gibt, kann man gegenseitige Konflikte nicht lösen. Sprenger widmet sich insbesondere der goldenen Regel, die, wie man heute sagen würde, eine globale Gültigkeit hat (Sprenger, 2003: 333 ff.; 2012: 101 ff.). Die Suche nach dem Maß des Rechts kann auch anderen Normen und Prinzipien nicht ausweichen (dazu gehören etwa der Dekalog, Ulpians tragende Rechtsgrundsätze, Grundmaßstäbe der Gerechtigkeit, Kants kategorischer Imperativ).

Was Sprenger besonders beschäftigt, ist, dass jedes gegenseitige Verhältnis eine *Entsprechung* haben muss, auf welche die Norm es lenkt. Die Entsprechung ist „angemessenes Antwort-Verhalten gegenüber dem Anderen" (Sprenger, 2003: 336). Die Offenheit und Flexibilität der goldenen Regel machen es möglich, dass „die Waage der Gerechtigkeit" das Gleichgewicht erreicht: *„Entsprechung als Antwort-Verhalten* ist „recht" (Sprenger, 2003: 334).

Entsprechung ist auch für Recht von Schlüsselbedeutung:

> „Recht hat ein bestimmtes äußeres Verhalten und Entsprechen innerhalb eines sozialen Gefüges zu gewährleisten, das sich aus typischen Situationen, Abläufen und Zweckkonstellationen des alltäglichen Miteinanders bestimmt." (Sprenger, 2003: 337)

Für das Recht ist es von wesentlicher Bedeutung, dass es Entsprechung „als Antwort-Verhalten" hat und sie ermöglicht. Wenn es keine Entsprechung gibt (z. B. zwischen dem Käufer und dem Verkäufer, zwischen dem Schädiger und dem Geschädigten, zwischen dem Steuerzahler und dem Fürsorgeempfänger), meldet sich das Rechtsgefühl zu Wort, das auf das Ausbleiben der Entsprechung mit Enttäuschung reagiert (Sprenger, 2003: 337; 2012: 105). Das Rechtsgefühl ist wesentlich sensibler, „als jeder positiv-rechtliche Maßstab, jedes juristische Begriffssystem und alle methodischen Bemühungen es je vermögen" (Sprenger, 2003: 337). Dass es tatsächlich so ist, zeigten lebendig und überzeugend der Schriftsteller Anatole France in seiner Erzählung *Crainquebille* sowie Professor Sprenger, der am Fall von Crainquebilles Geschichte seine Abhandlung über das Rechtsgefühl entwarf.

Und was hat das mit der Radbruchschen Unerträglichkeitsformel zu tun? Unmittelbar wenig, mittelbar jedoch sehr viel. Unmittelbar wenig deshalb, weil sich Sprenger nicht besonders mit der Unerträglichkeit selbst und mit konkreten Fällen von Unerträglichkeit befasst hat. Sprengers Stärke ist die Suche nach der Erträglichkeit von Recht, das, wenn es so sein will, auf „recht", das ins Rechtsgefühl von ehrlich fühlenden und denkenden Menschen eingewebt ist, beruhen muss. Je mehr sich positives Recht von den grundlegenden Elementen der Rechtlichkeit und vom grundlegenden Rechtsgefühl entfernt, desto eher ist es möglich, dass es illegitim und, wenigstens in einigen Segmenten, unerträglich wird.

---

21 Siehe Sprenger (2012: 101): „Unrecht aber meint hier: das Ausbleiben von Gegenseitigkeit."

Sprengers regulative Idee ist die Erträglichkeit (des Rechts). Am überzeugendsten spricht vielleicht darüber der Titel einer seiner Abhandlungen: Des Menschen Maß: der Andere (Sprenger, 1997a: 25-52).

## Literatur

Alexy, R. (1993). Mauerschützen. Zum Verhältnis von Recht, Moral und Strafbarkeit. In R. Alexy, H. J. Koch, L. Kuhlen und H. Rüßman, *Elemente einer juristischen Begründungslehre* (2003: 469-492). Baden-Baden: Nomos.

Alexy, R. (2009). Hauptelemente einer Theorie der Doppelnatur des Rechts. *Archiv für Rechts- und Sozialphilosophie*, 95 (2), 151-166.

Battis, U., Jakobs, G., Jensee, E. (1992). *Vergangenheitsbewältigung durch Recht. Drei Abhandlungen zu einem deutschen Problem*. Hrsg. von J. Isensee. Berlin: Duncker & Humblot.

Degan, V. Đ. (2000). *Međunarodno pravo (International Law)*. Rijeka: Pravni fakultet Sveučilišta u Rijeci.

Dreier, H. (1997). Gustav Radbruch und die Mauerschützen. *Juristen Zeitung (JZ)*. 52 (9), 421-434.

Dreier, R. (2011). Gustav Radbruchs Rechtsbegriff. In M. Mahlmann (Hrsg.), *Gesellschaft und Gerechtigkeit. Festschrift für Hubert Rottleuthner* (17-44). Baden-Baden: Nomos.

Hart, H. L. A. (1994). *The Concept of Law*. 2. Aufl. Oxford: Clarendon Press.

Hassemer, W. (2002). Naturrecht im Verfassungsrecht. In A. Donatsch, M. Forster und Ch. Schwarzenegger (Hrsg.), *Strafrecht, Strafprozessrecht und Menschenrechte. Festschrift für Stefan Trechsel zum 65. Geburtstag* (135-150). Zürich: Schulthess Verlag.

Kaufmann, A. (1984). *Rechtsphilosophie im Wandel. Stationen eines Weges*. 2. Aufl. Köln etc.: Carl Heymanns Verlag KG.

Kaufmann, A. (1995). Die Radbruchsche Formel vom gesetzlichen Unrecht und vom übergesetzlichen Recht in der Diskussion um das im Namen von der DDR begangene Unrecht. *Neue Juristische Wochenschrift*, 48 (2), 81-84.

Kaufmann, A. (1997). *Rechtsphilosophie*. München: Beck.

Kelsen, H. (2000). *Was ist Gerechtigkeit?* Stuttgart: Reclam.

Kelsen, H. (1934). *Reine Rechtslehre*. Nachdruck (1994). Aalen: Scientia Verlag.

Neumann, U. (2011). Leonid Pitamic, An den Grenzen der Reinen Rechtslehre. Herausgeber und Einführungsstudie: Marijan Pavčnik. Ljubljana 2009 (Erstausgabe 2005). *Archiv für Rechts- und Sozialphilosophie*, 97 (2), 279-281.

Paulson, S. L. (2006). On the Background and Significance of Gustav Radbruch's Post-War Papers. *Oxford Journal of Legal Studies*, 26 (1), 17-40.

Pavčnik, M. (2010). Die Frage der rechtlichen Grundnorm. Pitamic' Brief an Hans Kelsen. *Archiv für Rechts- und Sozialphilosophie*, 96 (1), 87-103.

Pavčnik, M. (2011). *Auf dem Weg zum Maß des Rechts. Ausgewählte Schriften zur Rechtstheorie*. Stuttgart: Franz Steiner Verlag.

Pavčnik, M. (2015). Gesetzliches (Un)Recht. In A. Brockmöller, S. Kirste, U. Neumann (Hrsg.), *Wert und Wahrheit in der Rechtswissenschaft*. Stuttgart: Franz Steiner Verlag, 41-60.

Philipps, L. (2007). Von Puppen aus Russland und einer Rechtslehre aus Wien. Der Rekursionsgedanke im Recht. *Slovenian Law Review*, 4 (1-2), 191-196.

Pitamic, L. (1956). Naturrecht und Natur des Rechtes. *Österreichische Zeitschrift für öffentliches Recht*. N. F., 7, 190-207. Nachdruck: Pitamic, 2005 (2009): 297-314.

Pitamic, L. (1960). Die Frage der rechtlichen Grundnorm. In *Völkerrecht und rechtliches Weltbild. Festschrift für Alfred Verdross*. Wien: Springer-Verlag (205-216). Nachdruck: Pitamic, 2005 (2009): 315-324.

Radbruch, G. (1914). *Grundzüge der Rechtsphilosophie*. Zitiert nach dem Nachdruck: GRGA II (1993). Heidelberg: C. F. Müller Juristischer Verlag.

Radbruch, G. (1934). Der Relativismus in der Rechtsphilosophie. In G. Radbruch, *Rechtsphilosophie III* (1990), GRGA III (17-22). Heidelberg: C. F. Müller Juristischer Verlag.

Radbruch, G. (1945). Fünf Minuten Rechtsphilosophie. Zitiert nach dem Nachdruck: G. Radbruch, 1999: 209-210.

Radbruch, G. (1946). Gesetzliches Unrecht und übergesetzliches Recht. Zitiert nach dem Nachdruck: G. Radbruch, 1999: 211-219.

Radbruch, G. (1948). Vorschule der Rechtsphilosophie. In G. Radbruch, *Rechtsphilosophie III* (1990), GRGA III (121-227). Heidelberg: C. F. Müller Juristischer Verlag.

Radbruch, G. (1949). Neue Probleme in der Rechtswissenschaft. In G. Radbruch, *Eine Feuerbach-Gedenkrede sowie drei Aufsätze aus dem wissenschaftlichen Nachlaß* (1952: 31-34). Tübingen: Verlag J. C. B. Mohr (Paul Siebeck). Nachdruck: GRGA IV (2002: 232-235). Heidelberg: C. F. Müller Juristischer Verlag.

Radbruch, G. (1999). *Rechtsphilosophie. Studienausgabe*. Hrsg. von R. Dreier, S. L. Paulson. Heidelberg: C. F. Müller.

Saliger, F. (1995). *Radbruchsche Formel und Rechtsstaat*. Heidelberg: C. F. Müller Juristischer Verlag.

Savigny, F. K. von (1840). *System des heutigen Römischen Rechts. I*. Berlin: Veit und Comp.

Sieckmann, Jan-R. (2001). Die „Radbruch'sche Formel" und die Mauerschützen. *Archiv für Rechts- und Sozialphilosophie*, 87, 496-515.

Smole, D. (2009). *Zbrano delo (Gesammelte Werke). II [Dramski spisi (Schauspiele) I, Antigona (Antigone)]*. Ljubljana: Založba ZRC. Zitiert nach der Übersetzung von Tomislav Blažev, *Antigone*. Wien: Copyright 1966 by Universal Edition AG.

Sprenger, G. (1976). *Naturrecht und Natur der Sache*. Berlin: Duncker & Humblot.

Sprenger, G. (1996). Vom Wert der Wahrheit und der „Wahrheit" des Wertes im Recht. In G. Haney, W. Maihofer, G. Sprenger, *Recht und Ideologie. Festschrift für Hermann Klenner zum 70. Geburtstag*. Freiburg, Berlin: Rudolf Haufe Verlag (190-222). Nachdruck: Sprenger, 2010: 11-43.

Sprenger, G. (1996a). Legitimation des Grundgesetzes als Wertordnung. Einige philosophische Anmerkungen. In W. Brugger (Hrsg.), *Legitimation des Grundgesetzes aus Sicht von Rechtsphilosophie und Gesellschaftstheorie*. Baden-Baden: Nomos, 219-247.

Sprenger, G. (1997). 50 Jahre Radbruchsche Formel oder: Von der Sprachnot der Juristen. *Neue Justiz*, 1, 3-7.

Sprenger, G. (1997a). Des Menschen Maß: der Andere.- *Gedanken zu Humanität und Recht*. In R. Gröschner, M. Morlok (Hrsg.), *Recht und Humanismus. Kolloquium für Gerhard Haney zum 70. Geburtstag*. Baden-Baden: Nomos (25-52). Nachdruck: Sprenger, 2010: 231-258.

Sprenger, G. (1998). Crainquebille – oder: die verweigerte Gegenseitigkeit. Zur Ontologie des Rechtsgefühls. *Teoria prawa. Filozofia prawa. Współczesne prawo i prawoznawstvo*, 1998, 291-314. Zitiert nach dem Nachdruck: Sprenger, 2012: 87-110.

Sprenger, G. (2000). Recht und Werte. Reflexionen über eine philosophische Verlegenheit. *Der Staat*, 39 (1), 1-22. Zitiert nach dem Nachdruck: Sprenger, 2010: 125-146.

Sprenger, G. (2000a). Od naravnega prava do človekovega dostojanstva – Preoblikovanje nemškega pravosodja po letu 1945 (From Natural Law to Human Dignity – Transformation of German Judiciary after the Year 1945). Übersetzung: A. Mergole. *Pravnik*, 55 (4-5), 197-213.

Sprenger, G. (2003). Rechtsgefühl ohne Recht. *Festschrift für Ernst-Joachim Lampe zum 70. Geburtstag*. Hrsg. von D. Dölling. Berlin: Duncher & Humblot. Nachdruck: Sprenger, 2010: 305-326.

Sprenger, G. (2010). *Von der Wahrheit zum Wert. Gedanken zu Recht und Gerechtigkeit*. Stuttgart: Franz Steiner Verlag.

Sprenger, G. (2012). *Literarische Wege zum Recht*. Baden-Baden: Nomos.

Steiner, G. (1984, Nachdruck: 2003). *Antigones*. New York: Oxford University Press.

Škrk, M. (2007). Odnos med mednarodnim pravom in notranjim pravom v praksi Ustavnega sodišča (The Relationship between International Law and Internal Law in the Case of the Constitutional Court). *Pravnik*, 62 (6-8), 275-311.

Türk, D. (2007). *Temelji mednarodnega prava (Fundamental Principles of International Law)*. Ljubljana: GV Založba.

## The Author

Prof. Dr. **Marijan Pavčnik**, Pravna fakulteta (Faculty of Law), Poljanski nasip 2, 1000 Ljubljana, Slovenia. (Email address: Marijan.Pavcnik@pf.uni-lj.si).

# The Concept of *Gewalt* in Walter Benjamin Philosophy of Law

Karla Pinhel Ribeiro and Milton Meira do Nascimento

## Abstract

The paper attempt to investigate the concept of *Gewalt* in the early works of Walter Benjamin, its origin in the language and its problems and developments in the area of ethics, aesthetics and law. The main argument is an interpretation of Benjaminian conception, towards the differences among law, justice and right in Christian Jewish tradition.

## Keywords

Philosophy; Law; *Gewalt*

> *„Und Gott ‚sah alles, was er gemacht, und siehe, es war sehr gut‘.*
> *Also hat das Wissen von dem Bösen gar keinen Gegenstand.*
> *Dies ist nicht in der Welt. „*
>
> Walter Benjamin, *Ursprung des deutschen Trauerspiels*

## Introduction

In this paper we divided the research topics in the reference of the German edition of the complete works of Walter Benjamin – GS – published at Surhkamp Verlag, organized by Rolf Tildemann.

We privileged this editorial order despite of chronology order to enhance the thematic survey by the editor, which contributed to the theme of the systematic vision to glimpse the importance and the concept of role in each specific area such as aesthetics – which the contribution of Walter Benjamin to the field of aesthetics is now undeniable, and their original writings stored at the Berlin Academy of Arts as a great treasure of the German language, its art and its culture. The recognition of the greatness and innovation of Benjamin's work in German literature is proof of its relevance to the study of language and German thought. Walter Benjamin's contributions to metaphysics, to ethics and politics

© Springer Fachmedien Wiesbaden GmbH, part of Springer Nature 2018
H. Kabashima et al. (Hrsg.), *The Idea of Justice in Literature*,
Wirtschaftsethik in der globalisierten Welt,
https://doi.org/10.1007/978-3-658-21996-3_15

are considered a breakthrough because are few studies and brief on the subject. In Portuguese, however, it is even greater.

The attempt therefore is towards the support based on Walter Benjamin philosophy of law, that is searching for interdisciplinary lesson of the right and understands the human being on its diverse aspects.

We that are in the thinking of our time still present Walter Benjamin contribution to the current dilemma between natural law and positivism, law and politics, and the core problem of violence.

## 1    Archaeological and Genealogical Conception of *Gewalt*

The meaning of the word *Gewalt,* its historical interpretation and understanding are not only means for German language readers and authors[1], according to the German dictionary *Deutsches Wörterbuch von Jacob und Wilhelm Grimm* written in 1854 to 1961, but only completed published in 1971. On that dictionary cited as a reference by Walter Benjamin at one of his books, for example, has the meaning of the word *Gewalt* on an entrance with proximity of 300 pages[2].

Originally understood towards on both sides, feminine and masculine, the concept of *Gewalt* has its origin through the radical *"Wald"* – forest -, which later on history was attributed only to masculine gender, as

---

1    See Arendt, Hannah: Macht und Gewalt. German translation of On violence, made by Gisela Uellenberg. München, Piper Verlag, 1970; Butler, Judith: „Kritik, Zwang und das heelige in Walter Benjamins Zur Kritik der Gewalt", in: Rationalitäten der Gewalt. Org. Krasmann, Susanne; Martschukat, Jürgen. Bielefeld, Transcript Verlag, p. 19-46; Nitsch, Patrick: Zum Begriff von Macht und Gewalt bei Hannah Arendt. Norderstedt, Grin Verlag, Studienarbeit.

2    Jacob Grimm e Wilhem Grimm. We utilized the eletronic version. The original reference, is the following: Deutsches Wörterbuch von Jacob und Wilhelm Grimm, with 32 volumen, written in Leipzig between 1854 until 1961, its index was only finished in Leipzig, 1971,with the followin order: 1 I A – Biermolke 1854 2 II Biermörder – D 1860 3 III E – Forsche 1862 4 IV,I,1 Forschel – Gefolgsmann 1878 5 IV,I,2 Gefoppe – Getreibs 1897 6 IV,I,3 Getreide – Gewöhniglich 1911 7 IV,I,4 Gewöhnlich – Gleve 1949 8 IV,I,5 Glibber – Gräzist 1958 9 IV,I,6 Greander – Gymnastik 1935 10 IV,II H, I, J 1877 11 V K 1873 12 VI L, M 1885 13 VII N, O, P, Q 1889 14 VIII R – Schiefe 1893 15 IX Schiefeln – Seele 1899 16 X,I Seeleben – Sprechen 1905 17 X,II,1 Sprecher – Stehuhr 1919 18 X,II,2 Stehung – Stitzig 1941 19 X,III Stob – Strollen 1957 20 X,IV Strom – Szische 1942 21 XI,I,1 T – Treftig 1935 22 XI,I,2 Treib – Tz 1952 23 XI,II U – Umzwingen 1936 24 XI,III U – Uzvogel 1936 25 XII,I V – Verzwunzen 1956 26 XII,II Vesche – Vulkanisch 1951 27 XIII W – Weg[zwitschern]-zwiesel 1922 28 XIV,I,1 Weh – Wendunmut 1955 29 XIV,I,2 Wenig – Wiking 1960 30 XIV,II Wilb – Ysop 1960 31 XV Z – Zmasche 1956 32 XVI Zobel – Zypressenzweig 1954 33 Quellenverzeichnis 1971. The electronic version of the dictionary is for disposition on-line, at a project of the Competence Center of Electronic Procession and Publication on Humanity from the University of Trier, together with Berlin-Brandenburg Academy of Ciences and the Hirzel Verlag Stuttgart. Sponsored by German Research Foundation.

"-wald *m. n.* (*power, strength, might, efficacy, empire, rule, dominion, mastery, sway, jurisdiction, government, protection, keeping, a bridle-bit, potestas, facultas, imperium, dictio, arbitrium, jus, cannus*). Bosworth 464a; weald, *power. ebenda* 1171b; altnordisch vald *n.* (*macht, gewalt, kraft, ursache*) Möbius *altnordisches glossar* 489; altsächsisch giwald *fem., friesisch* wald, mittelniederdeutsch wald *vgl. sp.* 4913. *die häufigkeit der verwendung und die ausdehnung des bedeutungsumfangs, die schon das erste litterarische auftreten kennzeichnen, haben sich bis in die neuere zeit nicht vermindert, sondern in hohem grade gesteigert, vgl.* Gewalt, *potestas, potentia, facultas, efficacitas, vis, violentia, injuria, indignitas, mandatum, plenipotentia, robur imperii, jurisdictio, potestas magistratus, casus fortuitus*".[3]

Later still, become a verb, included in proximity con the original noun meaning of *Waldan*. After this, now is considered a noun with a new meaning, with it was changing from its original meaning of *wald*, but today was modified towards to what we understand as *Gewalt* such as creation, human work and human power.

Exists, however, the same on the history of the German language from New Testament. the main influence and reference of the construction of the concept *Gewalt*, the approval of the idea that changes come from since the beginning from nature to God, turned into a concept attributed to the deeds and creations of humanity.

Its start, the concept of *Gewalt* appears in Paul's Second Letter to the Corinthians, but also in the Book of Lucas, 3, 14, is showing the archaeological and genealogical divine demostrando: "Gloria for God in the Heaven and peace to the humanity He loves."

Therefore, highlighted in the German language, its appearance in the poem Así, *Heliand*, word which in old German has the meaning of "The Salvator":

„eingeengter bedeutung (garda valdan 1. Tim. 5, 14 οἰκοδεσποτεῖν, dem haushalt vorstehen Kautzsch; ähnl. Lucas 3, 14), ebenso wie der Heliand: thar ic allun scalirminthiodun demos adêlien, than motun gi mid iwomu drohtine that selbon sittien endi môtunthera saca waldan: adêlien aftar iro dâdiun. 3317 Behaghel, ähnl. 1321."[4]

## 2    On Benjamin's Early Works

### 2.1    *Der Begriff der Kunstkritik in der deutschen Romantik*

The treatises of Benjamin, that is, in the works in which he exposes didactically about science and art, starting with *Der Begriff der Kunstkritik in der deutschen Romantik* appear references to the term "*Gewalt*". For example, the adjective "*gewaltig*" (GS, I, 1, 15), which appears in a footnote in the text. Then the term "*Gewaltsreich*" also appears in this same treaty (GS, I, 1, 98).

---

3  Op. cit., Vol. 6, p. 4911.

4  Idem.

## 2.2    *Goethes Wahlverwandtschaften*

In the treaty of Benjamin entitled *Goethes Wahlverwandtschaften*, the term *"Gewalt"* (violence, power) appears very often. In this paper, the term *"Gewalt"*, for example, first appears when Benjamin comes to the distance of history, as a departure from the *"Gewalt"* (GS, I, 1, 126). Also in the treatise on Goethe, the term *"Gewalt"* first appears as a reference *"mytischen Gewalten des Rechts"*, i.e, the mythic violence of law (GS, I, 1, 130). Benjamin deals with violence (*Gewalten*) existing in Goethe (GS, I, 1, 131), which presents an idea of relationship between humanity and violence of nature: *"Die Menschen müssen die selber Naturgewalt bekunden"* (GS, I, 1 , 133). In *Goethes Wahlverwandtschften*, Benjamin also developed a concept of *"Gewalt"* in relation to humanity and the world and its importance in daily life (GS, I, 1, 139). It deserves relevant observation also this text Benjamin his first presentation of an idea of the relationship between *"Gewalt"* and *"machte"* as in the following passage: *"die freilich schreckhaft deutlich die Gewalt uralter machte in dem Leben dieses zeigt Mannes, der doch nicht ohne sie zum größten Dichter seines Volks geworden ist"* (GS, I, 1, 151). In this treatise on Goethe, Benjamin emphasizes the importance of the term *"Gewalt"* in Latin conception of the world (GS, I, 1, 167). Again on Goethe, Walter Benjamin deals with the relationship between *"Gewalt"* and *"Macht"*, especially as regards the *"Gewalt"* in its relation with power of nature (GS, I, 1, 171). Continuing this theme – the *Gewalt* regarding the power of nature – when Benjamin comes on Goethe and the tragedy highlights the role of violence in life (GS, I, 1, 176).

Later, Benjamin insists this violent element in this tragedy. He describes the problem of critical violence, as this word in this genre as well as its character of moralizing.

> „Das ist die Ausdruckslose kritische Gewalt, welche Schein vom Wesen der Kunst in zwar nicht zu trennen vermag, aber ihnen verwehrt, sich zu mischen. Diese Gewalt hat es als moralisches Wort. Im Ausdruckslosen erscheint die erhabne Gewalt des Wahren, wie es nach der Gesetzen moralischen die Sprache der Welt wirklichen bestimmt. Dieses nämlich zerschlägt was in allem schönen Schein als die Erbschaft des Chaos noch überdauert: die falsche, irrende Totalität – die absolute.[5]" (GS, I, 1, 181)

Following Benjamin towards the issue of tragic violence, its explanatory character and how violence and beauty come together in this same literary and dramaturgical genre. The composition and representation of violence in tragedy as in the case cf. Hölderlin, for example, features Benjamin for an expressive, again (GS, I, 1, 181-182) appears next to not only beauty but also the harmony of the second life the tragic expression, which then has

---

5    „This is the expression of less critical violence, that can certificate the nature of art in not to separate, but denied them to mingle. This has violence is a moral word. In the inexpressible the sublime power of truth appears as after moral laws determines the language of the real world. This namely what smashes in particularly beautiful appearance as the inheritance of chaos still survives: the wrong, erring totality – the absolute".

the role of expressing perhaps what is right. As if the character of the tragic violence could teach us something, as in this case, what it is right or even what is beautiful.

Benjamin cites the example of Ottilie (GS, I, 1, 184), who with his brilliance and singular beauty on the one hand, but with sacrifice and struggle for another. Her example serves to explain the mythical and divine violence are while designing the tragic violence. Thus, Benjamin signals not only this double aspect of tragic violence as mythical and divine but also it is moralizing function.

Forward, Benjamin comments on the painful and violent death of Ottilie and also about his relationship with the violence contained in the legal proverbs: "*Sie vor dem Grund flüchten im Sprüche des Rechts, the über sie noch Gewalt hat.*" (GS, I, 1, 185). In sequence, Benjamin again addresses the importance of the relationship between beauty and violence within the tragedy, especially for Goethe: "*Ursprung an durch Musik im Innersten berührt und vor der Gewalt Lebender Schönheit gefeit sind. Ihr Wesenhaft: es zu erretten ist das Ringen Goethes*" (GS, I, 1, 192).. And still, dealing with the same relationship between beauty and violence to the essence of tragedy through the same example of Ottilie, but when placed in comparison with other Goethe's characters, as Helena and Lucianen, for example. (GS, I, 1, 193).

At the end, Benjamin explains the example of the violent death of heroes also violent death (or death destructive violence) of Ottilie, as if contained in their lives to her death, "*die ganze Leben wie es aus seiner Dauer seinen eigenen eigenen Tod hat. Ja darf man sagen, daß er in Wahrheit, wenn etwas für irgend, gerade hierfür blind war.*" (GS, I, 1, 198).

## 2.3 *Ursprung des deutschen Trauerpiels*

In his treatise "*Ursprung des deutschen Trauerpiels*" from its "Prologue Epistemological-Critical", we faced our first problem in translating the concept of "*Erkenntnis*" which was translated by John Muddy as "knowledge", however, in the original sense "*Erkenntnis*" also mean achievement, experience, and even more in this scientific sense, as in the translation of the Prologue as "epistemological-critical" the German word "*Erkenntniskritische*". So what Benjamin suggests is not only knowledge in the general sense, it could be the term chosen by Benjamin, "*Wissenschaft*". But, however, is not the concept that Benjamin uses. What Benjamin has, in my point of view, from the beginning is the relationship between Truth (*Wahrheit*) and the knowledge produced by science, so dealing with a specific type of knowledge. Then, and following in "*Philosophische Schöneit*" the necessity of art for that scientific knowledge makes sense and can achieve the beauty of truth.

In this context, the term "*Gewalt*" appears from the start, related to the philosophy and life of the thinking being (GS, I, 1, 207). Later, again returns to relate to this context truth and knowledge (GS, I, 1, 216).

But not only the term violence is constant in work *Ursprung des deutschen Trauerspiels* but also its opposite, non-violence or its absence. The importance of non-violent way or just a way that is absent of violence and its qualities are in the chapter on Baroque literature (GS, I, 1, 229).

These opposite forms are in the baroque tragedy, with its principles and history (GS, I, 1, 229). And so, both violent and non-violent forms are represented by it. (GS, I, 1, 235) Benjamin concludes the chapter on the representation of baroque tragedy highlighting their non-violent and violent forms of expression (GS, I, 1, 236-237).

However, even in *"Ursprung des deutschen Trauerspiels"* in the chapter on *"Theorie der Souveränität"*, the term *"Gewalt"* appears in a predominant form. Primarily in its political aspect, such as the term *"Exekutivgewalt"* and even in the actual construction of the concept of sovereignty by Benjamin:

> „Diese extreme Lehre von der Gewalt ist fürstlichen in ihren – trotz der Gruppierung der Parteien gegenreformatorischen – Ursprüngen geistvoller und tiefer gewesen als ihre neuzeitliche Umbildung. Wenn der auf eine moderne Souveränitätsbegriff höchste, Fürstliche Exekutivgewalt hinausläuft, entwickelt sich aus einer der barocke Diskussion des Ausnahmezustandes und zur macht wichtigsten Funktion des Fürsten, den auszuschließen."[6] (GS, I, 1, 245)

Continuing in this political context of violence, on its emergence factors, Benjamin presents the idea of catastrophe and the relationship of violence with the catastrophe in the divine sphere, that is, theological (GS, I, 1, 246).

Another interesting relationship of the term *"Gewalt"* in the book *"Ursprung des deutschen Trauerspiels"* is when Benjamin deals with the concepts and forms of tyrant and martyr (GS, I, 1, 251), also contextualizing with this ethical-political aspect.

When dealing with the aspect of the decision of disability *(Entschlußunfähigkeit)* of the "tyrant as a martyr and the martyr as a tyrant" (GS, I, 1, 251), Benjamin returns through poetic example of Baroque thought of the ancient Greeks and Romans and his epic concept of time:

> „Der Held … sun ein Exempel seyn aller vollkomenen Tugenden / und Freunde von der Untreue seiner / Feinde betrübet und werden; jedoch dergestalt / daß er sich in allen Begebenheiten großmütig erweise und den Schmertzen / welcher mit Seufftzen / Erhebung der Stimm und vielen Klagworten hervorbricht / mit Tapferkeit überwinde"[7] (Georg Philipp Harsdörffer cited in Walter Benjamin, in: GS, I, 1, 252).

---

6    „This extreme of the doctrine of sovereign power was in its origins – of contrareformist sense, despite the various positions of the parties – much sharper and deeper than in their modern versions. The modern concept of sovereignty tends to a supreme executive power assumed by the prince, the Baroque develops from the state of exception discussion, considering that the most important prince's function is to prevent it. One who exercises power is destined beforehand to be the holder of a dictatorial power in situations caused by war, riots or other disasters."

7    „The hero … must be a finished example (perfect) of all virtues, and grieve with the disloyalty of his friends and enemies. But this should happen so that he proves magnanimous in all situations and be able to boldly overcome the pain, (which) manifested in sighs, voice high and many regrets. „

Here Benjamin puts next to the ancient Greek epic example and Roman also the example of Christ's Passion as a representation of martyrdom, in the ideal sense of the philosophy of history, both the Old Testament and the New Testament (GS, I, 1, 259). This theological aspect of violence reappears in his thinking on Christian eschatology as well as his conception of *"Heilsgewalt"*, especially when applied to the world of life, not only just in his dramatic and tragic representation German:

> „Nirgends ist das deutlicher als im ‚Leben ein Traum‘, wo es im Grunde eine dem Mysterium adäquate Ganzheit ist, in der der Traum als Himmel waches Leben überwölbt. Sittlichkeit ist in ihm zuständig: ‚Doch sey's Traum, sey's Wahrheit eben: / Recht thun muß ich; wär' es Wahrheit, / Deßhalb, weil sie's ist; und wär' es / Traum, um Freunde zu gewinnen, / Wenn die Zeit uns wird erwecken‘. Nirgend anders als bei Calderon wäre denn auch die vollendete Kunstform des barocken Trauerspiels zu studieren. Nicht zum wenigsten die Genauigkeit, mit der ‚Trauer‘ und ‚Spiel‘ aufeinander sich stimmen können, macht seine Geltung – Geltung des Worts wie die des Gegenstandes – aus. – Die Geschichte des Spielbegriffs in der deutschen Ästhetik kennt drei Perioden: Barock, Klassik, Romantik."[8] (GS, I, 1, 260).

And even then, Benjamin continues to seek a definition in history for violence within the context of the German tragic drama origin:

> „Vom Zweifel hatten Optimismus der Geschichtsauffassung abgesehen – im Sinn der Mär-tyrerdramatik ist nicht sittliche Vergehung, sondern der Stand des kreatürlichen Menschen selber der Grund des Unterganges. Diesen typischen Untergang, der so verschieden von dem außerordentlichen des tragischen Helden ist, haben die Dichter im Auge gehabt, wenn sie – mit einem Wort, das die Dramatik planvoller als die Kritik gehandhabt hat – ein Werk als ‚Trauerspiel‘ bezeichnet haben. So ist's – ein Beispiel, dessen Autorität vergessen lasse, wie fern es übrigens dem Gegenstande liegt – nicht Zufall, wenn die „Natürliche Tochter", die weit entfernt ist, von der weltgeschichtlichen Gewalt des revolutionären Vorgangs, welchen sie umspielt, bewegt zu werden, ein „Trauerspiel" heißt. Insofern aus dem staats politischen Ereignis zu Goethe nur das Grauen eines periodisch nach Art von Naturgewalten sich re-genden Zerstörungswillens sprach, stand er dem Stoff wie ein Poet des XVII. Jahrhunderts gegenüber. Der antikische Ton drängt das Ereignis in eine gewissermaßen naturhistorisch verfaßte Vorgeschichte; um dessentwillen übertrieb der Dichter ihn, bis er in einem lyrisch ebenso unvergleichlichen wie dramatisch hemmenden Spannungsverhältnis zur Aktion stand."[9] (GS, I, 1, 268)

---

8    „In no other piece is this more evident than La vida es sueño, which is a unit in itself the mys-tery background, and which covers dream, like a veil, the waking life. It morality does assert their rights, ‚Mas, sea verdad o sueño, / obrar bien es lo que importa; / si fuera verdad, por serlo; / si no, por ganar amigos / para cuando despertemos.‘ It is in Calderón we can study the tragic drama of the Baroque in its most finished form (perfect). Its effectiveness – effectiveness of word and object – resulting, among other factors, the precision with which harmonize the size of ‚mourning‘ (Trauer) and ‚game‘ (Spiel). The story of the ‚game‘ concept in the German aesthetic meets three periods: Baroque, Classicism and Romanticism."

9    „Not to mention the dubious optimism of this conception of history, it should be noted that in the sense of the tragedy of martyrs, the cause of the disaster is not in moral transgression, but own specific state of man. It was this very form of catastrophe, so different from the exceptional

## Conclusion

Recalling the nature of violence, its origins in the human and natural world, Benjamin analyzes the work of Lohenstein, the origin of the tragic nature of violence, both in its natural sense, therefore, but also mythical and divine, without leaving aside also in this context his character *construct hominis*.

When Benjamin will analyze the tragedy more specifically, the violently appears next to the tragic hero who can only rely on his physical strength and his silence, so without language. Thus he writes, quoting Franz Rosenzweig, thus ushering in a meta-ethical perspective:

> „Die Unmündigkeit des tragischen Heiden, welche die Hauptfigur der griechischen Tra-
> gödie gegen jeden späteren Typus abhebt, hat die Analyse des >metaethischen Menschen<
> durch Franz Rosenzweig zu einem Grundstein der Tragödienlehre gemacht. „Denn das ist
> das Merkzeichen des Selbst, das Siegel seiner Größe wie auch das Mal seiner Schwäche: es
> schweigt. Der tragische Held hat nur eine Sprache, die ihm vollkommen entspricht: eben das
> Schweigen. So ist es von Anfang an. Das Tragische hat sich gerade deshalb die Kunstform des
> Dramas geschaffen, um das Schweigen darstellen zu können... Indem der Held schweigt, bricht
> er die Brücken, die ihn mit Gott und Welt verbinden, ab und erhebt sich aus den Gefilden
> der Persönlichkeit, die sich redend gegen andre abgrenzt und individualisiert, in die eisige
> Einsamkeit des Selbst. Das Selbst weiß ja von nichts außer sich, es ist einsam schlechthin.
> Wie soll es diese seine Einsamkeit, dieses starre Trotzen in sich selbst, anders betätigen als
> eben indem es schweigt? Und so tut es in der äschyleischen Tragödie, wie schon den Zeitge-
> nossen auffiel." Das tragische Schweigen, wie diese Worte es bedeutungsvoll vorstellen, darf
> doch vom Trotz allein nicht beherrscht gedacht werden. Dieser Trotz bildet vielmehr in der
> Erfahrung der Sprachlosigktlit ebenso sich heran, wie sie an ihm sich bestärkt. Der Gehalt
> der Heroenwerke gehört der Gemeinschaft wie die Sprache. Da die Volksgemeinschaft ihn
> verleugnet, so bleibt er sprachlos im Helden. Und der muß jedes Tun und jedes Wissen je
> größer, je weiter hinaus wirkend es wäre desto gewaltsamer in die Grenzen seines physischen
> Selbst förmlich einschließen. Nur seiner Physis, nicht der Sprache dankt er, wenn er zu seiner
> Sache halten kann und daher muß er es im Tode tun."[10] (GS, I, 1, 286-287)

---

fall of the tragic hero, the authors had in mind when classifying – with a term that playwrights have used more consistently than the critics – a work as „tragic drama" (Trauerspiel ). Thus, it is not the case – to quote an example whose authority can forget the distance that separates our specific object – that Die natürliche Tochter [The natural daughter] far as is to be moved by the historical violence of the revolutionary process to its back, it was designated Trauerspiel. To the extent that Goethe read in political events only the horror of a will to destroy periodically reactivated, like natural disasters, their relationship with the dramatic issue was that of a poet of the seventeenth century. The tone of the piece with echoes of ancient tragedy, refers to the events a prehistory designed almost like a natural history, and the poet is accentuated to the point of placing it in a tense relationship with action, unparalleled in its lyricism, but inhibitory dramatic point of view."

10    „Failure responsibility of the tragic hero, which distinguishes the protagonist of the tragedy
      of all kinds later, did the analysis of the ‚meta-ethical man' by Franz Rosenzweig a key stone
      of the theory of tragedy. ‚For this is the own brand of the self (Selbst), the stamp of greatness

Therefore, complete with himself, in *Schicksal und Charakter* on this moral nature of the tragedy:

> „Nicht das Recht, sondern die Tragödie war es, in der das Haupt des Genius aus dem Nebel der Schuld sich zum ersten Male erhob, denn in der Tragödie wird das dämonische Schicksal durchbrochen. Nicht aber, indem die heidnisch unabsehbare Verkettung von Schuld und Sühne durch die Reinheit des entsühnten und mit dem reinen Gott versöhnten Menschen' abgelöst würde. Sondern in der Tragödie besinnt sich der heidnische Mensch, daß er besser ist als seine Götter, aber diese Erkenntnis verschlägt ihm die Sprache, sie bleibt dumpf. Ohne sich zu beKönigtum und Tragödie kennen sucht sie heimlich ihre Gewalt zu sammeln ... Es ist gar keine Rede davon, daß die >sittliche Weltordnung< wieder hergestellt werde, sondern es will der moralische Mensch noch stumm, noch unmündig – als solcher heißt er der Held – im Erbeben jener qualvollen Welt sich aufrichten. Das Paradoxon der Geburt des Genius in moralischer Sprachlosigkeit, moralischer Infantilität ist das Erhabene der Tragödie."[11]
> (GS, I, 1, 288-289)

---

and also the sign of their own weakness: he shut up. The tragic hero has only one language that fully corresponds to it: precisely the silence... By staying silent, the hero breaks the bridges that connect to God and the world, rises and leaves the domain of personality that is defined and it is individualized in the intersubjective speech, to enter the icy solitude of self. This is nothing known to him, is the only lonely. How else he give expression to this loneliness, this uncompromising obstinacy with himself, unless falling silent? This is what happens in the tragedies of Aeschylus, as contemporaries themselves noticed.' The tragic silence, significantly illustrated in these words, can not however be thought of only in dependence on a stubbornness. This will be formed before the experience of silence in the same way that the latter is reinforced therein. The substance of heroic action belongs, as the language, the community. Once disowned by the community, it remains shattered the hero. And this has to circumscribe all their actions and all their knowledge, the greater the weight and reach, the more violently within the bounds of the physical self. Only your phýsis, not the language, it must the ability to stay true to its cause, and so it has to do so in death."

11  „It was not the right, but in the tragedy, the head of genius raised the first time the mists of guilt because it was a tragedy that broke with the demonic destiny. But that did not happen by replacing the chain, no end in sight of pagan perspective, guilt and atonement for the purity of man redeemed and reconciled with pure god, but because the tragedy pagan man realizes that it is better than their gods, although this recognition towel his tongue and let it stay silent. Without doing so openly, it looks secretly gather their forces... This is not restoring the ‚moral order of the world‘, but the will of the moral man, still silent, not yet responsible – and it is in that capacity that he hero calls – to rise amid the upheavals that plagued world. The sublime tragedy is the genius birth paradox in full nudity and moral childishness."

## References

ARENDT, Hannah. *Macht und Gewalt*. München: Piper Verlag, 1970.
BENJAMIN, Walter. *Gesammelte Schriften*. 17 Band. Frankfurt am Main: Suhrkamp Verlag, 1982.
BUTLER, Judith. *"Kritik, Zwang und das heelige in Walter Benjamins Zur Kritik der Gewalt"*, in: *Rationalitäten der Gewalt*. Org. Krasmann, Susanne; Martschukat, Jürgen. Bielefeld: Transcript Verlag.
NITSCH, Patrick. *Zum Begriff von Macht und Gewalt bei Hannah Arendt*. Norderstedt: Grin Verlag, Studienarbeit.

## The Authors

Karla Pinhel Ribeiro, Professor of Philosophy and Political Science at Centro Universitário Curitiba – UNICURITBA, Ph.D. from University of São Paulo – USP.
karlapinhelribeiro@gmail.com

Milton Meira do Nascimento, Professor of Philosophy at Universidade de São Paulo – USP.
milton@usp.br

Printed by Printforce, the Netherlands